FINANCING TERRORISM

Financing Terrorism *offers a unique examination of how and why terrorist groups raise money. The combination of innovative theory and rich case studies from leading academics and practitioners make this book an invaluable contribution to the study of terrorism.*

Seth G. Jones, RAND and Georgetown University, USA

T0300313

This book is dedicated to those around the world who have fought and died to make us safe.

Financing Terrorism
Case Studies

Edited by

MICHAEL FREEMAN
Naval Postgraduate School, USA

Routledge
Taylor & Francis Group

LONDON AND NEW YORK

First published 2012 by Ashgate Publishing

2 Park Square, Milton Park, Abingdon, Oxon OX14 4RN
711 Third Avenue, New York, NY 10017, USA

Routledge is an imprint of the Taylor & Francis Group, an informa business

First issued in paperback 2016

British Library Cataloguing in Publication Data
Financing terrorism : case studies.
  1. Terrorism--Finance. 2. Terrorism--Finance--Case
  studies.
  I. Freeman, Michael, 1973-
  363.3'251-dc23

Library of Congress Cataloging-in-Publication Data
Financing terrorism : case studies / [edited] by Michael Freeman.
    p. cm.
  Includes bibliographical references and index.
  ISBN 978-1-4094-4261-5 (hbk)
  1. Terrorism--Finance--Case studies. I. Freeman, Michael, 1973-
  HV6431.F572 2011
  363.325--dc23

2011046424

ISBN 978-1-4094-4261-5 (hbk)
ISBN 978-1-138-24992-9 (pbk)

Contents

List of Figures, Tables and Map

Figures

Tables

Map

List of Contributors

Celso Andrade-Garzon is a General in the Ecuadorian Army and Head of the Joint Command of Military Intelligence.

Eduart Bala is a Colonel in the Albanian Army and Chairman of the National Security Strategy Department, Albanian Defence Academy.

Saul Hiram Bandala is a Commander in the Mexican Navy and serves on the Mexican Navy General Staff.

Christopher L. Corley is a Lieutenant Colonel in the U.S. Air Force and Executive Officer to the Director of Security Forces, Deputy Chief of Staff for Logistics, Installations and Mission Support.

Michael Freeman is an Assistant Professor in the Department of Defense Analysis at the Naval Postgraduate School in Monterey, California.

Dan Furleigh is a Lieutenant Colonel in the U.S. Air Force and currently Commander of the 72nd Operations Support Squadron.

Wade A. Germann is a Major in the U.S. Army and currently a student at the U.S. Army Command and General Staff College (CGSC), Fort Leavenworth, Kansas.

Puay Hock Goh is a Lieutenant Commander in the Singapore Navy.

Eric Hartunian is a Major in the U.S. Army and is a Strategist and the Chief of Plans for the 101st Airborne Division.

Geoffrey Kambere is a Major in the Uganda People's Defence Forces.

Pranav Kumar is a Lieutenant Colonel in the Indian Army.

Christopher L'Heureux is a Major in the U.S. Army and is currently a student at the United States Army School of Advanced Military Studies at Fort Leavenworth, Kansas.

Krishnamurti Mortela is Lieutenant Colonel in the Philippine Army and is currently a student at the Command General Staff Course in the Philippines.

Fulgence Msafiri is a Colonel in the Tanzanian Army and is currently Military Assistant to the Chief of Staff of the Tanzania People's Defence Forces.

Doug Philippone leads the Department of Defense program for Palantir Technologies Inc. in Palo Alto, California.

Richard A. Polen is a Captain in the U.S. Army and is a Company Commander of a UH-60 Blackhawk Helicopter Company for the 1st Infantry Division.

Duke Pope is a Lieutenant Colonel in the U.S. Air Force and is Director of Operations, 18th Flight Test Squadron (FLTS), Hurlburt Field, Florida.

Justin Y. Reese is a Major in the U.S. Army.

Moyara Ruehsen is an Associate Professor at the Graduate School of International Policy and Management at the Monterey Institute of International Studies of Middlebury College in Monterey, California.

Stein-Fr Kynoe is a Lieutenant Colonel in the Norwegian Army and is serving at United States Central Command in Tampa, Florida.

PART I
Introduction

Chapter 1

Introduction to *Financing Terrorism: Case Studies*

Michael Freeman

After the unsuccessful World Trade Center attack of 1993, one of the conspirators, Ramzi Yousef, claimed that if he had had more money, he would have been able to purchase more explosives. With a bigger bomb, he might have been successful in toppling the tower into other buildings. But because of cash-problems, the attack failed, killing six people and injuring over 1,000.[1] This anecdote highlights the importance of money for terrorism.

How each terrorist group spends money varies, but typically organizations need money for recruitment, salaries, retirement pensions, guns, explosives, bribes, communication equipment, transportation, forged documents, and more. Without money, terrorists can neither function as organizations nor conduct attacks. Yet, questions remain: how vulnerable are terrorists to financial disruptions? Can states put pressure on their finances in meaningful ways or are they too resilient and adaptive to be affected by our state actions?

These and other questions about terrorism financing are vigorously debated by scholars and policymakers.[2] In fact, the subject of terrorism financing has received great interest since the attacks of September 11th. While there is ever-increasing literature on policy issues, strategies, and counter-measures, states must first understand their enemies before developing strategies to defeat them. So, instead of focusing on the state response, this book asks more foundational questions:

---

1 Statement of Dale Watson, Chief International Terrorism Section, National Security Division, Federal Bureau of Investigation, "Foreign Terrorists in America: Five Years after the World Trade Center," Senate Judiciary Committee Subcommittee on Technology, Terrorism, and Government Information, United States Senate, Washington, D.C., February 24, 1998, available at: http://cryptome.org/jya/fbi-fta.htm (accessed January 11, 2012).

2 Jeanne Giraldo and Harold Trinkunas, eds, *Terrorist Financing and State Responses: A Comparative Perspective* (Stanford, CA: Stanford University Press, 2007); Thomas Bierstecker and Sue Eckert, eds, *Countering the Financing of Terrorism* (New York: Routledge, 2008); Douglas Farah, *Blood From Stones: The Secret Financial Network of Terror* (New York: Broadway Books, 2004), R. Thomas Naylor, *Wages of Crime: Black Markets, Illegal Finance, and the Underworld Economy* (Ithaca, NY: Cornell University Press, 2004), Rachel Ehrenfeld, *Funding Evil: How Terrorism is Financed and How to Stop It* (Chicago, IL: Bonus Books, 2003); Loretta Napoleoni, *Modern Jihad: Tracing the Dollars Behind the Terror Networks* (London: Pluto Press, 2003).

How do different terrorist groups actually raise money? What are their budgets? What do their portfolios look like? How have they changed over time? What are the advantages and disadvantages of different sources of financing?

Chapter 2, "Sources of Terrorist Financing," addresses these questions from a conceptual vantage point. Freeman divides the sources of terrorist financing into four broad categories: state sponsorship, illegal activities, legal activities, and popular support. Each of these funding mechanisms has different advantages and disadvantages for the terrorist group as well as different opportunities for disruption. This chapter is intended to be an overview of the sources of funding, while the subsequent chapters, and the focus of the book, will look at individual case studies

The following chapters will look at 11 different cases of terrorist financing, divided into four regions: the Middle East (Iraq and Hezbollah), Asia (PKK, LeT, Taliban, Tamil Tigers, and the Philippines), Europe (Loyalists in Northern Ireland and Albania), and the Americas (FARC and ELN, both in Colombia). These cases cover a wide range of terrorist groups or countries facing terrorist threats. The motivations of the various groups include examples of religious, nationalist, and Marxist ideologies. Some groups are relatively small, while others enjoyed more popular support and were more insurgents than terrorists (with consequences for how they raised money). Similarly, there is variation between areas where groups have not yet even formed (Albania) to groups that are still active (Hezbollah, LeT, FARC, and others), to groups that have mostly been defeated (LTTE, Loyalists in Northern Ireland). Each case has different lessons for those interested in counterterrorism strategies.

Chapter 3, "Insurgent and Terrorist Finances in Iraq," by Freeman, L'Heureux, Furleigh, and Pope examines how various insurgent groups in Iraq—including nationalist, Sunni, and Shia groups—raise, move, and spend money for their causes. This chapter also identifies several challenges to addressing insurgent financing and recommends new policies and different priorities in counter-terrorist financing. Chapter 4, by Doug Philippone, addresses what many observers consider to be one the most challenging of all terrorist groups—Hezbollah. They are a group responsible for much violence, but also a group that is socially embedded within the Shia population of Lebanon and politically active in the legitimate governance of Lebanon. They are large and well organized and receive support from Iran and Syria as well as from diaspora communities in Africa and South America.

In Chapter 5, Moyara Ruehsen analyzes the multitude of methods used by the PKK to raise funds. As she argues, the PKK has done well to maintain its income as the larger fortunes of the organization have risen and fallen over time. The PKK has also exploited its geographic context by utilizing neighboring countries for safe havens and by taking advantage of the drug smuggling routes that go from central Asia into Europe through Turkey. Chapter 6, by Geoffrey Kambere, Puay Hock Goh, Pranav Kumar, and Fulgence Msafiri, examines the LeT's finances. Their reliance on sponsorship from Pakistan as well as charitable donations has enabled them to conduct some of the most noted recent terrorist attacks, including the 2008 coordinated and simultaneous attacks in Mumbai.

Justin Y. Reese examines the case of the Taliban in Chapter 7. The focus is mostly on the Taliban post-2001 when it became an insurgent group in Afghanistan and Pakistan and was no longer governing Afghanistan. As the chapter shows, the opium and black market economies of the region provide much of the funding for the Taliban. In Chapter 8, Christopher Corley discusses the methods by which the Tamil Tigers (LTTE) of Sri Lanka raised and moved funds. The LTTE had been a long-running ethnic separatist group that supported terrorist units, as well as militia-type conventional forces, as well as a nascent sea and air capabilities. Their revenues are diversified, coming from diaspora communities, illegal activities, and elsewhere. In the Philippines, several insurgent and terrorist groups have emerged, ranging from Marxist groups to Islamic separatist groups, and even criminal gangs. Chapter 9 by Germann, Hartunian, Polen, and Mortela's describes the background of the various violent opposition groups in the Philippines and recounts the various methods used by the different groups to raise funds.

Turning to Europe, Stein-Fr Kynoe in Chapter 10 addresses the methods used by the Loyalist groups in Northern Ireland. While the Provisional IRA and other Catholic/Republican groups dominate the discussions of terrorism in Northern Ireland, the Protestant-led Loyalist groups fighting to remain part of the United Kingdom are also worthy of analysis, in part because they relied on different sources of funding than the PIRA. Eduart Bala, in the chapter on Albania (11), offers a slightly different perspective on terrorist financing. Albania has not seen any active terrorist groups, yet it has seen an increase in the number of fundamentalist Muslim charities operating in the country trying to establish an ideological foothold there. Bala's chapter examines many of these charitable organizations and how the Albanian government has countered their increasing presence.

The last case study chapters (12 and 13), by Saul Hiram Bandala and Celso Andrade-Garzon, discuss the financing of two groups in Colombia—the FARC and ELN, respectively. Colombia has been racked by insurgent and terrorist violence for decades and these two groups, both Marxist, have been responsible for much of it. Both groups are heavily involved in drug (cocaine) trafficking, but also engage in other criminal activities, like kidnapping and ransom and extortion, to raise funds. Like with the Taliban's connection to the opium trade in Afghanistan, the ties between the FARC and ELN and the cocaine trade pose similar challenges for the government of Colombia. These challenges and opportunities for better countermeasures are addressed by both Bandala and Andrade-Garzon.

The final chapter (14), by Michael Freeman, summarizes many of the key points and themes brought up by the earlier case studies. More importantly it challenges our understanding of how to think about countering terrorist financing. Freeman asks, how much of a priority should this be? What strategies are most likely to achieve success? How should states organize to fight terrorist financing? How do we measure effectiveness and success?

Overall, this book seeks to provide detailed case studies on many of the most prominent and important terrorist/insurgent groups. While much has been written debating the relevancy and priority of counter-terrorism efforts and much has been

written about the overall profiles of these groups, this book offers a focused set of
case studies on just the financing of different terrorist groups. As readers will see,
terrorist groups tend to be fairly adaptive, flexible, and resilient in acquiring funds.
Each group has a different portfolio tailored to their needs and their environment.
All of this makes countering terrorist financing more challenging for the state. Yet
understanding these challenges is necessary if states are to do better at curtailing
terrorist financing.

Chapter 2

Sources of Terrorist Financing: Theory and Typology

Michael Freeman

Terrorism costs money. In fact, some experts have described money as "the lifeblood" of terrorist organizations.[1] Without money, these groups could neither conduct their operations nor exist as organizations. But how do they raise money? What are the possible sources of terrorist financing? The sheer variety of sources is impressive, ranging from state sponsorship to petty theft, from the international smuggling of drugs to the extortion of local businesses, and from dispersed diaspora communities giving charitable donations to wealthy private individuals using their personal wealth to fund the organization. These, among many others, are just a few of the ways that terrorist groups acquire funds. But why would terrorist groups use one of these sources and not others, or why a particular combination of sources? Understanding this variation requires a theory that explores and explains the relative advantages and disadvantages of each source of terrorist financing. In other words, from the terrorist organizations' perspectives, what are their goals when it comes to financing and how do they maximize these goals by picking the right combination of sources?[2]

While much has been written about terrorism financing, most of this literature addresses specific case studies of terrorist groups or addresses potential counter-measures that could be implemented to disrupt terrorist financing by targeting the movement of funding through charities, *hawalas*, or the official banking sector (by applying anti-money laundering regimes).[3] These studies are clearly valuable but do not offer explanations that theorize why terrorist portfolios vary as much as they do.

To construct a theory of terrorist financing, this chapter proceeds in several steps. The first (brief) section addresses why terrorists need money and how

---

1   Dipak Gupta, "Exploring Roots of Terrorism," in *Root Causes of Terrorism: Myths, Reality and Ways Forward*, edited by Tore Bjorgo (New York: Routledge, 2005), 28.

2   For the purposes of theory building, I assume terrorist organizations maximize their utility. In practice, however, they frequently make mistakes and miss opportunities.

3   For example, see Jeanne Giraldo and Harold Trinkunas, eds, *Terrorist Financing and State Responses: A Comparative Perspective* (Stanford, CA: Stanford University Press, 2007); Thomas Biersteker and Sue Eckert, eds, *Countering the Financing of Terrorism* (New York: Routledge, 2008); Sean Costigan and David Gold, eds, *Terrornomics* (Aldershot: Ashgate, 2007).

much money they actually need. The second section develops a theory of terrorist financing that identifies six key criteria by which we can evaluate the advantages and disadvantages of different sources of financing. These criteria are: quantity, legitimacy, security, reliability, control, and simplicity. The third section offers a typology of terrorist financing sources that identifies four broad sources: state sponsorship, illegal activities, legal activities, and popular support. This chapter will analyze the advantages and disadvantages of each type according to the criteria set out in the theory section. Finally, the fourth section will address the counterterrorism financing implications of understanding the rationale behind different sources of financing.

It should be noted however, that this chapter does *not* address the movement of money into, within, or out of a terrorist organization. Just as there are many possible sources of funding, terrorists exploit several methods of moving money including: formal banking, informal banking (e.g. *hawala*), trade-based money laundering, charities, cash-smuggling, and others. Understanding the movement of money is an important facet of terrorist financing, but one that is sufficiently different from the sources of money to warrant a different theory and a different typology.

The Need for Money

The costs of individual terrorist operations can be relatively low, even for "strategic" level attacks. For example, the 1993 World Trade Center attack was estimated to have cost about $19,000. The 2002 Bali bombings are thought to have cost $20,000, and the 2004 Madrid attacks, somewhere between $10,000 and $50,000. In comparison, the September 11th attacks were relatively expensive, costing between $350,000 and $500,000, but they involved at least 19 hijackers operating abroad, with several requiring expensive flight simulation training.[4]

Although the costs of specific *operations* may be relatively inexpensive (and even more so for low level attacks), terrorist *organizations* require much larger budgets to function. Organizations need to devote resources to recruiting new members. If they are operating in failed or sympathetic states, they need funds to build training camps, and sometimes must provide food and housing for their members. Organizations must acquire the equipment necessary for conducting acts of violence—guns, explosives, triggers, training simulators, as well as fake passports and other travel or identification documents—and communication devices such as phones and computers. They may need to bribe officials to turn a blind eye to their activities. Finally, many groups need funds to pay stipends to their "retired" veterans and the families of dead terrorists or suicide bombers.

---

4   Nikos Passas, "Terrorism Financing Mechanisms and Policy Dilemmas," in *Terrorist Financing and State Responses: A Comparative Perspective*, edited by Jeanne Giraldo and Harold Trinkunas (Stanford, CA: Stanford University Press, 2007), 31.

As a result of these expenses, terrorist groups have budgets that can range up to hundreds of millions of dollars per year, especially for the larger and more active groups. Although the following numbers are just estimates, they are indicative of the overall phenomenon: al-Qaeda's annual budget was estimated to be $30 million;[5] until the 1990s, the Provisional IRA had a budget of up to $15 million per year;[6] at its peak in the 1990s, the PKK was thought to have an annual budget of $86 million;[7] Hezbollah's budget is between $100 million and $200 million per year, and may range as high as $400 million;[8] the FARC in Colombia has an annual budget of somewhere between around $100 million and $1 billion;[9] the Afghan Taliban raises somewhere between $240 million and $360 million per year;[10] and all the different insurgent groups in Iraq collectively raised between $70 million and $200 million per year.[11] As these figures demonstrate, the organizations that are responsible for terrorist attacks are much more expensive to operate than is indicated by the cost of any individual attack. Acquiring tens or even hundreds of millions of dollars requires that the organization must pay a certain degree of attention to its own financial portfolio.

A Theory of Terrorist Financing: Six Criteria

What do terrorist organizations look for when they consider various sources of financing? What makes one source more attractive than others? Overall, terrorist groups might be concerned with the following six criteria: quantity, legitimacy, security, reliability, control, and simplicity. From a terrorist group's perspective, there is no perfect source; each has advantages and disadvantages across the following criteria.

---

5 Passas, "Terrorism Financing Mechanisms and Policy Dilemmas," 32.

6 John Horgan and Max Taylor, "Playing the 'Green Card' – Financing the Provisional IRA: Part 1," *Terrorism and Political Violence*, 11:2 (Summer 1999), 10.

7 Mitchel Roth and Murat Sever, "The Kurdish Workers Party (PKK) as Criminal Syndicate: Funding Terrorism through Organized Crime: A Case Study," *Studies in Conflict and Terrorism*, 30 (October 10, 2007), 906.

8 Matthew Levitt, "Hezbollah: Financing Terror through Criminal Enterprise," Testimony before the Hearing of the Committee on Homeland Security and Governmental Affairs, United States Senate, May 25, 2005, available at: http://www.washingtoninstitute.org/html/pdf/hezbollah-testimony-05252005.pdf.

9 Marc Chernick, "FARC-EP," in *Terror, Insurgency, and the State: Ending Protracted Conflicts*, edited by Marianne Heiberg, Brendan O'Leary, and John Tirman (Philadelphia, PA: University of Pennsylvania Press, 2007), 71.

10 Peter Kenyon, "Exploring the Taliban's Complex, Shadowy Finances," *National Public Radio*, March 19, 2010, www.npr.org/templates/story/story.php?storyId=124821049 (accessed January 13, 2012).

11 John Burns and Kirk Semple, "U.S. Finds Iraq Insurgency Has Funds to Sustain Itself," *New York Times*, November 26, 2006.

Quantity

Terrorist organizations want as much money as possible. Sources that offer the largest amount of money are clearly the most desirable. With more money, terrorist groups can conduct more frequent and more violent attacks, be more likely to be able to offer social services to a constituent population, can better protect themselves from the state's security forces, can offer more incentives to potential recruits, and so on. Put simply, more money allows terrorist groups to be stronger and more effective; sources of financing that provide larger quantities are better than those that do not.

Legitimacy

Terrorist groups need legitimacy if they are to sustain themselves. If the ideology of a terrorist group is seen as illegitimate, they will have little popular support and few recruits (which is often the case). Likewise, if their strategies or tactics are seen as illegitimate (e.g. attacking targets that even their supporters see as innocent), then they will also lose support. Particular financing sources, as one type of tactical decision, can also impact the legitimacy of a group in several ways. First, they can be an indicator of legitimacy, especially if groups get large sums of money from a broad support base (e.g. diasporas and religious contributions). Second, certain fund-raising methods are often seen as illegitimate and might be avoided by a terrorist group or, when used, prove counterproductive. Involvement in the drug trade, for example, is often avoided or reluctantly embraced by terrorist groups for this reason. Finally, the legitimacy of a terrorist group can be undermined if members use their fundraising methods to acquire personal wealth (e.g. Abu Sayyaf and kidnapping for ransom).[12] Not only does this distract members of the organization from their mission, it also may lead to perceptions, perhaps justified, of corruption within the organization. Both these distraction and corruption dynamics can undermine the legitimacy of the group. Everything else being equal, then, terrorist groups will look for sources of funds that demonstrate their legitimacy, that are themselves seen as legitimate, and that keep members focused on their mission rather than leading to distraction or corruption.

Security

Terrorist groups generally operate clandestinely, hiding from the security forces of the state to organize, plan, recruit, and train. Meanwhile, the state is looking for avenues to infiltrate the organization or gain intelligence on them. As a result, terrorist groups will often employ specific sources of funding that allow them to stay off the state's intelligence "radar screen." Some sources of financing, like

---

12   Robert Trager and Dessislava Zagorcheva, "Deterring Terrorism: It Can Be Done," *International Security*, 30:3 (Winter 2005/2006), 118.

criminal activities for example, may draw unwanted attention from the police and others. They may also make it easier for the security forces to infiltrate someone into the terrorist organization, especially because the terrorist group may have more interactions with organized crime organizations, members of which may be easier to turn.[13]

Reliability

Sources of financing that are predictable and consistent are better for terrorist groups than those that fluctuate inconsistently. Whether or not a particular source of financing is reliable often depends on factors of geography and demographics. For example, a terrorist group that wants a reliable revenue stream that is tied to the drug trade needs to be near the source of the drug (e.g. FARC and cocaine, Taliban and heroin), located along a trafficking route (PKK and heroin), or have access to a domestic population with sufficient numbers of drug users (especially Western Europe, but to some degree everywhere). Likewise, demographics matter because a group relying on a diaspora community for funding, for example (like the LTTE), must have access to and control of the diaspora community in order to extort contributions or be able to receive voluntary assistance.

Control

Money is often associated with influence and power. Different sources of financing can threaten or strengthen a terrorist group's control over its members and operations. Terrorists do not want to be beholden to external sponsors because these sponsors (states, private donors) will often use their funding to influence the nature of the terrorist campaign. The sponsor could encourage the terrorist group to commit acts it otherwise would not do, or might discourage them from committing acts they might otherwise do. Another concern for terrorist groups is the possible lack of command and control within the organization itself, especially if small units or local commanders are responsible for their own financing. When this is the case, the decentralization of funding may mean that the central command has less control over its subsidiary units. A different issue is that often funding sources can create competition from rival organizations operating within the same political space. For example, if charities are supporting a broad cause (Palestinian independence, for example), there may be multiple actors all vying for funding, thereby creating competition and threatening any one actor's control over the political space. Lastly, terrorists will also want to control the timing and speed of their financing, especially if they need to raise funds quickly for a future attack.

---

13   Phil Williams, "Terrorist Financing and Organized Crime: Nexus, Appropriation, or Transformation?" in *Countering the Financing of Terrorism*, edited by Thomas Biersteker and Sue Eckert (New York: Routledge, 2008).

Simplicity

Terrorists groups, like any organization, want their methods of financing to be as simple as possible. Methods that require fewer specialized skills, that require as little effort as possible, that have simpler processes, and that have fewer inherent costs will be more desirable than other methods. For example, petty theft and extortion require fewer skills than cyber-crimes and are simpler processes than elaborate, multi-stage, and multi-actor drug smuggling operations. Also, for example, terrorist groups that receive external support will have to exert less effort than those groups that have to actively acquire funding.

With all of these criteria for evaluating the sources of terrorist financing, clearly terrorist groups will face tradeoffs. One source—for example, state sponsorship—might be advantageous for bringing in large sums of funding, but may be disadvantageous because the terrorist group may be beholden to the state sponsor's agenda and so lose some control over how their organization functions. These types of tradeoffs will be explored in more detail in the following section.

Because there are tradeoffs, terrorist groups must prioritize among the different criteria. Is getting more money worth the loss of control? Or is some loss of legitimacy worth the gains in acquiring more reliable funds (for example, through extortion)? How, then, would these six criteria be ranked? At a general level we might be able to hypothesize a prioritization list for the criteria, perhaps with quantity and legitimacy at the top. However, in practice, terrorist groups prioritize their needs according to their own situational context. Any particular ordering of the criteria would probably only explain a handful of cases. Overall, though, groups that are "better" will manage these tradeoffs more efficiently while less capable groups might make more mistakes, mistakes that the state can encourage and exploit (more on this in the final section).

Sources of Financing: Four Types

The range of terrorist financing sources is broad, ranging from state sponsorship to petty theft. To make some sense of this phenomenon, the different sources are divided into four general categories: state sponsorship, illegal activities, legal activities, and popular support.

State Sponsorship

One of the primary sources of funding for terrorist organizations is state sponsorship. With a few notable exceptions, state sponsorship has decreased significantly in recent years.[14] It was much more common during the Cold War years, when Marxist groups around the world were allegedly supported by

---

14   Passas, "Terrorism Financing Mechanisms and Policy Dilemmas," 24.

the Soviet Union, Cuba, and North Korea.[15] The U.S. also supported its own collection of groups; a number of these, such as the Mujahedin in Afghanistan and the Contras in Nicaragua, could be considered terrorist organizations. Many Arab states financed the PLO, providing at least $100 million per year during its early years, and possibly upwards of $250 million a year in the 1970s and 1980s.[16] In the 1980s, Libya gave aid and financial support to many groups, including Abu Nidal, the Red Brigades, the IRA, the PLO, the ETA, the Japanese Red Army, and Baader-Meinhof.[17]

Today, Iran is perhaps the most active state sponsor of terrorism, providing Hezbollah with an estimated $100 million per year—approximately half of the organization's annual budget.[18] Syria is also an important sponsor of terrorism. It provides weapons, safe havens, and financial support to Hezbollah and seven other groups on the U.S. State Department's list who have headquarters in Syria, including Hamas and Palestinian Islamic Jihad. Pakistan's Inter-Services Intelligence agency (ISI) sponsors the Afghan Taliban[19] as well as groups that are fighting for Pakistani control of Kashmir, including the Lashkar-e-Taiba, Harakat ul-Mujahidin, and the Hizbul Mujahideen.[20]

From the perspective of a terrorist organization, state sponsorship is advantageous because of the quantity of funds it can provide and the simplicity by which the terrorists can get them. The budgets of nation-states dwarf that of a terrorist group, making it an incredibly inexpensive proposition for a state like Iran to fund Hezbollah, and with a quantity of funds that Hezbollah would have a hard time replacing with other methods. From the terrorist perspective, state sponsorship is also relatively simple because it provides high returns for almost no effort.

State sponsorship has disadvantages for terrorist groups in terms of control and reliability. First, a state can use its financial support to control the group's activity, compelling the group to act as a proxy for the state's interests. The state may attempt to constrain the terrorist group, or force it to escalate its efforts, or require it to change its tactics. As a result, the group may be compelled to engage in activities that it would not otherwise undertake. The second disadvantage of state sponsorship is that states and their policies change. In some cases, states

---

15   Claire Sterling, *The Terror Network: The Secret War of International Terrorism* (New York: Holt, Rinehart, and Winston, 1981).

16   James Adams, *The Financing of Terror* (London: New English Library, 1986), 42, 73-5.

17   Adams, *The Financing of Terror*, 81.

18   Jeanne Giraldo and Harold Trinkunas, "The Political Economy of Terrorism Financing," in *Terrorist Financing and State Responses: A Comparative Perspective*, edited by Jeanne Giraldo and Harold Trinkunas (Stanford, CA: Stanford University Press, 2007), 10.

19   Ron Moreau, "With Friends like These ..." *Newsweek*, August 9, 2010, 24.

20   MIPT database entry for each group is available at: www.tkb.org.

disappear, which is why many Marxist groups lost much of their funding when the Soviet Union dissolved in the early 1990s. In other cases, states may change their policies and stop funding terrorist groups, which Libya has done in response to international pressure.

Illegal Activities

Because state sponsorship can be unreliable and constrain terrorist behavior, terrorist groups have increasingly sought funding through illegal activities. These have typically included activities such as extortion or "revolutionary taxes," kidnapping and ransom, theft, smuggling, petty crime, and pirating and counterfeiting goods. However, scholars and policymakers are concerned that terrorists will turn to more technologically sophisticated forms of crime, such as using online social networks or cyber-extortion, as methods of raising funds.

Terrorist groups often impose what they call "revolutionary taxes" on a population, forcing the population to provide funds for the group. Some notable groups that have used this method include the Shining Path in Peru, the FARC and ELN in Colombia, the Tupamaros of Uruguay, and the ETA in Spain, among many others. The Pakistani Taliban, as a specific example, publishes a "tax schedule" that lists various fees for different activities.[21] Extortion, although similar to "revolutionary taxes," is usually directed at particularly vulnerable targets who are threatened with violence unless some sum of cash is paid. For example, the PLO extorted $5 to $10 million a year from airlines in the 1970s and allegedly extorted $100 to $220 million from OPEC.[22] The Protestant Loyalists in Northern Ireland were also quite adept at extortion. They would simply approach local business owners and offer to protect them from violence for a fee. Of course, they were the ones who would be committing the violence. The business owner could even claim 40 percent of these expenses as a tax deduction, until the British government realized that it was essentially funding the terrorists and changed the laws. Before the laws were changed, extortion was the primary source of funding for the Loyalist groups.[23]

Kidnapping powerful officials or wealthy businessmen and holding them for ransom not only provides publicity for terrorist organizations, but it is also is one of their most profitable sources of financing.[24] Groups that are or were heavily

---

21   Arabinda Acharya, Syed Adnan Ali Shah Bukhari, and Sadia Sulaiman, "Making Money in the Mayhem, Funding Taliban Insurrection in the Tribal Areas of Pakistan," *Studies in Conflict and Terrorism*, 32:2 (2009), 98.

22   Napoleoni, *Modern Jihad*, 34.

23   Andrew Silke, "In Defense of the Realm: Financing Loyalist Terrorism in Northern Ireland—Part One: Extortion and Blackmail," *Studies in Conflict and Terrorism*, 21 (1998), 336.

24   John Picarelli and Louise Shelley, "Organized Crime and Terrorism," in *Terrorist Financing and State Responses: A Comparative Perspective*, edited by Jeanne Giraldo and

engaged in kidnappings include the Abu Sayyaf Group in the Philippines, the FARC in Colombia, the Italian Red Brigade, the Tupamaros of Uruguay, and insurgent groups in Iraq, the Pakistani Taliban, among many others. The ransoms paid for the safe return of kidnapped individuals may run in the millions of dollars; the record seems to belong to the Monteneros of Argentina, who received $60 million for the release of Juan and Jorge Born.[25]

Sometimes terrorist groups simply steal cash or valuables to finance their operations. The more notorious of these thefts include: the PLO/Christian Phalange robbery of the British Bank of the Middle East, which netted somewhere between $20 and $600 million in 1976;[26] the Jemaah Islamiyah bank robberies, which yielded five pounds of gold that were used to finance the Bali bombings;[27] the 1963 Tupamaros raid on a rifle club, yielding 28 guns that were used to jumpstart the organization's campaign of terrorism;[28] the ongoing theft of oil from pipelines in Iraq by insurgent groups;[29] numerous bank robberies conducted by the Pakistani Taliban;[30] and bank robberies carried out by the Symbionese Liberation Army.[31]

Smuggling is a profitable activity for anyone engaged in it. Terrorists smuggle almost anything, including drugs, diamonds, cigarettes, cash, people, and even animals, in order to finance their organizations and operations. The link between drugs and terrorism has garnered a lot of attention in recent years, and has spawned the term, "narco-terrorists." Some of the more notable organizations involved in the drug trade include the FARC in Colombia, the PKK in Turkey, and the Shining Path in Peru.[32] The Afghan Taliban profits from

---

Harold Trinkunas (Stanford, CA: Stanford University Press, 2007), 44.

25   Paul Lewis, *Guerrillas and Generals: The "Dirty War" in Argentina* (Westport, CT: Praeger, 2001), 57.

26   *TIME*, "Top Ten Brazen Heists," March 11, 2010, http://www.time.com/time/specials/packages/article/0,28804,1865132_1865133_1865218,00.html (accessed January 12, 2012); LebaneseForces.com, "Historical Fact: Arafat's Bank Robbery," http://www.lebaneseforces.com/blastfromthepast001.asp (accessed April 14, 2011).

27   "Jemaah Islamiyah in South East Asia: Damaged but Still Dangerous," International Crisis Group Asia Report No. 63, 26 August 2003, http://www.seasite.niu.edu/indonesian/islam/ICG-JI%20Damaged%20but%20Dangerous.pdf.

28   Michael Freeman, *Freedom or Security* (Westport, CT: Praeger, 2003), 88.

29   Robert Worth and James Glanz, "Oil Dollars Fund the Insurgency, Iraq and U.S. Say," *New York Times*, February 5, 2006; Burns and Semple, "U.S. Finds Insurgency Has Funds to Sustain Itself," Richard Oppel, Jr., "Iraq's Insurgency Runs on Stolen Oil Profits," *New York Times*, March 16, 2008.

30   Acharya et al., "Making Money in the Mayhem," 100.

31   Public Broadcasting Service, "The Rise and Fall of the Symbionese Liberation Army," February 16, 2005, http://www.pbs.org/wgbh/amex/guerrilla/peopleevents/e_kidnapping.html (accessed January 13, 2012).

32   Picarelli and Shelley, "Organized Crime and Terrorism," 42.

the opium trade, making between $70 million and $400 million per year.[33] While terrorist groups may be involved in the growing and selling of drugs, they are more commonly involved in their distribution and transit through or out of a country. For example, the PKK is heavily involved in the heroin traffic from Southwest Asia into Europe, with some estimating that 80 percent of the drugs in Europe have some connection to the PKK.[34] The profits are large; a kilogram of heroin that costs $1,000 to $2,000 in Thailand is worth $6,000 to $8,000 in Turkey, and has a street value of $200,000 in Germany.[35] Additionally, terrorists often provide drug dealers with protection from security forces in exchange for a cut of their profits.

Terrorist groups also are reportedly heavily involved in the smuggling of commodities. For example, there are some reports that al-Qaeda engaged in the smuggling of diamonds from West Africa and Tanzanite from Tanzania.[36] Likewise, Hezbollah has also been implicated in gold and diamond smuggling. For terrorist groups, the appeal of these commodities is that they are small, yet highly valuable, secure in their value, and hard to trace. Smuggling is often common in places with differential tax rates. For example, a Hezbollah bought cigarettes in North Carolina, where the taxes were low, then sold them at a discount in Michigan, where taxes were higher. It has been estimated that they raised approximately $3.7 million dollars over the course of several years, and sent at least a portion of their profits back to Lebanon.[37]

Terrorists also engage in human smuggling. For example, the PKK is reportedly heavily involved in the smuggling of people from Iraq and elsewhere in Asia into Europe, usually through Italy. Interpol estimates that the PKK receives between 2,000 and 3,000 Euros per individual. The exact number of people smuggled per year is unknown, but there was a single operation connected to the PKK in which 9,000 Kurds were smuggled into Europe.[38]

In one of the more odd cases of smuggling, the IRA raised $2 million in one year by smuggling pigs across the border between Northern Ireland and the Irish Republic border. The IRA would openly export the pigs to the British side of the border, collect the export subsidy (eight pounds per pig), then smuggle the pigs back into Ireland and repeat the whole operation with the same pigs. As one scholar

---

33   Eric Schmitt, "Many Sources Feed the Taliban's War," *The New York Times*, October 19, 2009. Kenyon, "Exploring the Taliban's Complex, Shadowy Finances," cites an estimate that the Taliban earns between $90 million and $160 million from opium.

34   Roth and Sever, "The Kurdish Workers Party (PKK) as Criminal Syndicate," 908.

35   Roth and Sever, "The Kurdish Workers Party (PKK) as Criminal Syndicate," 907.

36   Picarelli and Shelley, "Organized Crime and Terrorism," 42.

37   Tom Diaz and Barbara Newman, *Lightning Out of Lebanon* (New York: Ballantine Books, 2005), 87.

38   Roth and Sever, "The Kurdish Workers Party (PKK) as Criminal Syndicate," 909.

notes, this produced "a considerable amount of cash and some very tired pigs."[39] Besides cigarettes and pigs, almost any good could be and has been smuggled across borders to take advantage of the differences in taxes or subsidies.[40]

Petty crime is also an important source of terrorist financing. This category can include almost any criminal activity that might be used by terrorists to raise funds. For example, Ahmed Ressam, the Millennium bomber, stated during his interrogation that while living in Montreal, he stole from tourists, sold passports for cash, robbed a currency exchange, and engaged in credit card fraud.[41]

Last (although this is far from an exhaustive list), terrorists have been known to deal in pirated and counterfeit goods and currencies. For example, the Tri-Border area between Paraguay, Brazil, and Argentina is well known as a market for pirated goods, and Hezbollah is believed to be heavily involved there.[42] The Provisional IRA and Loyalist groups in Northern Ireland are known to deal in counterfeit clothing, compact disks, perfume, videos, currency, etc. and have raised around a million pounds for both sides combined.[43] The PKK is known to deal in counterfeit stamps and banknotes.[44]

For the terrorist group, there are several advantages to illegal activities as a source of funding.[45] First, illegal activities provide a reliable source of income because, as Picarelli and Shelly put it, "crime provides cash on a rapid and repeatable basis."[46] Extortion, for example, can be used repeatedly and expanded as needed. The diversity and availability of illegal activities means that they can take place anywhere. Commercial activities that can be exploited, or scarce resources that can be smuggled, traded, or stolen, can be found all over the world, and terrorists of all kinds take advantage of these opportunities to finance their organizations.

Another benefit of illegal activities is that they can enhance the legitimacy of the terrorist group, or at least undermine the legitimacy of the state. When groups engage in extortion and the population does not report the activity to the authorities, the terrorists have achieved at least the passive support of the population. Ideally, they would want strong, active support, but their ability to engage in extortion to

---

39   Loretta Napoleoni, *Modern Jihad: Tracing the Dollars Behind the Terror Networks* (London: Pluto Press, 2003), 31.

40   For example, in Roth and Sever, "The Kurdish Workers Party (PKK) as Criminal Syndicate," 912, the authors discuss the PKK smuggling blood.

41   Marc Sageman, *Understanding Terror Networks* (Philadelphia, PA: University of Pennsylvania Press, 2004), 100; Picarelli and Shelley, "Organized Crime and Terrorism," 44-5.

42   Picarelli and Shelley, "Organized Crime and Terrorism," 44.

43   Andrew Silke, "Drink, Drugs, and Rock'n'Roll: Financing Loyalist Terrorism in Northern Ireland—Part Two," *Studies in Conflict and Terrorism*, 23 (2000), 120.

44   Roth and Sever, "The Kurdish Workers Party (PKK) as Criminal Syndicate," 912.

45   See Picarelli and Shelley, "Organized Crime and Terrorism," 46-7, for a chart on the costs and opportunities of various methods.

46   Picarelli and Shelley, "Organized Crime and Terrorism," 40.

the extent that they do indicates that either the population does not feel loyalty to the state or lacks confidence in the state's ability to exert control. In other words, extortion shows that the terrorists may not have fully won over the population, but at least they have taken them out of the state's area of control. This also undermines the legitimacy of the state. By engaging in these practices, the terrorists show that the state cannot control its own territory. In a world that is "zero-sum," a loss for the state can be seen as a win for the terrorists.

Illegal activities are also often relatively easy. Depending on the type, illegal activities may require only minimal levels of skill in order to be carried out successfully. For example, robbing a bank or store requires a weapon and nerve, but not much else. Likewise, extortion is a relatively simple process, especially compared to many other methods of raising money.

A final advantage to the terrorist group in engaging in illegal activities is that they can maintain more control, especially if these activities allow them to be independent of state sponsors. The collapse of the Soviet Union was what led many terrorist organizations to shift their funding from state sponsorship to illegal activities.

Engaging in illegal activities also has some disadvantages for the terrorist groups. For some activities (like extortion, for example), there are limits to how much they can take from a population, thereby impacting the total quantity available from this source. The terrorists are essentially in a parasitic relationship; they want to feed off their host, but they cannot kill it without dying themselves. If they force a business to pay more than it makes in profits (at least for some extended period of time), that business will have to close down, and the terrorists will lose it as a source of income.

For terrorist groups concerned with legitimacy, several types of illegal activity may alienate the terrorist group's constituent population. Groups engaging in kidnappings, extortion, or drug smuggling may antagonize the community, costing a terrorist group some of its popular support. Many organizations stay away from these types of activities in order to avoid a public-relations disaster. The Provisional IRA, for example, has refused to become involved in Northern Ireland's drug trade for precisely this reason. Also, having access to large amounts of money from criminal enterprises may result in corruption among members of the organization, who may be tempted to take some of the profits for themselves.[47] Illegal activities will often be kept a secret even within the organization, and the funds generated by such activities are not easily tracked or accounted for. For example, Yasser Arafat is believed to have skimmed off between $900 million and $1.3 billion from the PLO's coffers.[48]

In terms of security, illegal activities are risky. The state and its police force are already looking for and trying to stop these activities, so the danger of capture

47   Picarelli and Shelley, "Organized Crime and Terrorism," 50.
48   Gideon Alon and Amira Hass "MI Chief: Terror Groups Trying Hard to Pull off Mega-attack," *Haaretz*, August 14, 2002.

is high. A cost/benefit analysis may lead an organization to conclude that illegal activities carry too high a risk when compared to other avenues for acquiring funds. Additionally, when the state does become aware of illegal activity conducted by terrorist groups, government security forces may use that information to track and disrupt the group. A small, clandestine organization is more likely to "fly under the radar" if it does as little as possible to challenge the state.[49]

Finally, terrorist groups may lose control when they engage in illegal activities. When a group is profitably engaged in criminal activity, it may grow more interested in pursuing profits than in attacking the state. This can be a particular problem when the illegal activities are carried out by peripheral cells of the organization. Self-sufficient cells that are capable of financing themselves may feel free to act independently of the leadership if they disagree with the organization's strategy.

Legal Activities

Terrorist groups do not just engage in criminal activity; they often operate totally legal businesses for a profit. For example, while al-Qaeda was in the Sudan between 1992 and 1996, the organization operated many legitimate businesses, including farms where peanuts were grown and honey was produced, several trading companies, a tannery, a furniture-making company, a bakery, and an investment company.[50] Elsewhere, al-Qaeda cells ran a construction and plumbing company, a company that fixed and sold used cars, a fishing business, and a manufacturing company.[51] The Aum Shinrikyo group in Japan operated a similarly large host of legitimate businesses, running a copy shop, a noodle shop, a computer software company, and a real estate business, among others.[52]

The Provisional IRA and Loyalist groups in Northern Ireland have also used legitimate businesses to finance their organizations. Both have operated drinking clubs or pubs; although these did begin as illegal operations, the groups then went on to obtain the proper licenses, and reported their income to the government (but usually not all of it). They also operated gaming machines—only some of which were legal—in the drinking clubs. Some scholars contend that these clubs were the single greatest source of income for these groups in the 1980s.[53] Both groups

---

49   Picarelli and Shelley, "Organized Crime and Terrorism," 51.

50   Jason Burke, *Al-Qaeda: The True Story of Radical Islam* (London: I.B. Tauris, 2003), 145.

51   Paul Smith, "Terrorism Finance: Global Responses to the Terrorism Money Trail," in *Countering Terrorism and Insurgency in the 21st Century*, vol. 2, edited by James Forest (Westport, CT: Praeger, 2007), 146.

52   Daniel Metraux, *Aum Shinrikyo's Impact on Japanese Society* (Lewiston, NY: Edwin Mellen Press, 2000).

53   Andrew Silke, "In Defense of the Realm: Financing Loyalist Terrorism in Northern Ireland—Part One: Extortion and Blackmail," *Studies in Conflict and Terrorism*, 21 (1998), 108.

also operated taxi services, with the IRA owning two companies of up to 600 taxis and the Loyalists operating over 90 cabs.[54] Because of their cash-based operations, both the pubs and the taxi services provided channels through which the groups could launder money that had been obtained from other illegal sources. As a last example, both sides in Northern Ireland also ran security firms that guaranteed the safety of companies and their workers, although these security firms often crossed the line into outright extortion.

For the terrorist group, engaging in legal activities to raise money is especially advantageous in terms of security. Because the activity is entirely legal, there is little the state can do to target the activity or those engaged in it. To do so would require the state to rewrite its laws in a way that might be seen as discriminatory or illegitimate.

Nevertheless, there may be some disadvantages to engaging in legal activities for the terrorist group. In terms of security, even legal activities may draw unwanted attention from the authorities. This would be particularly problematic if the terrorist group is trying to remain secret or clandestine while still in the planning stages. The use of legal businesses may give the authorities greater insight into the terrorist network or organization. A legal business may act as a beacon that offers the authorities a door into the terrorist group, and might allow them to trace back communication or flows of money into the "dark" side of the organization. Legal businesses are also required to keep records and can be audited, both of which provide the state with possible avenues to gather intelligence on the terrorist group.

Second, legal activities are not necessarily simple; they require that terrorist groups have good business skills if they are to make a profit. They will be competing in the market with all the other businesses who are also trying to make a profit. For terrorist groups that lack business skills illegal activities would become more attractive.

Lastly, in terms of quantity, legal activities may yield lower profits than other funding sources. Legal businesses have to compete in the marketplace, and doing so drives down profits. Illegal activities, in contrast, may yield higher profits, in part because of the risk premium attached to them.

Popular Support

Many terrorist groups rely on the support of a sympathetic population or constituency as a source of funding. Charitable donations comprise a large portion of the revenue for many Islamic groups in particular. Terrorists might also tap into sympathetic diaspora communities living overseas, or rely on membership dues to fill their coffers.

Many groups receive money in the form of charitable donations. This is a well-known and well-documented phenomenon for many Islamic groups. As examples,

---

54   James Adams, *The Financing of Terror* (London: New English Library, 1986), 214-16.

the Global Relief Foundation and the al-Wafa organization have been associated with al-Qaeda; the Holy Land Foundation for Relief and Development and the Quranic Literacy Institute have given money to Hamas; Benevolence International has been tied to Chechen groups; and the Islamic Concern Project and the World and Islam Studies Enterprises have sent funds to Palestinian Islamic Jihad.[55] Much of the money collected comes from Saudi Arabia and other Gulf states, where there are many wealthy donors sympathetic to these causes. Iraqi insurgents also received some funds from wealthy donors from the Gulf region; some Iraqi insurgent leaders had arrangements with the imams in the mosques where the money was collected.[56] The Afghan Taliban also receives money from charities located in the Gulf countries estimated at between $150 million and $200 million per year.[57]

Some groups also receive financial support from their diaspora communities. (The difference between this support and charitable donations is that support from the diaspora is based more on ethnic or racial connections and less so on religious ones.) For example, 50 percent of the IRA's revenue in the 1970s came from donations collected by NORAID from Irish-Americans. Likewise, many Palestinians living abroad would send five to seven percent of their salaries back to the PLO. Similarly, the LTTE raises $7 to $22 million a year from the Tamil diaspora in Canada, while many Lebanese expatriates around the world send money back to Hezbollah.[58]

As a final category, popular support can also come from membership dues or donations by members directly to the organization. Osama bin Laden has probably donated much of his personal wealth, for example, to al-Qaeda, although the estimates of the size of his fortune have probably been exaggerated. As another example, members of Aum Shinrikyo would usually give the organization all of their wealth upon joining the group.[59]

For terrorist groups, acquiring funds through popular support can be tremendously advantageous. First of all, it can be a clear signal of their legitimacy. By providing a clear and concrete demonstration that people support the cause, widespread financial backing is both a boon for the organization and a blow to the state. Moreover, some terror groups use the contributions they receive to conduct social welfare activities, thereby further undermining the legitimacy of the state and gaining supporters for their own cause.

---

55 Passas, "Terrorism Financing Mechanisms and Policy Dilemmas," 25.

56 Caleb Temple, "Financing of Insurgency Operations in Iraq," testimony before the House Armed Services Committee, July 28, 2005, available at: http://financialservices. house.gov/media/pdf/072805ct.pdf.

57 Kenyon, "Exploring the Taliban's Complex, Shadowy Finances."

58 Smith, "Terrorism Finance," 144.

59 David Kaplan and Andrew Marshall, *The Cult at the End of the World* (New York: Crown Publishers, 1996).

In terms of simplicity, popular support is relatively easy. Terrorist groups do not have to devote a lot of resources to acquiring funds; instead, they can simply "sit back" and wait for the money to come in. This is similar to the advantage coming from state sponsorship.

Popular support can offer a terrorist group a reliable source of income because charities, specifically, give the terrorist group more geographical flexibility. Not only can groups solicit donations from anywhere—for example, Hamas collected $13 million from the U.S. through the Holy Land Foundation—but they can also operate anywhere. Charities can go to remote parts of Indonesia, Iran, or Lebanon and, by providing aid on behalf of opposition movements, gain the trust and support of those populations.

Although receiving financial resources from donations and charities is generally advantageous, there are several disadvantages for the terrorist group. One possible disadvantage is a loss of control. Popular support can affect the terrorists' behavior, much like state support does. It could lead terrorists to moderate their behavior if they fear that their actions could undermine their popular support. Conversely, popular support could force them to escalate their behavior if their constituent population is more "hawkish" than they are. It could also cause them to escalate their operations if they are in a competitive environment for funding. For example, Hamas and Palestinian Islamic Jihad rely on more or less the same population base for support; if one of them is seen as less active, it may lose some of its financial revenue. Additionally, popular support may create a competitive environment in which new groups form in order to take advantage of the widespread sympathy and support available to organizations that espouse a particular cause. As in the business world, new companies form and move into areas where there are large profits to be made.

Popular support may also be disadvantageous in terms of the quantity of funds raised because popular support depends on the overall health of the economy. If people are struggling to meet their own needs, they will be less likely to donate money to a charitable cause.

Countering the Sources of Terrorist Financing

Different sources of financing have different vulnerabilities that can be exploited. This is good news for a state that is trying to cut the financial resources of terrorist groups; it is also a warning that countermeasures must be specifically tailored not only to the particular group being targeted, but also to the way in which that group acquires financial resources. For example, the countermeasures most likely to be successful against the Iraqi insurgents would vary depending on whether they are receiving state sponsorship from Saudi Arabia and Iran, or whether they rely on kidnappings and extortion. This is made more complicated by the fact that terrorists often use a wide portfolio of sources and that no two terrorist groups will have the same profile of funding. As a result, there can be no single strategy for addressing the sources of terrorist financing; instead, strategies must be tailored to different groups and their different portfolios of fundraising.

In addition, terrorists adapt. Although the categories discussed in this chapter are meant to capture the best known sources of funding, terrorist groups have proven themselves adept at finding new and creative ways of financing their organizations, and it is therefore possible that there are other categories of funding not known at this time. When the state cracks down on particular paths of support, terrorist groups are sometimes able to respond by financing their operations through less risky or more lucrative arenas.[60] For example, the funding sources of Iraqi insurgents have shifted over time; they were originally financed by regime loyalists, and then got the bulk of their money from foreign fighters who smuggled cash into Iraq; and then were self-financing through crime, extortion, and donations.[61] As a result, there cannot be a fixed strategy; instead, strategies for countering terrorist financing must be as flexible and adaptable as the terrorists' strategies.

We should also recognize that there is no easy strategy to disrupt the sources of terrorist financing. Typically, states are reasonably well organized to counter the movement of money (through anti-money laundering measures, financial oversight and regulation, etc.), but are less capable of going after the sources of funds. While almost all recommendations require a more intensive dedication of resources, resources are always scarce. Many states are already attempting to improve their intelligence gathering, enhance their police forces, improve their governance, or provide more social welfare goods.

Despite these difficulties, the theory of terrorist financing articulated above offers an important way of thinking about how better countermeasures can be developed. Ultimately, states need to reverse the logic behind the six criteria. If terrorists want to acquire money in large quantities, legitimately, securely, reliably, simply, and in a way that they can control, then states must reduce the quantity of funds and make their acquisition illegitimate, dangerous, unreliable, distracting, and complicated. The following suggestions are just some ways this might be done. (These options focus on the first three criteria [reducing quantity, legitimacy, and security] as these are more open to manipulation by the state. The reliability, simplicity, and control aspects of various sources may vary, but are harder to impact externally.)

To reduce the large quantities of money terrorists receive from state sponsors, states can impose economic sanctions or embargos; they can offer incentives to induce sponsor states to change their behavior, essentially "bribing" them to stop supporting terrorism; they can apply diplomatic pressure in an attempt to

---

60   Note that shifts in terrorist fundraising can also be seen as insights into the terrorist organization. When al-Qaeda in Iraq began robbing merchants, that might have been a sign that they had lost legitimacy and popular support and so were no longer able to rely as much on private donations and charities.

61   Burns and Semple, "U.S. Finds Iraq Insurgency Has Funds to Sustain Itself."

convince the sponsor states to behave; or they can attack and invade the countries that support terrorism. Although international pressure can work—it has been effective in convincing Libya to change its ways—sanctions, diplomacy, and military action can sometimes have little impact. U.S. attacks on Libya in 1986 and Afghanistan in 1998 failed to deter those countries' support for terrorism, and Iran continues to support Hezbollah. Charities, too, provide large quantities of funds to terrorists and countering this source requires that states can do a better job of monitoring where and how charities raise money. In Saudi Arabia, for example, the government has recognized since 2003 the role that charities play in financing terrorism, and has responded by creating more oversight and legal constraints on how charities operate within the kingdom.[62]

Addressing the terrorists' desire for legitimacy is sometimes hard, especially if they rely on charities for funds. Charities are rarely entirely devoted to financing terrorist organizations; rather, they may distribute most of their money to other, legal causes, including other charities. Additionally, even the money that does go to terrorist groups is often spent on social welfare programs and not on violent activities. Both Hamas and Hezbollah are well known examples of groups that engage in robust social welfare activities where the government is incapable or unwilling to do so.[63] If the government provided better governance—and this might require more international aid—it would undermine popular support for the terrorist organizations. Additionally, the state could, for example, use information operations to publicize the connections between charities and terrorist groups. Oftentimes, donors are unaware of how their donations are distributed, and may be less likely to support a charity if they know that its funds are used to support terrorism.

To make terrorists less secure in the methods used to acquire funds, the state can also improve its police, domestic intelligence agencies, and legal prosecution organizations to put more pressure on terrorist organization.[64] For example, the state could focus more of its resources on prosecuting criminals, especially those who might be tied to terrorist groups. Additionally, the state could increase the punishments for terrorists who are convicted of engaging in such illegal activities. For example, if the punishment for smuggling drugs is five years, it could be increased to 10 years if the person is also affiliated with a terrorist group. Also, devoting more resources to the police should have the effect of lowering crime overall, which should lower the rate of terrorist related crime as well. Lastly, there needs to be greater information sharing between police and intelligence agencies. Better information sharing would allow

---

62   Christopher Blanchard, "Saudi Arabia: Terrorist Financing Issues," *Congressional Research Service*, September 14, 2007.

63   Alexus Grynkewich, "Welfare as Warfare: How Violent Non-State Groups Use Social Services to Attack the State," *Studies in Conflict and Terrorism* 31 (2008).

64   Picarelli and Shelley, "Organized Crime and Terrorism," 54.

authorities to tie together disparate pieces of information in order to identify and counter terrorist organizations.

These recommendations are not an exhaustive list; rather they are meant to be illustrative suggestions for how we might think about addressing the sources of terrorist financing. There are no easy solutions to disrupt the sources of terrorist financing; nevertheless, more can be done. Since money *is* the lifeblood of terrorist organizations, attacking it in better and smarter ways will result in a more effective fight against terrorism overall.

PART II
Middle East

Chapter 3

Insurgent and Terrorist Finances in Iraq

Michael Freeman, Christopher L'Heureux, Dan Furleigh,
and Duke Pope

This chapter will examine the financial elements of the insurgency in Iraq. We will begin with a brief discussion of the insurgency and the operational environment in Iraq. Then we will undertake a detailed examination of the major Sunni and Shiite insurgent organizations and their funding. Finally, we will present recommendations aimed at improving the coalition's ability to interdict insurgent financing in Iraq.

Background

While the precise beginning of the insurgency remains in doubt, most reports agree the initial motivation was to rid Iraq of the United States and its coalition partners.[1] As early as mid-March and early April 2003, a chaotic environment and lawlessness on the streets set the preconditions for the insurgency. Insurgent groups quickly emerged from numerous sectors of Iraqi society, and across the entire landscape of the country. The intensity of the insurgency can be measured using the number of attacks per week as a guide.

Groups

The insurgency in Iraq is complex and not easy to categorize. One defense research organization lists 33 distinct insurgent groups.[2] While the list is not exhaustive and reflects some groups that have been co-opted by the counter-insurgents as 'Sons of Iraq', it does illustrate the multifaceted nature of the insurgency.[3] There

---

1   Ahmed S. Hashim, *Insurgency and Counter-Insurgency in Iraq* (Ithaca, NY: Cornell University Press, 2006); Ali Allawi, *The Occupation of Iraq: Winning the War, Losing the Peace* (New Haven, CT: Yale University Press, 2007).

2   GlobalSecurity.org, "Iraq Insurgency Groups," http://www.globalsecurity.org/military/ops/iraq_insurgency.htm (accessed November 30, 2008).

3   For additional information regarding the Sons of Iraq and the Sunni Awakening, see Farook Ahmed, "Backgrounder #23, Sons of Iraq and Awakening Forces," The Institute

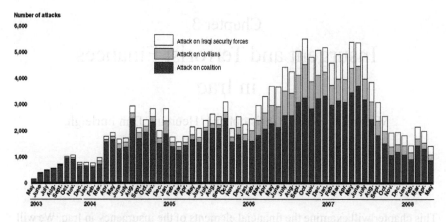

Figure 3.1   Overall Weekly Iraq Attack Trends: May 2003-May 2008

Source: United States Government Accountability Office, Securing, Stabilizing, and Rebuilding Iraq: Progress Report: Some Gains Made, Updated Strategy Needed, June 2008, http://www.gao.gov/new.items/d08837.pdf.

are, however, two broad themes found within the insurgent groups: their desire to expel the foreign occupiers—the United States;[4] and/or their religious nature. With this in mind, the insurgency can be divided into three general categories: the nationalists, the Sunni Islamic extremists, and the Shia militias.

Nationalists

In the beginning of the insurgency, nationalist groups made up of former regime elements (FRE) were most dominant, although they never coalesced into a coherent organization or groups of organizations.[5] They recruited from the Fedayeen Saddam, the Republic Guard, the *Mukhabarat* (secret police), the Baath party, the military, and others loyal to the Hussein regime.[6] They fought the United States simply because it was an occupying force.[7] Many of

for the Study of War, February 28, 2008, http://www.understandingwar.org/files/reports/Backgrounder%2023%20Sons%20of%20Iraq%20and%20Awakening%20Forces.pdf.

   4   Eric Schmitt and Thom Shanker, "The Conflict in Iraq: Rebels; Estimates by U.S. See More Rebels With More Funds," *New York Times*, October 22, 2004.

   5   The Memorial Institute for the Prevention of Terrorism (MIPT.org) lists Khatibat al-Fursan (Knights Brigade) and Dhi Qar as former loyalist groups, but both of these organizations were responsible for only single attacks.

   6   Hashim, *Insurgency and Counterinsurgency in Iraq*, 99.

   7   David Hawkins, "Iraqi Fighters: Yankees Go Home," *CBS News*, July 23, 2003, http://www.cbsnews.com/stories/2003/07/21/eveningnews/main564357.shtml (accessed January 13, 2012).

these groups were, or could have been, labeled as religious/Sunni ones as well because they sought to establish a Sunni state in Iraq after they rid Iraq of foreign influences. A few of the most prominent nationalist groups included the Salahuddin al-Ayyubi Brigades (JAMI, the military wing of the Iraqi Islamic Resistance Front or IFIR), which was anti-coalition but also anti Shia; Kata'ib Thawrat al-Ishreen (the 1920 Revolution Brigade), which was also listed as a Sunni group; and Al-Jaish al-Islami fi al-Iraq (Islamic Army in Iraq or IAI).[8] Some reports argue that the "main pillar" of the insurgency came from these Iraqi nationalists among the traditional Sunni tribes and that "Sunni nationalism seems to be the strongest contributing factor fueling the unrest."[9]

These nationalist groups were well-funded, equipped and manned. Saddam's regime began preparing for an insurgency well before the U.S. invasion. He trained his forces in guerrilla tactics and instructed them to cache money, weapons, and supplies.[10] When the nationalist insurgency developed, their funding came mostly from Hussein officials who had appropriated funds before the regime fell and funneled them back into Iraq.[11] Qusay Hussein himself took out $1 billion in cash as the invasion was in progress.[12] Other regime officials fled to Syria, Jordan, Saudi Arabia, Iran and the United Arab Emirates and "established financial bases to fund the insurgency."[13] In 2004, the U.S. thought that "about a half-billion dollars that once belonged to the former Iraqi government, along with funds from individuals and religious groups in Saudi Arabia, [was] being funneled through Syria and used to fund insurgents."[14] These former regime loyalists were dealt a blow with the seizure of $3.6 billion of assets by an American led effort. Coupled with the increasing realization that the Baathists would not return to power, especially after Saddam's capture and execution, this segment of the insurgency led by former regime elements declined.[15] Many of the former regime elements shifted their allegiances to Islamist causes.

---

8   Anthony Cordesman, "Iraq's Sunni Insurgents: Looking Beyond Al-Qa'ida," Center for Strategic and International Studies, July 16, 2007.

9   Nawaf Obaid and Anthony Cordesman, "Saudi Militants in Iraq: Assessment and Kingdom's Response," Center for Strategic and International Studies, September 19, 2005, 6 and 7.

10   Hashim, *Insurgency and Counterinsurgency in Iraq*, 12, 168; Caleb Temple, "Financing of Insurgency Operations in Iraq," testimony before the House Armed Services Committee, 28 July 2005, http://financialservices.house.gov/media/pdf/072805ct.pdf.

11   Thomas Ricks, "Rebels Aided by Allies in Syria," *Washington Post*, December 8, 2004. Schmitt and Shanker, "The Conflict in Iraq."

12   John Burns and Kirk Semple, "U.S. Finds Insurgency Has Funds to Sustain Itself," *New York Times*, November 26, 2006.

13   Caleb Temple, "Financing of Insurgency Operations in Iraq."

14   Cnn.com, "U.S.: Saddam regime funds financing Iraq insurgency," October 22, 2004.

15   John Burns and Kirk Semple, "U.S. Finds Insurgency Has Funds to Sustain Itself," *New York Times*, November 26, 2006; *Jane's Intelligence* entry for Former Regime Elements.

Sunni

The insurgency became much more dominated by Sunni religious extremists to include al-Qaeda in Iraq (AQI), the Mujahideen Shura Council (MSC), the Islamic State of Iraq (ISI), Al-Jaish al-Islami fi al-Iraq (Islamic Army in Iraq or IAI) and many others.[16] The particularly Sunni nature of the insurgency was reflected in an ABC News Poll from March, 2007, in which 51 percent of Iraqis said "that violence against U.S. forces is acceptable" but that, among Sunnis, this number was higher than 90 percent.[17] Supporting this trend, by 2005, approximately 90 percent of the insurgents were Iraqi Sunni Arabs, not former regime elements.[18] In broad terms, these groups received some portion of their funding from wealthy Gulf State donors and some from donations collected at mosques. The rest is obtained through extortion, smuggling and other criminal activities.

Foreign fighters bringing cash to the radical Sunni groups like AQI was also a prominent source of funding for the insurgents.[19] However, the influx of foreign

---

16 AQI (Tanzim Qa'idat al-Jihad fi Bilad al-Rafidayn (Organization of Jihad's Base in the Country of Two Rivers), formerly Tawhid and Jihad (Monotheism and Holy Struggle) combined with Jaish al-Taifa al-Mansoura (Victorious Army Sect); al-Ahwal Brigades (Calamities Brigade); Islamic Jihad Brigades; al-Ghuraba Brigades; Saraya Ansar al-Tawhid (Partisans of Monotheism Brigades); Jaish al-Sunna Wal Jama'a to form the Shura Council. On October, 15, 2006, the MSC joined with Jaish al-Fatiheen (Army of the Conquerers); Jund al-Sahaba (Army of the Prophet's Companions); Ansar al-Tawhid wal-Sunna; Jamaat al-Murabitin; Fursan al-Tawheed; and Jund Milllat al-Ibrahim to form the ISI. Other Sunni groups would include Jaish Ansar al-Sunnah (Army of the Followers of Tradition or JAS), a mixed Kurdish and Arab group formed out of the Ansar al-Islam group in northern Iraq; Jaish al-Mujahedeen: Kata'ib Thawrat al-Ishreen (The 1920 Revolution Brigade); Jaish al-Rashideen (Army of First Four Calpihs); Asa'ib al-Iraqi al-Jihadiya (Jihad Factions of Iraq or The Clans of the People of Iraq); Abu Nakr al-Siddiq Army; al-Qassas Brigade; Saraya al-Dawa wal Ribat (Missionary and Frontier Guarding Movement); Saraya al-Ghadhab al-Islami (Islamic Anger Brigades); Saraya Usud al-Tawhid (Lions of Monotheism Brigades); and Saraya Suyuf al-Haqq (Swords of Justice Brigades), among others. There are 12 more groups listed by MIPT not included here. This is a compilation of entries from the MIPT database, www.tkb.org/Home.jsp; Evan Kohlmann, "State of the Sunni Insurgency in Iraq: 2006," www.globalterroralert.com, December 29, 2006; "In their Own Words: Reading the Iraqi Insurgency," International Crisis Group, February 15, 2006.

17 MSNBC.com, "Poll: Iraqis pessimistic on war's outcome," March 19, 2007.

18 FoxNews.com, "Report: Saudis Bring Money, Fighters to Iraq's Insurgency," September 20, 2005.

19 See Brian Fishman, ed., *Bomber, Bank Accounts, and Bleedout* (Harmony Project at the Combating Terrorism Center at West Point, 2008). "Al-Qaeda Turns More to Extortion, Abductions to Fund Fight, U.S. Says," San Diego Union-Tribune, July 30, 2008 notes that foreign fighters provided up to 70 percent of AQI's budget in one sector. John F. Burns and Kirk Semple, "US Finds Iraq Insurgency Has Funds to Sustain Itself," *New York Times*, November 26, 2006.

fighters dropped due to several factors: Iraqi tribes have turned against them; U.S. and Iraqi efforts within the country have made it difficult for them to operate; and other governments like Saudi Arabia and Morocco have put pressure on the smuggling networks.[20] As a consequence, AQI and other groups turned to criminal activities, like extortion and kidnapping, to raise funds. Overall, the Sunni insurgency was "self-sustaining financially" and did not rely on outside sources of funding for its continued level of operations.[21]

Shia

In April 2004, Shiite militias first surfaced as a serious threat in the form of the anti-U.S. cleric Muqtada al-Sadr and the Mahdi Army, or Jaysh al-Mahdi (JAM). At the time, Coalition forces were heavily engaged and primarily focused on the threat posed by FREs and Sunni foreign fighters who had developed a stronghold in Fallujah. But even in 2004-2006, Shiite militias participated in the insurgency; regularly attacking coalition forces and moderate Shiites, and retaliating against Sunni groups. By July 2007, the threat posed by Shiite militias was too great to ignore. According to U.S. General Ray Odierno, second in command in Iraq, Shiite militias "carried out 73 percent of the attacks that killed or wounded American troops in Baghdad."[22]

When analyzing Shiite militias in Iraq, two principal organizations dominate the discussion; the aforementioned JAM and the Badr Organization (also known as the Badr Brigade or Badr Corps). Again, Muqtada al-Sadr is considered the leader of JAM, although his control over the entire organization has been questioned. When sectarian violence plagued the Iraqi countryside following the al-Askari mosque in 2006, JAM gained legitimacy by providing needed security to Shia population centers.[23] Bruce R. Pirnie and Edward O'Connell of the RAND Corporation credited al-Sadr with developing JAM into "an organization comparable to Hezbollah, providing social services in addition to security."[24] Accurate membership estimates of JAM are difficult to pin down. A June 2008 Government Accountability Office report to Congress estimated JAM has "a combined nationwide strength of approximately 25,000 to 40,000 active

---

20   "Al-Qaeda Turns More to Extortion, Abductions to Fund Fight, U.S. Says," San Diego Union-Tribune.

21   Burns and Semple, "U.S. Finds Insurgency Has Funds to Sustain Itself."

22   Michael R. Gordon, "U.S. Says Iran-Supplied Bomb Kills More Troops," *The New York Times*, August 8, 2007.

23   Anthony H. Cordesman and Jose Ramos, "Sadr and the Mahdi Army: Evolution, Capabilities, and a New Direction," Center for Strategic & International Studies, August 4, 2008, 8.

24   Bruce R. Pirnie and Edward O'Connell, *Counterinsurgency in Iraq (2003-2006)*, RAND Corporation, 2008, 32.

members supported by a large body of non-active supporters."[25] *The Iraq Study Group Report* put the number as high as 60,000 JAM fighters.[26]

The Badr Organization is the armed wing of the Supreme Islamic Iraqi Council (SIIC). Lionel Beehner of the Council on Foreign Relations asserts the Badr Organization was 10,000 members strong.[27] The SIIC was previously known as the Supreme Council for the Islamic Revolution in Iraq (SCIRI), among other names.[28] In 1982, during the Iran-Iraq War, SCIRI was established in Iran by exiled Iraqi Shiites. SCIRI has had strong financial ties and military backing with Tehran since its establishment. When Saddam's regime fell to the U.S.-led Coalition, SIIC and Badr Organization leaders quickly asserted themselves and their party as a political force in Iraq.

On July 13, 2003, Sayyed Abdul Aziz al-Hakim, the leader of SIIC and one-time leader of the Badr Organization, was appointed to the Interim Governing Council (IGC) by the CPA. With predominantly Shia influences like al-Hakim's advising on governance matters, it is no surprise Sunni Arab opposition spiked in response to the IGC. In his book *War Journal: My Five Years in Iraq*, Richard Engel describes the prominent role al-Hakim played in the debate which took place during the drafting of the Iraqi constitution in 2005. According to Engel, al-Hakim joined forces with Ahmed Chalabi, a Shia elite from Baghdad and co-member of the IGC. Together, these men pushed for greater regional authority, and they hoped to create "'Shiastan,' a mini-state on the border with Iran, rich in oil and with control over access to the Persian Gulf. It would be powerful, wealthy, strategically located, and pro-Iranian."[29] The "pro-Iranian" position of SIIC and the Badr Organization played heavily into the financial portfolio of the group, which is detailed later in the paper.

In April 2005, the Shia Beyan Jabr was appointed as the position of Minister of Interior. Before the U.S.-led invasion, Jabr was the head of the SCIRI office in Damascus. He was a known Badr Organization official, and is considered by many reports responsible for enabling the Badr Organization to infiltrate the Iraqi National Police corps. Ken Silverstein of Harper's Magazine referred to Jabr as the "minister of civil war." He claims Jabr quickly purged the ministry of Sunnis and placed members of the Badr Brigade into the Iraqi National Police and other

---

25   GAO-08-837 Report to Congressional Committees, "Securing, Stabilizing, and Rebuilding Iraq: Progress Report: Some Gains Made, Updated Strategy Needed," *Government Accountability Office*, June 2008, 22.

26   James A. Baker, III, and Lee H. Hamilton, Co-Chairs, *The Iraq Study Group Report* (New York: Vintage Books, 2006), 5.

27   Lionel Beehner, "Shiite Militias and Iraq's Security Forces," The Council on Foreign Relations, November 30, 2005.

28   Literature concerning the Supreme Iraqi Islamic Council (SIIC) refers to previous names used by the organization. Those names include: the Supreme Council for the Islamic Revolution in Iraq (SCIRI); and the Islamic Supreme Council of Iraq (ISCI).

29   Richard Engel, *War Journal: My Five Years in Iraq* (New York: Simon & Schuster, 2008), 216.

paramilitary units.[30] While Jabr served as the Iraqi Minister of Interior, numerous secret detention facilities were uncovered. In November 2005, Brigadier General Karl Horst, U.S. Army, discovered the al-Jadiriyah Bunker, where 169 detainees were found. Most of the detainees had been tortured, and 166 of the 169 were Sunni.[31] Thus, despite a 2003 promise by the Badr Organization to devote itself to peaceful purposes, many assume the SIIC and its military wing, the Badr Organization, have contributed to the insurgency through direct action and corrupt government practices. However, it is worth mentioning recent accounts of the situation in Iraq reflect the Badr Organization had very little, if any, confrontations with coalition or Iraqi government forces. Since 2007, most reported engagements involving the Badr Organization reflect a struggle for power and control in southern Iraq with JAM affiliated forces.

Expenditures

In terms of expenditures, most of the funds raised by the different insurgent groups was probably spent on travel, food, lodging, payments to the families of dead insurgents, and bribes, while some money also went into the personal coffers of the insurgent leaders.[32] Spending on munitions was minimal as stockpiles of weapons are fairly plentiful. Also, payments to foot soldiers to conduct attacks were fairly low; the costs of paying someone to plant IEDs was reportedly between $40 and $100, while payments for more elaborate attacks cost somewhere between $100 and $2,000.[33]

For JAM, a key portion of their expenditures was tied to militia recruitment. Hashim likened JAM to a "social movement" as he explains Sadr's militia was "made up largely of disgruntled and unemployed young Shi'a men."[34] Sadr City, one of the poorest districts of Baghdad and home to over 2 million Shiites, was an early bastion of strength for JAM.[35] Unlike the Badr Organization which has existed since the 1980s, JAM was established in the aftermath of the U.S.-led invasion and subsequent occupation. Engel explains, "Now the Mahdi Army had

---

30   Ken Silverstein, "The Minister of Civil War: Bayan Jabr, Paul Bremer, and the Rise of the Iraqi Death Squads," *Harper's Magazine*, August 2006.

31   Frontline, "Gangs of Iraq: Interviews," April 17, 2007, http://www.pbs.org/wgbh/pages/frontline/gangsofiraq/interviews/horst.html (accessed January 12, 2012).

32   Caleb Temple, "Financing of Insurgency Operations in Iraq;" Jacob Shapiro, "Bureaucratic Terrorists: Al-Qa'ida in Iraq's Management and Finances," in *Bomber, Bank Accounts, & Bleedout*, edited by Brian Fishman, 74.

33   Evan Thomas and John Barry, "A New Way of War, *Newsweek*, August 20, 2007. Robert Looney, "The Business of Insurgency: The Expansion of Iraq's Shadow Economy," *The National Interest*, Fall 2005, 2.

34   Hashim, *Insurgency and Counter-Insurgency in Iraq*, 254-5.

35   Cordesman and Ramos, "Sadr and the Mahdi Army," 16.

decided to fight Sunnis, it needed cash to keep its members loyal."[36] According to the *Telegraph*, a "field report" written by a British officer claimed JAM "used money from Iran to recruit and pay young unemployed men up to $300 a month to carry out attacks."[37]

Shiite militias also provided social services ("maintaining security, collecting taxes and dispensing justice") where the Iraqi government could not.[38] Social services may have accounted for an even greater portion of the pie in 2008 and onwards as Muqtada al-Sadr announced a reorganization of JAM on June 13, 2008 with the largest wing transitioning to a "civilian movement dealing with religious, social and cultural affairs."[39] This development in JAM's structure reminded many U.S. officials of the continued influence of Iran as it pushes the militia more in line with Lebanese Hezbollah.

Source of Funding

Economic Environmental Factors

Aspects of Iraq's civil society, the country's poor economic situation and the nation's level of crime and corruption contributed to the ease in which insurgents were able to raise, spend and move funds. Years of dictatorship and the importance of social linkages within Arabic culture affected the way the government, the insurgency and the Iraqi population interacted. Over the last 35 years the authoritarian regime created a system of norms that propagated "cronyism and parochial, sectarian, ethnic, and tribal discrimination."[40] Robert Looney described Iraq under Saddam Hussein as a "family-party state dominated by close family members and tribal associates."[41]

Corruption was entrenched and has a longstanding history in Iraqi society.[42] Amnesty International ranked Iraq as one of the three most corrupt nations in the world in 2008.[43] The Iraq Study Group estimated that corruption accounts for

36   Engel, *War Journal*, 255.

37   Sean Rayment, "Iran 'Paid Iraq Insurgents to Kill UK Soldiers,'" *Telegraph*, May 25, 2008, http://www.telegraph.co.uk/news/worldnews/middleeast/iran/2022631/Iran-'paid-Iraq-insurgents-to-kill-UK-soldiers'.html (accessed August 7, 2008).

38   Hashim, *Insurgency and Counter-Insurgency in Iraq*, 254.

39   Cordesman and Ramos, "Sadr and the Mahdi Army," 23.

40   Ahmed S. Hashim, "Saddam Husayn and Civil-Military Relations in Iraq: The Quest for Legitimacy and Power," *Middle East Journal*, 57:1 (Spring, 2003), 28-9.

41   Robert E. Looney, "The Business of Insurgency: The Expansion of Iraq's Shadow Economy," *The National Interest* (Fall, 2005), 1-6.

42   Robert E. Looney, "Impediments to Stability in Iraq: The Illusive Economic Dimension," *Middle East Review of International Relations*, 12:1 (March, 2008), 30.

43   Iraq was tied with Myanmar and Somalia was worse. Corruption Perception Index 2008, *Transparency International*, http://www.transparency.org/policy_research/surveys_indices/cpi/2008 (accessed January 13, 2012).

$5-7 billion in costs annually.[44] Corruption is found in most sectors of the Iraqi economy and government. Oil revenues accounted for 70 percent of Iraq's formal GDP but up to 22 percent was reportedly stolen annually.[45] Iraqi reconstruction programs were inundated by corruption and mismanagement and the Ministry of Interior, which managed a large portion of the Iraqi Security Forces, was reportedly infiltrated by militia and plagued by corruption.[46] Large amounts of the Ministry of Defense budget was siphoned into the pockets of influential officials and contractors.[47] The crime and corruption in Iraq gave the insurgency a relatively permissive environment in which to conduct financial operations. Not only did the crime provide background noise in which to operate but the corruption ensured there was a means to obtain almost any end.

Iraq also had a weak banking sector. Iraqis deposited little money in banks and those that did preferred to hold their money in foreign institutions.[48] Familial links also manifested themselves in the widespread nepotism and patronage that plagued Iraq.[49] Many Iraqis expected the process of patronage to continue.[50] There was a dependence on informal and familial social links which ultimately reduces the effectiveness of government oversight, regulation and institutions.

Working within this economic environment, the insurgent groups in Iraq collectively raised between $70 and $200 million per year to finance their activities, according to a classified, but leaked National Intelligence estimate from 2006.[51] Insurgent funding came from a multitude of sources, including, but not limited to: illegal activities (oil smuggling, kidnapping and ransom, counterfeiting, and extortion), legal activities, popular support through charitable donations, and state sponsorship.[52]

Illegal Activities

Oil smuggling accounted for $25-$100 million of insurgent revenue per year according to the 2006 leaked NIE report. Iraqi Oil and Finance ministers claimed

---

44   Baker and Hamilton, *The Iraq Study Group Report*, 20.

45   Baker and Hamilton, *The Iraq Study Group Report*, 20.

46   Baker and Hamilton, *The Iraq Study Group Report*, 13.

47   Hashim, *Insurgency and Counterinsurgency in Iraq*, 317.

48   Robert Looney, "Postwar Iraq's Financial System: Rebuilding from Scratch," *Middle East Policy*, 22:1 (Spring, 2005), 34-47.

49   Looney, "Impediments to Stability in Iraq," 27.

50   Hashim, *Insurgency and Counterinsurgency in Iraq*, 106, 255.

51   Burns and Semple, "U.S. Finds Insurgency Has Funds to Sustain Itself." To put this number in perspective, the Provisional IRA was thought to have an annual budget of $15 million, AQ raised about $30 million per year prior to 2001, and Hezbollah receives somewhere between $100 million and $200 million per year, around half of that coming from Iran. See Jeanne Giraldo and Harold Trinkunas, eds, *Terrorism Financing and State Responses* (Stanford, CA: Stanford University Press, 2007).

52   Burns and Semple, "U.S. Finds Insurgency Has Funds to Sustain Itself."

that 10-30 percent of the $4-5 billion in oil imports are smuggled out for resale and insurgents receive about half of those profits (approximately $200 million).[53] From the Baiji refinery alone, Iraq's largest, 70 percent of its $2 billion in fuel production went to the black market in 2007; at least one-third of its production was still being diverted to black markets in 2008.[54] At one point, al-Qaeda in Mesopotamia is estimated to have received $50,000 to $100,000 a day in smuggled profits from the Baiji refinery.[55]

Other non-oil smuggling operations provided another lucrative flow of cash for the insurgents. For example, the smuggling of antiquities provided a steady stream of money for Shiite insurgent groups. Additionally, Lebanese Hezbollah implemented an "underground tariff system" on the antiquities smuggling operations, which hints at further involvement by Shiite militias due to their suspected connections with Hezbollah.[56]

The insurgency was also loosely tied to drug smuggling. Iraq had a burgeoning narcotics trade, run by organized crime.[57] In July 2006, U.S. soldiers destroyed a marijuana farm in an area supportive of al-Qaeda in the Ninewa province and during summer 2008, U.S. Marines battled cocaine smugglers in al-Anbar.[58] Although no direct evidence links insurgent groups with drug smuggling, some degree of interaction was inevitable as they both operated in dark networks and occupied the same geographical space.

Since 2004, kidnapping and ransoms accounted for 70 percent of all reported crime and became the primary source of funds for both criminal organizations and insurgent groups.[59] They accounted for approximately $36 million dollars per year, with $30 million of that allegedly paid by the French

53 Robert Worth and James Glanz, "Oil Dollars Fund the Insurgency, Iraq and U.S. Say," *New York Times*, February 5, 2006; Burns and Semple, "U.S. Finds Insurgency Has Funds to Sustain Itself;" Richard Oppel, Jr., "Iraq's Insurgency Runs on Stolen Oil Profits," *New York Times*, March 16, 2008.
54 Oppel, "Iraq's Insurgency Runs on Stolen Oil Profits."
55 Oppel, "Iraq's Insurgency Runs on Stolen Oil Profits."
56 Elena Becatoros, "Smuggled Antiquities Funding Iraq Extremists, U.S. Says," *National Geographic News*, March 19, 2008, http://news.nationalgeographic.com/news/pf/53096116.html (accessed January 13, 2012).
57 Hashim, *Insurgency and Counterinsurgency in Iraq*, 340.
58 CPT Christopher L'Heureux commanded the U.S. unit that seized the narcotics with Iraqi Police and Kurdish Regional Government forces. "US troops, Iraqi police seize marijuana plants," *Stars and Stripes*, Mideast edition, July 8, 2006, http://www.stripes.com/news/u-s-troops-iraqi-police-seize-marijuana-plants-1.51332 (accessed January 13, 2012).
59 In January 2004 an average of 2 kidnappings occurred per day. By March 2006 this number jumped to 30 to 40 per day. Michael E. O'Hanlon and Jason H. Campbell, *Iraq Index: Tracking Variable of Reconstruction & Security in Post-Saddam Iraq*, The Brookings Institution, available at: http://www.brookings.edu/fp/saban/iraq/index.pdf; 23; Chester G. Oehme, III, "Terrorists, Insurgents, and Criminals—Growing Nexus?" *Studies in Conflict & Terrorism* 31 (2008), 85.

and Italian governments in 2005.[60] Often, kidnappers were simply criminals who ransomed the victims for economic gains. One anecdotal example occurred in October 2006:

> A U.S. platoon was approached by a distraught Kurdish woman claiming her husband was kidnapped in the Karradah district of Baghdad. After describing the assailants as members of the Shia militia group Jaish al-Mahdi (JAM), she led the U.S. soldiers to her husband's captors. In actuality, the man was held by a prostitute and what can best be described as two street thugs. The group confessed that it was only loosely affiliated with JAM; a portion of the ransom was to be paid to the Shia militia for the ability to operate within their area.[61]

This method of fundraising had a particularly destabilizing effect on the population by undermining support for the Iraqi government, which was seen as incapable of protecting its citizens.[62]

Unknown amounts were also raised by counterfeiting and theft.[63] One marine unit indicated the biggest issue within their area of responsibility came from criminal groups.[64] These groups thrived in areas with weak government and some cooperated with insurgent groups.[65] Crime was no longer the sole purview of criminals. Insurgents looking for income could easily tap into the vast sources of money derived through criminal activity.

Some reports claim that hundreds of thousands of dollars have been extorted from U.S. rebuilding funds in Anbar province alone. In some cases, insurgents demanded contractors and transporters pay up to 50 percent of the value of their contract in return for their safety, and often just take the goods themselves.[66] In Mosul, insurgents extorted "5 to 20 percent of the value of contracts local businessmen get from the government" in 2008.[67] The absence of government-provided security and services proved to be an especially great enabler for Shiite militias. Early on, the militias successfully filled the security vacuum and protected Shia populations from Sunni terrorists. Later, the militias exploited and threatened the same populations they were defending. Reporting for *The*

---

60 Burns and Semple, "U.S. Finds Insurgency Has Funds to Sustain Itself."

61 CPT Christopher L'Heureux commanded the unit that detained the kidnappers.

62 Looney, "The Business of Insurgency," 4.

63 Caleb Temple, "Financing of Insurgency Operations in Iraq."

64 Rear Admiral Patrick Driscoll, "Department of Defense Bloggers Roundtable Teleconference," July 31, 2008, http://www.defenselink.mil/DODCMSShare/BloggerAssets/2008-09/09110812495020080911_RearAdmDriscoll_transcript.pdf (accessed November 30, 2008).

65 Baker and Hamilton, *The Iraq Study Group Report*, 11.

66 Hannah Allam, "Insurgents extort U.S. aid, Iraqis say," *Columbus Dispatch*, August 8, 2007.

67 Oppel, "Iraq's Insurgency Runs on Stolen Oil Profits."

New York Times, Sabrina Tavernise described JAM's stranglehold on numerous cities across Iraq, including major portions of Baghdad:

> At the peak of the militia's control last summer, it was involved at all levels of the local economy, taking money from gas stations, private minibus services, electric switching stations, food and clothing markets, ice factories, and even collecting rent from squatters in houses whose owners had been displaced. The four main gas stations in Sadr City were handing over a total of about $13,000 a day, according to a member of the local council.[68]

Assuming the dollar amount provided by the local council member is accurate and this activity occurred on a daily basis, JAM was collecting over $4.7 million per year from its extortion of just four gas stations in Baghdad.

Legal Activities

Legal transactions also provided a source of insurgent financing. According to interviews with Iraqi officials, there are reports of insurgent groups financing their activities by simply selling off the assets of members. In one incident, an insurgent financier raised cash for an operation by selling off some furniture. There are also examples of insurgents using trade to move funds into and around the country. Instead of trying to smuggle cash, which is still the norm, groups can buy and ship merchandise and resell it at another location. Iraqi officials noted that they witnessed insurgent-affiliated businessmen selling cars and shirts to raise cash in a particular region or neighborhood.[69]

Popular Support

Charities have also provided funding to the insurgents. According to Caleb Temple, mosques in Iraq itself, but also in Iran and the Gulf states collected funds for the insurgents. Sometimes the imams were "openly sympathetic" to the insurgents, while in other cases the insurgents paid the imams to allow them to raise money in their mosques.[70] According to official counts, however, very few charities or NGOs supported the insurgency. The interagency report found that only 10-15 of the 4,000 NGOS in Iraq supported the insurgents.[71] The extent of this foreign support is debated, however. A U.S. defense official claimed in 2004 that money was raised in Saudi Arabia, funneled through charities, and

---

68   Sabrina Tavernise, "A Shiite Militia in Baghdad Sees Its Power Wane," *The New York Times*, July 27, 2008.

69   Personal interviews by Michael Freeman, Baghdad, March 2008.

70   Caleb Temple, "Financing of Insurgency Operations in Iraq."

71   Burns and Semple, "U.S. Finds Insurgency Has Funds to Sustain Itself."

then passed through Syria into Iraq.[72] Anthony Cordesman disputed these claims, noting that very little evidence has been produced to support them.[73]

State Support

There are some allegations that outside states were also providing support to insurgents.[74] In particular, Iran was believed to be providing money, training, and supplies to the main Shia insurgent groups, the Mahdi Army (Jaish al-Mahdi or JAM) led by Moqtada al-Sadr.[75] In March 2006, U.S. Secretary of State Condoleezza Rice said, "Iran has been the country that has been in many ways a kind of central banker for terrorism in important regions like Lebanon through Hezbollah in the Middle East, in the Palestinian Territories, and we have deep concerns about what Iran is doing in the south of Iraq."[76] According to Mark Kukis of *Time* magazine, few doubted Iran was providing support to JAM and the Badr Organization.[77] While U.S. government officials have often detailed the training and weapons support Iran provided Iraqi militias, specifics regarding the financial assistance supplied to the militias from Iran are extremely rare. On September 28, 2006, CNN reported, "A Shiite Muslim militia ... has received 'millions of dollars' and an assortment of weaponry from Iran, a senior U.S. military official says."[78] Nearly a year later on July 2, 2007, Brigadier General Kevin Begner provided even more insight when he told reporters Iran is funneling up to $3 million per month to militias in Iraq.[79] According to a classified report leaked to the *New York Times*, "Iran's Islamic Revolutionary Corp-Quds Force is providing professionally-built EFPs (explosively formed penetrators [or projectiles]) and components to Iraqi Shia militants."[80] In addition to EFPs, Cochrane notes the "Special Groups" of JAM used "advanced weapons provided by Iran, including

---

72 John Lumpkin, "Insurgents infiltrating Iraq have cash," *USA Today*, October 21, 2004.

73 Lumpkin, "Insurgents infiltrating Iraq have cash."

74 International Crisis Group, "Iran in Iraq: How Much Influence?" March 21, 2005 is generally skeptical of these claims.

75 *Jane's Intelligence* entry for JAM notes that a London-based newspaper claimed Iran sent $80 million to the Sadr-led organization. For more on JAM and al-Sadr see the International Crisis Group's reports, "Iraq's Muqtada al-Sadr: Spoiler or Stabiliser?" July 11, 2006 and "Iraq's Civil War, the Sadrists and the Surge" February 7, 2008.

76 Greg Bruno, "State Sponsors: Iran," *Council on Foreign Relations*, October 7, 2010, http://www.cfr.org/publication/9362/ state_sponsors.html (accessed January 13, 2012).

77 Mark Kukis, "Is Iran Aiding Iraq's Militias?" *Time*, August 15, 2007.

78 *CNN.com*, "Military Official: Iranian Millions Funding Insurgency," September 28, 2006, http://www.cnn.com/2006/WORLD/meast/09/28/iraq.iran/index.html (accessed January 12, 2012).

79 Kenneth Katzman, "Iran's Activities and Influence in Iraq," Congressional Research Service, January 24, 2008, 3.

80 Quoted in Michael Gordon, "Deadliest Bomb in Iraq is made in Iran, U.S. Says," *New York Times*, February 10, 2007.

light and heavy mortars, 107-mm rockets, and 240-mm rockets."[81] Cordesman and Ramos annotated the existence of "a growing concern of weapon technology being transferred from Iran to Shi'a militias."[82] American officials have also claimed that Iranian-sponsored Hezbollah trained 1,000-2,000 fighters from the Mahdi Army and other groups in Lebanon.[83] In General Petraeus's report to Congress, this Hezbollah unit was identified as Department 2800 and worked closely with the Quds Force to train Shia militants.[84]

Although Saudi officials denied that their country was a financial source of support, there is evidence that $25 million went to one top Iraqi Sunni cleric to purchase a Strela Russian AA missile. On November 27, 2006 an American F-16 crashed while flying in support of operations in Anbar province; there are claims that a Strela AA missile was responsible.[85] Also, the Associated Press interviewed several drivers describing how truck drivers delivered boxes of cash to Iraqi addresses and bus drivers witnessed cash movement during pilgrimage activities, a convenient and effective cover for illicit transfers from Iran into Iraq.[86]

Movement

Both Sunni and Shia groups moved funds into Iraq from neighboring countries. For the Sunnis, the Sinjar records, captured in the eponymous town in the northwest of Iraq between spring 2006 and summer 2007, contained information on the foreign fighters' personal background, group affiliation, travel to Syria, and intended role in Iraq, and were released by the West Point Combating Terrorism Center (CTC) in a paper titled *Bombers, Bank Accounts and Bleedout: Al-Qa'ida's Road in and out of Iraq*.[87] While some records had considerably more detail than others did, these records detailed the operations of the Syrian ratlines through personal records of foreign fighters crossing into Iraq, AQI contracts for suicide bombers, fighters leaving Iraq, plus financial records with narratives written by smugglers.

The CTC's analysis provides an interesting view inside the sources and movement of threat financing in the Sunni insurgency. First, the ratlines into Iraq were a Sunni resistance lifeline supplying a steady and dependable source of people and money. Second, there was a tremendous amount of Saudi nationals and Saudi money involved. Additionally the Saudi involvement was highly desirable. Third,

---

81   Marisa Cochrane, *Iraq Report: Summer, 2007-Summer, 2008 Special Groups Regenerate*, The Institute for the Study of War, August 29, 2008, 4.

82   Cordesman and Ramos, "Sadr and the Mahdi Army," 16.

83   Michael Gordon and Dexter Filkins, "Hezbollah Said to Help Shiite Army in Iraq," *New York Times*, November 28, 2006.

84   "Rise of a Secret Unit," *Newsweek*, October 1, 2007.

85   "Rise of a Secret Unit," *Newsweek*.

86   "Rise of a Secret Unit," *Newsweek*.

87   Fishman, ed., *Bomber, Bank Accounts, & Bleedout*.

radical jihadis viewed Iraq as a favorable place to fight and commit martyrdom, and AQI marketed it as such.

Similarly, the movement of weapons from Iran to Shiite militias operates on a well-established smuggling network through central and southern Iraq. Bill Roggio of *The Long War Journal* details the "ratlines" utilized by the Iranian Ramazan Corps to supply Iraqi militias with explosively formed penetrators (EFPs).[88] According to Marisa Cochrane of the Institute for the Study of War, EFPs were "the hallmark weapon of Special Groups," militia cells that receive funding, training, and weapons from Iran.[89] It is not too large of a leap to believe cash, as well as people, can move along these "ratlines" as easily as EFPs and other weapons.

Countermeasures

How vulnerable, in general, are insurgent finances to disruption? What countermeasures can be implemented to exploit their vulnerabilities? One element of the insurgent financing that may be vulnerable is their increasing reliance on criminal activity and extortion as sources of funds, which are often unpopular among the insurgents own constituency.[90] For example, Zarqawi's operations alienated the Sunni tribes of al-Anbar, which led to the 'Sunni Awakening.'[91] As the tribes began to support the Iraqi government, they began to resist forced taxation and ceased donating money to the insurgency. A captured *communiqué* believed to be from Zarqawi cited a lack of funds as a cause of his lower operational tempo.[92] As the external sources of funding became increasingly scarce, the insurgency had to devote progressively more time and resources to local fundraising to maintain their organizations.[93] This led insurgents to form closer ties with criminal organizations, which was also unpopular.[94] To exploit this vulnerability, information operations might have been able to highlight the

---

88 Bill Roggio, "Iran's Ramazan Corps and the Ratlines into Iraq," *The Long War Journal*, December 5, 2007, http://www.longwarjournal.org/archives/2007/12/irans_ ramazan_corps.php (accessed January 12, 2012).

89 Cochrane, "Iraq Report," 4.

90 "Al-Qaeda Turns More to Extortion, Abductions to Fund Fight, U.S. Says," San Diego Union-Tribune notes that AQI's "funding scheme could drive an even deeper wedge between the terrorist organization and the Iraqi tribes."

91 "Al-Qaeda Turns More to Extortion, Abductions to Fund Fight, U.S. Says," San Diego Union-Tribune, 182.

92 "Al-Qaeda Turns More to Extortion, Abductions to Fund Fight, U.S. Says," San Diego Union-Tribune, 188.

93 Steven Metz and Raymond Millen, "Insurgency in Iraq and Afghanistan: Change and Continuity," Strategic Studies Institute, http://www.dni.gov/nic/PDF_GIF_2020_ Support/2004_05_25_papers/insurgency.pdf, 4.

94 Burns and Semple, "US Finds Iraq Insurgency Has Funds to Sustain Itself."

criminal or extortive nature of the insurgency to highlight how these activities should be seen as illegitimate and so separate the insurgents from some of their popular support. For example, information operations could have publicized that many insurgent leaders were corrupt and used organizational resources for their own benefit.[95] Also, because extortion, kidnapping and ransom, smuggling, and drug dealing were all predatory behaviors that were generally unpopular, the ties to criminal activity and/or organized crime groups will erode the legitimacy of the insurgent group among its supporters. In fact, this occurred as AQI's "coercive fundraising backfired" in Sinjar.[96] AQI was aware of its image problem and issued its own announcement disavowing these types of activities and those who engaged in them.[97] In sum, terrorists do not want to be seen as criminals and criminals do not want to be seen as terrorists—and this dynamic can be better exploited by the state.

Insurgent finances can also be curtailed by improving the overall level of security and governance in Iraq. As governance spreads and becomes more pervasive, the conditions that enable criminal activity of any kind will be reduced and the larger black market economy will shrink.[98] For example, *The New York Times* recently reported, "The Mahdi Army's decline also means that the Iraqi state, all but impotent in the early years of the war, has begun to act the part, taking over delivery of some services and control of some neighborhoods."[99] Increasing the capacity of the Iraqi government will be a key element to halting insurgent operations conducted by militias. Improving security may not be explicitly intended to curb insurgent funding; nevertheless, as general security increases, smuggling, extortion, kidnapping, and other criminal activities can be diminished.[100]

Overcoming the entrenched corruption and unregulated economy is also necessary and will require patience and persistence in many counterinsurgencies.[101] In Iraq, rampant unemployment, subsidies, and the high cost of imported goods contributed to this unregulated and unseen economy that accounted for as much as 65 percent of Iraq's GDP.[102] This equated to approximately $66 billion in 2007.[103] The black market provided insurgent groups with the means to obtain supplies without government interference and potentially a large revenue stream.

---

95   Shapiro, "Bureaucratic Terrorists," 70.
96   Shapiro, "Bureaucratic Terrorists," 70.
97   Shapiro, "Bureaucratic Terrorists," 72.
98   See Looney, "The Business of Insurgency."
99   Tavernise, "A Shiite Militia in Baghdad Sees Its Power Wane."
100   "Al-Qaeda Turns More to Extortion, Abductions to Fund Fight, U.S. Says," San Diego Union-Tribune, notes that as Iraq becomes wealthier and more stable, Iraq will have wealthier citizens that would make more lucrative targets for extortion and kidnapping.
101   Transparency International, *Annual Report 2007*, June 2008, 27.
102   Looney, "Impediments to Stability in Iraq: The Illusive Economic Dimension," 28.
103   According to the CIA the GDP (purchasing power parity) was estimated at $102.4 billion in 2007. The World Fact Book, "Iraq—Economy," *Central Intelligence Agency*, https://

Both the abundance of cash and the shadow economy afforded the insurgency tools that facilitated financing.

Improving the economic conditions (mitigating unemployment, a lack of electricity and other fuels, and a weak banking system) in the poor neighborhoods of Baghdad and other Iraqi cities may help undercut support for groups like JAM, which recruit from these neighborhoods.[104] As Robert Looney writes, "We neglect the economic roots of the Iraqi insurgency at our peril."[105] Reviving the Iraqi economy is one of the coalition's primary goals in Iraq but the task is enormous and progress is slow. One former advisor to Paul Bremmer said, "They don't have a reliable, robust banking system over there. It's still a cash economy."[106] As of summer 2008, it was still common for businessmen and contractors to fly into Iraq with large amounts of cash.[107] Although the United States has begun to use electronic funds transfers for amounts in excess of $50,000, the majority of all transactions in the country are still cash-based.[108] The country is awash in cash, making it easy to move, hide and extort large amounts of money without arousing suspicion. The weak formal banking system and the large amount of cash in circulation encourage the use of the relatively untraceable *hawala* system for moving money.[109]

The external sponsorship of the insurgent groups provides its own set of challenges. Nevertheless, there have been some successes; General David Petraeus somewhat effectively applied an 'anaconda strategy' that choked off the majority of resources arriving from neighboring countries.[110] This affected the insurgency as a whole, including the Shia militias that were not pitted against the coalition. By restricting external financial sources and continuing to target fiscal assets, the insurgency was forced to turn more inward to fund its operations.[111] To go even further in eroding this source of funding would require

---

www.cia.gov/library/publications/the-world-factbook/geos/iz.html (accessed November 30, 2008).

104 Hashim, *Insurgency and Counter-Insurgency in Iraq*, 255.

105 Looney, "The Business of Insurgency," 6.

106 Brian Beutler, "Ambassador Crocker's Kooky Economics," The Media Consortium, September 14, 2007, http://www.themediaconsortium.com/reporting/2007/09/14/ambassador-crockers-kooky-economics/ (accessed January 13, 2012).

107 "Iraqi Banking Sector Shows Signs of Health," *The New York Times*, July 23, 2008.

108 "Iraqi Banking Sector Shows Signs of Health," *The New York Times*.

109 Robert E. Looney, "Preventing Terrorist Finance in Iraq" (briefing, Naval Postgraduate School, Washington, D.C., April 5, 2005).

110 Rear Admiral Patrick Driscoll, "Department of Defense Bloggers Roundtable Teleconference," July 31, 2008, http://www.defenselink.mil/DODCMSShare/BloggerAssets/2008-09/091108124950200809l1_RearAdmDriscoll _transcript.pdf.

111 Robert C. Martinage, "The Global War on Terrorism: An Assessment," The Center of Strategic and Budgetary Assessment, 2008, available at: http://www.csbaonline.org/wp-content/uploads/2011/02/2008.02.23-The-Global-War-on-Terrorism.pdf, 189.

persuading, compelling, or deterring Iran from changing its support for Shia militants will require the full range of diplomatic, military, economic, legal, and financial tools within the U.S. arsenal. Moreover, the issue of insurgent financing is just one issue that must be appropriately prioritized within the U.S.–Iranian relationship. It may need to take a back seat to negotiations over Iranian political support for the government of Iraq, Iranian involvement in Afghanistan, Iranian–Israeli relations, and Iranian support for Hezbollah, for instance. Countering the support for insurgents coming from Saudi and gulf state private citizens and charities has also been problematic. This issue has been an ongoing source of tension between the United States and Saudi Arabia, not just related to Iraq, but to the larger effort in the global war on terrorism.[112] While Saudi officials claimed that they are taking measures to curb the finances coming out of the Kingdom, it remains an issue.[113]

Conclusion

For any type of financing countermeasure, there are several confounding issues. First is the issue of capacity and resources. The classified interagency report "paints an almost despairing picture of the Iraqi government's ability, or willingness, to take steps to tamp down the insurgency's financing."[114] Without the resources that improve Iraqi capabilities and with continued corruption that makes leaders unwilling to target insurgent financing, little will be accomplished.[115] Second, even with the capabilities and will, the insurgents have an inherent advantage because of the nature of the insurgency, which is "opaque and complex."[116] The insurgents were and are secretive, making any assessment of where they get their financing or how they move and spend their resources difficult. Critics of the interagency report note that U.S. officials are "just guessing ... they really have no idea [because] they've been very unsuccessful in penetrating these organizations."[117] In addition, insurgents financed their operations from diverse sources, they were highly adaptive to pressures and constraints, and proved regenerative after seeming coalition successes.[118] All of

112   Alfred B. Prados and Christopher M. Blanchard, "Saudi Arabia: Terrorist Financing Issues" Congressional Research Service, March 1, 2005.

113   "Initiatives and Actions Taken by the Kingdom of Saudi Arabia to Combat Terrorism," September 2003, http://www.saudiembassy.net/archive/2003/news/page141. aspx (accessed January 13, 2012).

114   John Burns and Kirk Semple, "U.S. Finds Insurgency Has Funds to Sustain Itself."

115   Looney, "The Business of Insurgency," 2, points out that Iraq is the most corrupt country in the Middle East and 129th out of 145 countries globally.

116   Burns and Semple, "U.S. Finds Insurgency Has Funds to Sustain Itself."

117   W. Patrick Lang, quoted in Burns and Semple, "U.S. Finds Insurgency Has Funds to Sustain Itself."

118   Caleb Temple, "Financing of Insurgency Operations in Iraq."

this points to the conclusion that efforts to counter insurgent financing may have only limited or marginal effects and that addressing the funding, by itself, will be unlikely to defeat the insurgents.

Chapter 4

Hezbollah: The Organization
and its Finances

Doug Philippone

While most of the world's attention has been focused on al-Qaeda and its many affiliated forms, one terrorist organization of global reach that deserves special emphasis is Hezbollah. CIA director George Tenet, the Director of the Central Intelligence Agency, testified in 2003 that "Hezbollah, as an organization with capability and worldwide presence, is [al-Qaeda's] equal, if not a far more capable organization. I actually think they're a notch above in many respects."[1] Deputy Secretary of State Richard Armitage echoed that opinion by stating, "Hezbollah may be the A team of terrorists," while "al-Qaeda is actually the B team."[2] Armitage followed those words with a statement that most Americans may have forgotten, "they [Hezbollah] have a blood debt to us and ... we're not going to forget it."[3] To be specific, Hezbollah was responsible for more American deaths than any other terrorist organization prior to the 9/11 attacks.

In order to counter Hezbollah, its history, organizational structure, alliances, and goals must be understood. One of the many techniques being employed to counter terrorist networks is the targeting of financial support for terrorists. The theory is that if financial and material support for a network can be disrupted, the network will be unable or less able to operate. Hezbollah understands this concept very well and to ensure its continued existence, it has become one of the most diversified and well-funded of all terrorist networks in the world. Hezbollah currently receives funding from state sponsorship, individual remittances, crime networks, and drug profits. Why does Hezbollah need such a vast network of funding and what do they use the money for? A quick look at the organization will help us understand the organization and how to ultimately change their behavior or defeat them altogether.

---

1 U.S. Senate Committee on Armed Services, "Current and Future Worldwide Threats to the National Security of the United States," February 12, 2003.

2 Daniel Byman, "Should Hezbollah Be Next?" *Foreign Affairs*, November/December 2003.

3 Byman, "Should Hezbollah Be Next?"

Background

Hezbollah was founded in 1982 during the Lebanese Civil War (1975-1990).The Palestinian Liberation Organization (PLO) took advantage of the chaos from the civil war and used southern Lebanon as a staging ground for attacks on Israel. Israel invaded southern Lebanon to defeat the PLO and eliminate its safe haven. In response to Israel's occupation of southern Lebanon, a militia of Shia followers of the Ayatollah Khomeini, which were backed and trained by Iran, came together to form Hezbollah. Their initial goals were to install an Islamic government and drive Israel out of southern Lebanon.[4]

Over time, Hezbollah proved its lethality in multiple terrorist attacks against the United States and other Western powers. Hezbollah is responsible for the 1983 Beirut Marine barracks bombing in which 241 American servicemen were killed and 60 Americans were injured and the bombing of the U.S. embassy in Lebanon in 1983 and 1984. In 1985 three members of Hezbollah hijacked TWA flight 847 and killed a Navy diver on board. Throughout the 1980s Hezbollah conducted multiple kidnappings of westerners, including Terry Anderson, William Buckley and Richard Higgins. In these cases the captive was either killed or held for ransom.[5]

With its regional influence on the rise in the late 1980s, Hezbollah sought to export its successful terror network across the globe. In 1989, Spanish authorities arrested ten members of Hezbollah as they attempted to smuggle 18 pounds of plastic explosives into Valencia, Spain. The Hezbollah operatives were thought to be planning to attack U.S. and other western targets within Western Europe. During that same year, a bombing of UTA (French airline Union des Transports Aériens) flight 772 in West Africa killed 171 people.[6] French intelligence authorities believed "cells of pro-Iranian Shiite extremists played "a prominent role" in the bombing."[7] In 1992 and 1994, Hezbollah conducted operations in South America with the bombings of the Israeli Embassy and a community center in Argentina, respectively. Since 2000, Hezbollah has been a sponsor of suicide bombings of civilian targets throughout Israel. For example, according to Daniel Byman, "Hezbollah has provided guerrilla training, bomb-building expertise, propaganda, and tactical tips to Hamas, Palestinian Islamic Jihad, and other anti-Israeli groups. There are also reports that Hezbollah is trying to establish its own Palestinian proxy, the Return Brigades."[8] During its 2006

---

4   Augustus Richard Norton, *Hezbollah* (Princeton, NJ: Princeton University Press, 2007).

5   Norton, *Hezbollah*.

6   Robin Wright, "Hezbollah Seen Setting Up Terror Network in Africa," *The Los Angeles Times*, November 27, 1989, A1.

7   Wright, "Hezbollah Seen Setting Up Terror Network in Africa," A1.

8   Byman, "Should Hezbollah Be Next?"

war with Israel, Hezbollah was accused of war crimes against civilians. Human Rights Watch declared:

> Hezbollah forces in Lebanon fired thousands of rockets into Israel, causing civilian casualties and damage to civilian structures. Hezbollah's means of attack relied on unguided weapons that had no capacity to hit military targets with any precision. It repeatedly bombarded cities, towns, and villages without any apparent effort to distinguish between civilians and military objectives. In doing so, Hezbollah, as a party to an armed conflict governed by international humanitarian law, violated fundamental prohibitions against deliberate and indiscriminate attacks against civilians.[9]

Organizational and Financial Needs

Hezbollah's current goals include: the removal of Israeli influence within Lebanon (although this goal has essentially been realized with the 2000 withdrawal of Israeli occupation forces, except for the issue of Shebaa Farms), and Shia empowerment within Lebanon. The organization has morphed from a simple militia to a fully-fledged semi-state with a political wing, social welfare organization, military organization and a modern media outlet. This transformation is the result of hundreds of millions of dollars of financing, such that Hezbollah is now a direct competitor to the established Lebanese government in many areas of Lebanon. In a classic example of the problems created by ungoverned areas or weak nation-states, Hezbollah initiated the 2006 war with Israel from inside Lebanese borders. After the massive Israeli retaliation, National Public Radio reported "Hezbollah has promised to provide housing and furniture for the next year to each of the tens of thousands of families whose homes were destroyed by the month-long Israeli bombing campaign. Hezbollah spokesmen say the funding will come from foreign donors, including Iran, and it will be disbursed directly, not through the Lebanese government."[10]

The ability to filter and distribute international funding within Lebanese borders causes a significant challenge to the authority of the Lebanese government. The fact that Hezbollah actually holds seats in the Lebanese Parliament makes this relationship even more problematic because it provides Hezbollah with significant international legitimacy. To further Hezbollah's influence in the region, it funds and operates 50 hospitals throughout Lebanon. One hospital, the Al Janoub

---

9   Human Rights Watch, "Civilians under Assault: Hezbollah's Rocket Attacks on Israel in the 2006 War," August 2007, http://hrw.org/reports/2007/iopt0807/2.htm (accessed January 13, 2012).

10   National Public Radio, "Hezbollah Takes the Lead in Rebuilding Lebanon," August 17, 2006, http://www.npr.org/templates/transcript/transcript.php?storyId=5662485 (accessed January 13, 2012).

hospital receives $100,000 per month from Hezbollah.[11] While these social welfare programs are obviously expensive, they provide Hezbollah with support from the local population and act as a showpiece for propaganda messages distributed through their media machine. In early 1991, Iran donated one million dollars to Hezbollah to start al-Manar Television. This television channel has become the voice of Hezbollah and now operates on an estimated budget of $15-50 million a year and reaches approximately 200 million people across the world.[12]

The complexity of Hezbollah's organization has enabled the military wing to flourish. The Washington Post called Hezbollah "the best guerrilla force in the world."[13] The military wing of Hezbollah possesses modern unmanned aerial vehicles, anti-tank, anti-aircraft and ultra modern anti-ship missiles.[14] Hezbollah's military wing is first rate by any standard and uses a significant portion of its budget to stockpile all types of missiles and rockets for use against Israel. Hezbollah used approximately $50 million to establish military training camps for multiple terrorist organizations, including al-Qaeda, in the Baka'a valley.[15] Hezbollah continues to operate the camps to this day.

State Sponsorship

Hezbollah receives state funding in arms, training and money from both Syria and Iran, with the largest monetary contributions coming from Iran. Most large expenditures, including the founding of training camps in the Baka'a valley and the start up of al-Manar TV, come from Iranian seed money. In some situations, Iran may have a vested interest in increased activity or instability. During these periods, Iran has been noted to make lump sum payments of as much as $22 million to disrupt peace talks or foment instability within Israel and Palestine.[16] Hezbollah would then source out the money to groups for action. According to

11   Scott Wilson, "Lebanese Wary of a Rising Hezbollah," *The Washington Post*, December 20, 2004.

12   Steven Stalinsky, "Terrorist TV: Hezbollah's Al-Manar TV Should be shut down," *National Review*, April 4, 2006, http://www.nationalreview.com/articles/217228/terrorist-tv/steven-stalinsky (accessed January 13, 2012).

13   Edward Cody and Molly Moore, "The Best Guerrilla Force in the World," *The Washington Post*, August 14, 2006.

14   Dan Darling, "Hezbollah's Arsenal: It's more lethal than everyone thought," *The Weekly Standard*, July 21, 2006, 11:43.

15   *The 9/11 Commission Report: Final Report of the National Commission on Terrorist Attacks Upon the United States*, 61.

16   "Iran Expands Its Palestinian Control; Offers al-Khadoumi Five Million Dollars," *Al-Watan* (Kuwait), December 13, 2004, quoted in House Committee on International Relations, Subcommittee on the Middle East and Central Asia, Subcommittee on International Terrorism and Nonproliferation, *Iranian State Sponsorship of Terror: Threatening U.S. Security, Global Stability, and Regional Peace.*

Palestinian officials, they had "intercepted e-mail communications and bank transactions indicating that Hezbollah has increased its payments to terrorists. 'Now they are willing to pay $100,000 for a whole operation, whereas in the past they paid $20,000, then raised it to $50,000'."[17]

In addition to monetary support from Iran and Syria, Hezbollah also receives significant arms shipments and training on new weapon systems from both countries. These shipments include thousands of short range rocket systems and ballistic missiles. Syria built and transferred the 220mm rockets used in the deadly attack on Haifa in 2006.[18] Syria also supplies RPG-29s, Kornet-E, Sagger2 and Metis-M anti tank missiles for Hezbollah to use in volley fire against Israel's top of the line main battle tank, the Merkava III. Hezbollah was able to disable several of these key Israeli vehicles as a result of this important state support; without it, Hezbollah would be at a serious disadvantage.[19] Hezbollah also received a very sophisticated C-802 anti-ship cruise missile along with an Iranian training team. This system is an Iranian version of the Chinese Silkworm missile and with assistance from Iran; Hezbollah successfully attacked an Israeli warship.[20] Hezbollah also took delivery of up to 12 unmanned aerial vehicles (UAV) and began to fly them over Israel in late 2004.[21] While Syria does not offer the monetary support that Iran does, it provides a transfer point for all Iranian arms shipment into the country and facilitates the logistical and technological support for the organization.

Countering state sponsorship will require a consensus of nations to stop Iran and Syria from meddling in the affairs of Lebanon and to halt their proxy war against Israel. One of the largest obstacles to accomplish this is the designation of Hezbollah as an international terrorist organization. Currently only four nations consider Hezbollah a terrorist organization and two other nations consider only the military wing terrorists.[22] As long as most of the international community continues to recognize Hezbollah as a legitimate organization, it will be hard to stop Iran and Syria from supporting it.

Ultimately, the international community must move to support the Lebanese government and fill the ungoverned southern areas with a strong Lebanese or

---

17   U.S. Congress, Committee on International Relations, "Iran: A Quarter Century of State Sponsored Terror," February 16, 2005, 14.

18   The   Israel   Project,   http://www.theisraelproject.org/site/c.hsJPK0PIJpH/ b.2904001/k.ED3B/An_Inside_Look_at_Hezbollahs_Iranian_and_SyrianSponsored_ Arsenal.htm (accessed January 13, 2012).

19   Cody and Moore, "The Best Guerrilla Force in the World."

20   Mark Mazzetti and Thom Shanker, "Arming of Hezbollah Reveals U.S. and Israeli Blind Spots," *The New York Times*, July 19, 2006.

21   Jim Kouri, "Hezbollah's UAVs concern Israel and United States security experts," Renew America, September 5, 2006, http://www.renewamerica.us/columns/kouri/060905 (accessed January 13, 2012).

22   The United States, Canada, Israel, and the Netherlands designate the entire organization as a terrorist group. Australia and the United Kingdom only designate the military wing.

international rule of law and government. Hezbollah flourishes in southern Lebanon because it provides crucial services to the people. If the international community can support the Lebanese government to provide these same services, Hezbollah's benefits will be diminished and their cost to the people will be amplified. Of course, this will not be easy.

Individual Remittances

Each one of Hezbollah's funding streams has its benefits, but also constraints. While state sponsorship is Hezbollah's largest single source of funding at an estimated $200 million,[23] Hezbollah leaves itself accountable to the wishes of the donor state. If a state sponsor, in this case Iran, does not agree with Hezbollah's tactics, the state may withhold sponsorship or, on the flip side, the state sponsor may instruct Hezbollah to operate in a manner that does not suit Hezbollah's internal goals. As a result, Hezbollah has diversified to reduce these constraints.

Since the time of the Phoenicians, Lebanese society has been one of movement and migration. Years of civil war and fighting between Hezbollah and Israel has led to a further wave of migration to North and South America, Africa, other Gulf States and Europe. Some estimates claim as much as 80 percent of all Lebanese people live outside Lebanon.[24] As these large groups of Lebanese citizens settle across the world, many of them send money home to support their families or other organizations within Lebanon, including Hezbollah. According to Nassib Ghobril, the head of research and analysis for a large bank in Beirut, "these migrants supply Lebanon with about $1,400 per capita every year," one of the highest rates of remittances in the world.[25]

Getting a piece of this large inflow of money is very important to Hezbollah. Al-Manar TV and other propaganda efforts are key tools used by Hezbollah to spread its message and entice people to donate money to the cause. In a case from North Carolina, Lebanese migrants were using Hezbollah-produced videos to gather support from the local Arab community to donate money to Hezbollah. The group would meet every week for "prayer meetings," watch al-Manar produced videos, read letters from Hezbollah leaders and solicit donations of support to send back to Hezbollah in Lebanon.[26]

---

23   Wilson, "Lebanese Wary of a Rising Hezbollah." Global Security and Anthony Cordesman believe they are exaggerated and put the number lower, in the $25-$50 million range.

24   Impressions Staff, "Lebanese Diaspora," *Impressions*, 2007, http://impressions-ba.com/features.php?id_feature=10280 (site discontinued).

25   Robert F. Worth, "Home on Holiday, the Lebanese Say, What Turmoil?" *The New York Times*, December 24, 2007.

26   Rachel Ehrenfeld, "Funding the Party of God," *Journal of International Security Affairs*, 6, Winter 2004, 46.

Hezbollah also receives individual donations from the Tri-Border Area (TBA) in South America. This area is the shared border of Paraguay, Brazil and Argentina and is the home of a very large Lebanese and Arab population. In one case, the National Police of Paraguay seized paperwork indicating more than $700,000 had been transferred from the TBA to Lebanon.[27] This case mirrors the North Carolina example. They both employ solicitation of Lebanese expatriates by a Hezbollah linked patron, in the TBA case Ali Khalil Mehri, by using propaganda tapes and videos produced by al-Manar TV.

This technique of soliciting ex-patriots is also used in West Africa. Two public cases indicate the massive scope of West African support for Hezbollah: an intercept of $1.7 million dollars in donations from Senegal and the unfortunate crash of an airliner carrying over $2 million in donations bound for Beirut. These two incidents, in 1998 and 2003 respectively, support claims by Israeli intelligence that Hezbollah raises several hundred thousand dollars every year from this part of the country.[28] According to Arab news articles uncovered by Hezbollah expert Matthew Levitt, the crash of UTA flight 141 killed a "foreign relations official of the African branch of the Lebanese Hezbollah party and two of his aides,"[29] as well as destroying the $2 million in cash. The Lebanese communities in West Africa control much of the successful business and commerce in the area and provide a critical support node for Hezbollah's operations. It is estimated that as many as 300,000 Lebanese immigrants live across West Africa and they are viewed as the wealthiest social group in the area because of their domination of the import-export businesses along the coast.[30] Maintaining this support was so important to Hezbollah that they sent envoys to the region to console the survivors and the families of victims while doing as much damage control as possible.[31]

While much of the individual support for Hezbollah is donated directly to the organization through couriers or liaisons, a large portion of the support is funneled through charitable organizations. Charities pose a difficult problem to agencies that are involved in cutting off Hezbollah financing. Illicit financing is difficult to detect and easy to legitimize. There are hundreds of charities sending money into the region and much of the money goes to legitimate arms of Hezbollah. For example, organizations such as the Islamic Institution for Education and Teaching

27 Francesc Relea, "'Commandos' terrorists take refuge in the triple border: Dozens of Arabs buy false papers at the crossroads between Brazil, Argentina and Paraguay," *El País International*, September 11, 2001, in Spanish http://www.elpais.com/articulo/internacional/Comandos/terroristas/refugian/triple/frontera/elpepiint/20011109elpepiint_21/Tes/ (accessed January 13, 2012).

28 Matthew Levitt, "Hizbullah's African Activities Remain Undisrupted," *Washington Institute for Near East Policy*, March 2004.

29 Levitt, "Hizbullah's African Activities Remain Undisrupted."

30 "How the Lebanese conflict affects West Africa," *Jane's Islamic Affairs Analyst*, September 1, 2006.

31 Miriam Karouny, "Benin Plane Crash Deaths Rise to 111," *Reuters*, December 26, 2003.

legitimately funnel money into local schools, which then preach jihad against the West and recruit for Hezbollah.[32] According to the principal of one of the eight schools that receive money from the Institution, "we have the same aims and goals as Hezbollah."[33] The ability to intertwine social, political and military causes and still leave the ability to deny of unsavory activities gives Hezbollah an effective ability to raise money and support. Many people donate money unknowingly to charities such as the Goodwill Charitable Organization or the Lebanese Welfare Committee with no idea that the donation will either be used directly or indirectly to fund terrorism. Another difficult problem for authorities is the possibility of incorrectly shutting down a legitimate charity. If an organization can show the good deeds produced by their charity dollars and disassociate itself with terror, it is often very hard to prove a case against an illicit organization. Even if authorities can prove the case and shut down a charity, the organization may simply move its staff and structure to another area and start over with a new name.

While countering individual remittances is very difficult, several actions may be effective at slowing the donations. Using the legitimacy of Hezbollah's political wing against itself may lead to a slowdown in terror. Since Europe and several other key areas consider the political and social wings of Hezbollah legitimate organizations, they should require Hezbollah to provide detailed accountability of all funds entering the organization and indicate how those funds are dispersed to maintain that legitimate status. The United States should also raise the regulatory requirements for detailing exactly how money is transferred, provide specific accounts and names of recipients, and ensure complete accounting of the end use of the funds. The United States should also increase the criminal penalties for working in a charity that supports terror and require registration and background checks for all employees of charities that move money outside the United States and should also require more detailed and thorough accounting on wire transfers and movement of funds outside the United States. Obviously, these last few recommendations will require new database management and filter tools to be developed, more infrastructure and manpower, and may slow down the legitimate transfer of funds.

Crime Networks

One of the most extensive and profitable sources of funding for Hezbollah is their global crime network. Most estimates put Hezbollah's yearly crime profits in the hundreds of millions of dollars. In fact, according to two sources, General James T. Hill, commander of the U.S. Southern Command and Paraguayan interior minister Julio Cesar Fanego, Hezbollah generates as much as 500 million dollars a year

---

32   William Samii, "Iran: Teheran Supports Hezbollah in Lebanon," *Radio Free Europe*, November 10, 1999.
33   Samii, "Iran: Teheran Supports Hezbollah in Lebanon."

Map 4.1   Map of the Tri-Border Area

Source: The Library of Congress.

from crime and drug activity from just of the Tri-Border Area of South America.[34] While this sum seems high, multiple researchers and government agencies have documented the wide-spread crime and drug activity in the area and the extensive links in the region to Hezbollah.

The Tri-Border Area of South America is the border between three cities: Ciudad del Este (Paraguay), Puerto Iguazu (Argentina), and Foz de Iguazu (Brazil).

According to a Library of Congress research report, Ciudad del Este, the largest city in the Tri-Border Area, was generating "$12 to $13 billion in cash transactions annually, making it the third city worldwide behind Hong Kong and Miami."[35] This large flow of dollars is linked to massive money laundering from drug proceeds and crime profits, a small portion of which then makes its way back to Hezbollah accounts in Lebanon. Initial Hezbollah links in the area were detected during investigations into a well known businessman in the area, Ali Khalil Mehri. In February 2000, Paraguayan police raided his home for allegedly selling millions of dollars worth of pirated software and funneling the proceeds back to Hezbollah. During the raid, police uncovered Hezbollah propaganda videos, fund-raising forms for terrorist organizations and records of money transfers to known Hezbollah locations worth

---

34 "U.S. General: Islamic Rebels Get Cash from Latin America Gangs," *Orlando Sentinel*, March 10, 2003, A9.

35 Rex Hudson, "Terrorist and Organized Crime Groups in the Tri-Border Area (TBA) of South America," The Library of Congress, July 2003, 3.

$700,000.[36]As investigators uncovered more of the Hezbollah organization in the Tri-Border Area, Assad Ahmad Barakat emerged as the clear leader of Hezbollah's financial network in the area. According to Carlos Cálcena, Asunción's public prosecutor for drug trafficking and terrorism, "Barakat's remittances to Hezbollah are believed to have totaled up to $50 million dollars since 1995."[37] According to the U.S. Treasury, Barakat is the deputy of Hezbollah's financial director, Ali Kazan, and the primary liaison in the Tri-Border Area for Hezbollah's Secretary General Shaykh Hasan Nasrallah.[38] In addition to these claims, several personal letters from Nasrallah were seized by investigators, which specifically thanked Barakat and his tri-border network for his financial contributions.[39] The investigation and later collaborations between the United States and the tri-border nations have yielded much success against Hezbollah and Barakat, resulting in many of his subordinates now being imprisoned. However, Barakat's network was so large and profitable that Hezbollah will likely try to leverage its contacts in the area to continue to raise funds there.

In late 2004, the Unites States formalized its collaborative efforts with the tri-border nations and entered the 3+1 Group on Tri-Border Area security. This type of effort should continue and be used in other parts of the world to shut down ungoverned areas and empower local governments. This indirect approach allows the U.S. to achieve its aims without alienating foreign nations and seems to have had significant success in the Tri-Border Area. According to the 2006 Country Report on Terrorism, the 3+1 Group appears to have aided significantly in the reduction of Hezbollah's presence in the area. The largest challenges in the area are the bolstering of Paraguay's legal system and the enforcement of immigration and customs laws.[40] Both of these areas can be improved with U.S. financial support and training programs.

While South America has clearly been a hot spot for illicit financing, Hezbollah's networks have also made it into North America as well. Operation "Smoke Screen" unveiled an elaborate crime network linking a Hezbollah cell in North Carolina to operatives in Canada and back to Lebanon.[41] Thirty suspects were linked to the cell and charged with providing "currency, financial services, training, false documentation and identification, communications equipment,

36 Blanca Madani, "Hezbollah's Global Finance Network: The Triple Frontier," *Middle East Intelligence Bulletin*, 4:1, January 2002.

37 Madani, "Hezbollah's Global Finance Network."

38 U.S. Department of Treasury, "Treasury Designates Islamic Extremist, Two Companies Supporting Hizballah in Tri-Border Area," June 10, 2004, http://www.treasury.gov/press-center/press-releases/Pages/js1720.aspx (accessed January 13, 2012).

39 Marc Perelman, "U.S. Hand Seen in Paraguay's Pursuit of Terrorism Suspect," *The Jewish Daily Forward*, January 17, 2003.

40 U.S. Department of State. *Country Reports on Terrorism*, Chapter 2, 2006.

41 Tom Diaz and Barbara Newman, *Lightning out of Lebanon: Hezbollah Terrorists on American Soil* (New York: Balantine Books, 2006).

explosives and other physical assets to Hezbollah."[42] The group used a cigarette smuggling scheme to exploit the tax difference between cigarettes sold in North Carolina and Michigan. Over a year and a half period, the Hezbollah cell was able to generate an estimated $7.9 million dollars by taking advantage of the 70 cent tax difference per pack of cigarettes and driving them across state lines.[43] In addition to direct financial contributions to Hezbollah, the group used proceeds from its criminal activity to purchase night vision and global positioning devices, mine detection equipment, laser range finders and other high technology equipment not readily available to Hezbollah in Lebanon.[44] These purchases were made through an elaborate network throughout the U.S. and Canada, which ultimately ended with direct conversations between the U.S. cell and the Hezbollah military commander in Beruit, Sheik Abbas Harake.[45] Twenty-five of the 30 Hezbollah cell members were convicted, while five others are still at large. This particular case is not an anomaly; several other unrelated Hezbollah arrests have occurred in the United States in which operatives were either attempting to purchase thermal imaging gear or shipping weapons and ammunition to Lebanon.[46]

Success against Hezbollah's crime network will take significant interagency efforts and the ability of multiple organizations to share information and work together. Continuous legislative pressure will be needed to push law enforcement, intelligence and other government agencies to work together against a common enemy. Without such efforts our ability to successfully prosecute the cell members and dismantle the networks will be seriously degraded.

Conclusion

In order to counter Hezbollah, efforts need to span several dimensions. International cooperation is required to slow state sponsorship. The international community should ban Hezbollah's military wing altogether, support the legitimate Lebanese government enough to eliminate the non-governed area in southern Lebanon and closely tie sanctions to all international support to Hezbollah. Improved governance within Lebanon would also help to undermine Hezbollah's local legitimacy. A cohesive government that has a real presence in southern Lebanon would undermine the need for Hezbollah to exist as a provider of social services. With enhanced funding and training of judiciaries and security forces, particularly police and other law enforcement agencies in places like the TBA and Western

---

42   *United States v. Mohamad Youssef Hammoud et al.*, case no. 00-CR-147, March 28, 2001.

43   Rachel Ehrenfeld, Funding *Evil* (Chicago, IL: Bonus Books, 2005), 138.

44   Matthew Levitt, "Banning Hibzallah Activity in Canada," January 6, 2003, http://www.washingtoninstitute.org/templateC05.php?CID=1576 (accessed January 13, 2012).

45   Ehrenfeld, *Funding Evil*, 138.

46   Levitt, "Banning Hibzallah Activity in Canada."

Africa, Hezbollah's crime networks could be better targeted. Better interagency relationships and information sharing within the United States might reduce the bureaucratic issues that could interfere with the U.S. ability to track and disrupt networks operating within U.S. borders. Ultimately all of these measured maybe not sufficient if Hezbollah's underlying legitimacy is not addressed because the perceived legitimacy of Hezbollah is one of the key reasons individuals and charities are so successful in raising funds for the organization. In other words, their financing operations could be viewed more as a symptom or result of their legitimacy and cannot adequately be addressed unless and until Hezbollah's legitimacy is undermined.

PART III
Asia

PART III

Asia

Chapter 5
Partiya Karkeren Kurdistan (PKK)

Moyara Ruehsen

This chapter examines how the Kurdish separatist group, PKK (Partiya Karkeren Kurdistan) or Kurdistan's Workers Party, funded itself over three decades as it evolved from a political separatist group to an armed insurgency using terrorist tactics. The group has raised funds from a variety of sources including state sponsorship, voluntary contributions, extortion rackets, kidnapping, drug trafficking, and human trafficking. In recent years, governments have begun to cooperate in their efforts to cut off these funding sources by way of financial sanctions targeted at key members.

Background

The PKK was founded in 1978 by a group of Marxist-Leninist activists, led by Abdullah Ocalan, who dreamed of an independent Kurdistan in Eastern Anatolia. Classified by most countries as a terrorist organization, the PKK has not hesitated to target innocent civilians when it served the organization's purpose of harming the Turkish state. Except for a relative lull in activity from 1999-2004, over the past 33 years more than 35,000 people have died in the crossfire of armed confrontations between PKK fighters and the Turkish military, and in PKK-planned terrorist attacks around the world.[1]

In the early years of the PKK, the organization's activities were largely political, with small-scale violence, the occasional assassination of political rivals, protests, and confrontations with the military junta in Turkey in their quest for an independent Kurdistan in Eastern Anatolia. With more of their members targeted for arrest, the PKK sought refuge in neighboring states, particularly in Syria. Iran, Russia, and Greece are also alleged to have provided safe havens,[2] but the PKK leadership largely resided in and around Damascus and in Lebanon's Bekaa Valley, openly training its members in training camps and running the organization through local offices.

---

1 Numerous estimates range from 30,000 to 40,000, with most official sources claiming 35,000 deaths.

2 Anil Karaca, *Disrupting Terrorists Networks: An Analysis of the PKK Terrorist Organization*, Master's Thesis, Naval Postgraduate School, December 2010, 46-50, citing a Turkish publication by Sehirli.

Some of the PKK's operatives also fled to Europe. With Turkey's new constitution in the early 1980s outlawing the protection and development of non-Turkish cultures and languages (including Kurdish),[3] the plight of the Kurds generated sympathy among many Europeans. PKK-affiliated cultural clubs operated openly, especially in Germany where there was a large population of Turkish *Gastarbeiter*, or guestworkers. Although there is no evidence of official state sponsorship from any of the northern European countries with large Kurdish populations, there is strong evidence that until the past decade, those governments turned a blind eye to the organization's activities.

Syrian protection of the PKK continued through 1998, when Turkey threatened to go to war with Syria unless they stopped sheltering the organization. With no safe place to hide, Abdullah Ocalan was soon captured (in Kenya) by Turkish forces, imprisoned and put on trial. Initially sentenced to death, Ocalan called for his forces to give up the struggle. Some of the PKK leadership fled to Europe, and many members fled to Iraqi Kurdistan. The organization was in some disarray for a few years, and the suicide bombings of the 1990s finally came to an end. With a feeling of victory and relief that the PKK's campaign of violence was finally over, and eager to convince euroskeptics that their human rights record was improving, the Turkish government commuted Ocalan's death sentence to life imprisonment. He remains to this day in an isolated prison on the island of Imrali and is only able to communicate with the outside world by way of his lawyers.

Celebrations of the PKK's demise proved to be illusory. Various PKK affiliates throughout Europe continued to raise funds from voluntary donations, extortion rackets, illicit narco-trafficking, and other criminal enterprises. Affiliates like the PJAK in Iran also emerged to take up the mantle. All the while, Ocalan's former lieutenants laid low in temporary hibernation, but their goal of keeping the dream of an independent Kurdistan alive never faded. Only the tactics and leadership were in flux.

The U.S. invasion of Iraq created new opportunities for the PKK with the eventual establishment of a semi-autonomous Kurdish region in the oil-rich north of Iraq. Now, with "friends" along the Turkish-Iraqi border where most of Turkey's Kurdish population resides, PKK fighters were able to establish bases outside the territorial jurisdiction of the Turkey military.

With a new lease on life, the organization changed its name in 2003 from PKK to Kongra-Gel, short for *Kongra Gelê Kurdistan* (People's Congress of Kurdistan), but it continues to be called PKK among international policy makers. It also briefly called itself KADEK.

After years of relative quiet, deadly attacks resumed, with deadly bombings targeting resorts in Cesme and Kusadasi in 2005, tourism centers in Antalya, Marmaris, and Istanbul in the summer of 2006, and a deadly bombing in Ankara in May 2007. After 2007, most of the PKK's attacks were aimed at Turkish military

---

3   Aliza Marcus, *Blood and Belief: The PKK and the Kurdish Fight for Independence* (New York: New York University Press, 2007), 85.

Partiya Karkeren Kurdistan (PKK)   65

targets. By fall 2009, the Turkish government implemented several important reforms designed to placate the Kurdish population, but the PKK concluded that this was too little, too late. In June 2010, the organization threatened to launch more violent attacks. That was quickly followed by a ceasefire declaration, possibly suggesting internal dissent within the organization. Unfortunately, the ceasefire ended with a deadly bomb attack in Istanbul in October 2010, and attacks on Turkish military targets have continued since then.

There have not been any major acts of PKK violence in Europe since 2007 when the organization was responsible for at least 14 arson attacks against Turkish targets in Germany.[4] With renewed international cooperation and sanctions tools, the governments of Belgium, France, Germany, the Netherlands, Slovakia and Belgium have been making more arrests, charging PKK leaders with a variety of offenses including "terrorism financing via drug trafficking."[5]

Meanwhile, the PKK bases in northern Iraq remain a thorn in Turkey's side. The Iraqi Kurd leaders in the north may have once been willing to provide safe haven to the group, but with increased border shelling from Turkish military units, the Iraqi Kurds have largely come to the conclusion that the PKK may be more trouble than it is worth. The PKK is also facing more political competition among the Kurdish population in eastern Turkey as other Kurdish groups, without a reputation for violence, gain in popularity.

Sources of Funding

The PKK has its hand in many criminal activities, especially in Europe. One U.S. State Department official compared the group to an "octopus reaching out to many criminal areas to raise funds."[6] Turkey's Ministry of Foreign Affairs website on Terrorism, also confirms that the organization generates most of its revenue in Europe and cites the following sources:[7]

- Extortion.
- Revenues obtained from special events.
- Sales of publications.
- Revenues from commercial establishments.
- Drug trafficking.

---

4   The PKK admitted to 14 of these arson attacks, but the German security forces hold them responsible for 15 attacks, which took place between February and March 2007. Europol's *TE-SAT 2008: EU Terrorism Situation and Trend Report*, 29-30.

5   Europol's *TE-SAT 2008: EU Terrorism Situation and Trend Report*, 31.

6   U.S. Department of State News & Events "Urbancic Highlights U.S. Efforts to Combat PKK Networks in Europe," February 14, 2008.

7   Available at http://www.mfa.gov.tr/financing-of-its-activities.en.mfa (accessed January 13, 2012).

- Arms-smuggling.
- Trafficking in human beings.

Estimates of the PKK's annual income vary depending on the source and time period. In the 1990s, the organization was generating as much as $50 million each year in Europe just from voluntary donations, festivals, concerts, plays, and magazine subscriptions.[8] And the organization's criminal activities were generating an estimated $86 million annually.[9] According to the deputy chief of Turkey's General Staff, speaking at an international terrorism conference in March 2008, the group earns 400-500 million euros annually from its various criminal activities and voluntary donations. He went on to add that most of this was from criminal activity; specifically 200-250 million euros from drug dealing, 100-150 million euros from smuggling (primarily arms and people), and only 15-20 million euros from voluntary donations.[10]

State Sponsorship and Safe Havens

State sponsorship is a controversial term to define. Does it mean providing a designated terrorist group with funding, weapons, or other forms of tangible assistance? Or can it mean the mere provision of safe haven or turning a blind eye to the group's activities?

Several European countries such as Germany, Denmark, Sweden, and Belgium have been accused of ignoring PKK activism within their borders, but this has changed in recent years with several sting operations and trials discussed at the end of this chapter.

Greece and Cyprus, by contrast, have been accused of more than tacit approval and tolerance of the PKK. Turkish sources have alleged that the Greek government "provided political and military training to PKK militants on the island of Kos, and at two more camps in close proximity to Athens,"[11] and assisted with fundraising campaigns and diplomatic support. For example, when Abdullah Ocalan fled to Kenya before his arrest, he was briefly sheltered in the Greek Ambassador's private villa.[12] Cyprus also provided support to the organization in the 1980s and

---

8   Marcus, *Blood and Belief*, 230. Of this $50 million, $20 million is estimated to come from the cultural centers, and $30 million from donations.

9   Mitchell Roth and Murat Sever, "The Kurdish Workers Party (PKK) as Criminal Syndicate: Funding Terrorism through Organized Crime, A Case Study," *Studies in Conflict and Terrorism*, October 2007, 906.

10   "PKK revenues reach 500 mln euros," *Today's Zaman*, 12 March 2008.

11   Karaca, *Disrupting Terrorists Networks*, 46-7.

12   Marcus, *Blood and Belief*, 277-8.

1990s, and when he was captured Ocalan allegedly was carrying a Greek Cypriot passport.[13]

Syria's support for the PKK was much more explicit. Ocalan and other PKK leaders for most of the 1980s and 1990s lived under Syrian protection, first in Lebanon's Bekaa Valley, then later in Damascus. As one former PKK member confided, "We were finished as an organization after 1980. We had no strength in Europe, in Turkey we were in prison. But in Syria we could gather ourselves together."[14] At various camps throughout Syria itself and in the Syrian-controlled Bekaa Valley, PKK fighters trained with secular Palestinian groups like Yasir Arafat's Fatah, Nayif Hawatmah's Democratic Front for the Liberation of Palestine, George Habash's Popular Front for the Liberation of Palestine, Samir Ghosheh's Palestinian Popular Struggle Front, and the Lebanese Communist Party.[15] Perhaps because of their tense rivalry with Turkey, "Syria took no steps to limit PKK training, recruitment, or organizational work. Nor did it try and hamper Ocalan's activities."[16] The Syrian government even helped arrange for PKK militants to obtain Arab identity cards, which also gave the Syrians plausible deniability of their presence in the country.[17] Syria's support ended in 1998 when Turkey threatened to go to war over the matter.

Russia and Iran have also been accused of offering safe harbor to PKK separatists. According to translated Turkish sources, not only did the organization operate two training camps not far from Moscow, but the group held its Third Congress in Moscow in 1995. There was also alleged involvement in gambling and prostitution activities in Moscow.[18] However, in 1999, shortly before his capture, Russia refused to provide asylum to Abdullah Ocalan.[19] And there is no evidence that Russia has provided safe haven to any members of the group since then.

In 1987, the PKK was given permission to use Iranian territory as a safe haven, where they were granted "secure meeting spots for senior commanders, places to hold political training for new recruits, and centers to treat wounded rebels."[20] And many militants were even given Iranian identity cards. But there was a price. Iran demanded that new recruits provide intelligence on Turkish and U.S. military installations.[21] Eventually, this relationship backfired on Iran, when a PKK affiliate, the PJAK (Free Life Party of Kurdistan) established itself within

---

13   Roth and Sever, "The Kurdish Workers Party (PKK) as Criminal Syndicate," 905, and Tevfik Zehni, "Turkey and PKK Terrorism," MA Thesis, Naval Postgraduate School, June 2008, 33.

14   Zehni, "Turkey and PKK Terrorism," 58.

15   Zehni, "Turkey and PKK Terrorism," 57.

16   Zehni, "Turkey and PKK Terrorism," 99.

17   Zehni, "Turkey and PKK Terrorism," 59-60.

18   Karaca, *Disrupting Terrorist Networks*, 48-9.

19   Michael M. Gunter, *The Kurds Ascending: The Evolving Solution to the Kurdish Problem in Iraq and Turkey* (New York: Palgrave Macmillan, 2008), 60.

20   Marcus, *Blood and Belief*, 120.

21   Marcus, *Blood and Belief*, 121-2.

Iranian borders, sowing seeds of dissent among Iran's own Kurdish population. They have been engaged in open armed conflict with Iranian government forces throughout the 2000s.[22]

After the U.S. invasion of Iraq, and the establishment of a relatively safe Kurdish autonomous zone in the north, the PKK found yet another safe haven. The group has set up multiple camps throughout the Kandil mountains along the Iraqi-Turkish border, from which it can stage attacks on Turkish military targets near the border. Their new location also allows the PKK easier access to the Iraqi black market in weapons, mostly comprising former military stocks.[23] But this is far from a safe haven. Although the local Kurdish government in northern Iraq turns a blind eye to the group's activities, Turkey has for several years now been mounting air attacks across the border against suspected PKK bases.[24] It is, however, by no means an easy task for the Turkish military. The Turkish army has suffered many casualties in skirmishes with the PKK. In 2009 a television crew from Dubai's Al-Aribiya station ventured into the Kandil Mountains to interview PKK fighters, and filmed fighters shooting down a Turkish helicopter.[25] How long the PKK can take refuge in Northern Iraq, however, remains to be seen. According to one academic expert, "There's nothing [Iraqi Kurds] would like more than to get rid of the PKK, but they are looking for a way that is acceptable to them and their own public and which doesn't involve fighting other Kurds."[26]

Karaca argues that the value of safe havens should not be underestimated.[27] The monetary value of such protection is difficult to measure, to be sure, but the protection these countries have provided undoubtedly lowered the organization's operational costs, and enabled them to raise funds more openly.

Charitable Giving vs. Extortion

According to a report entitled "PKK 2008," prepared by Turkey's National Intelligence Organization (MİT), "the bulk of its funding is donations and monthly payments," adding that "the PKK extorts money from businessmen of Kurdish origin as well as collecting '*fitre*' and '*zekat*', charity donations that

---

22   Gunter, *The Kurds Ascending*, "Intelligence report on PKK alarms Turkey," *Today's Zaman*, October 11, 2007, and Aliza Marcus, "Turkey's PKK: Rise, Fall, Rise Again?" *World Policy Journal*, Spring 2007.

23   Lt.Col. Perry Clark, "Reassessing U.S. National Security Strategy: The Kurdistan Worker's Party (PKK)" *Strategy Research Project*, U.S. Army War College, March 2008, 8.

24   Clark, "Reassessing U.S. National Security Strategy," 6.

25   Al-Arabiya TV in Arabic, as summarized by the BBC Monitoring Service, April 9, 2009.

26   Professor Henry Barkey, quoted in "Turkey Sharpens Response to Upsurge in Kurd Violence," *The Christian Science Monitor*, August 29, 2006.

27   Karaca, *Disrupting Terrorist Networks*, 53.

are obligatory in Islam, from citizens of Kurdish background."[28] Distinguishing between voluntary donations and extorted "donations" is difficult, as it is difficult to determine whether Kurdish households and businesses make the donations out of obligation and pressure, or because they truly support the PKK's cause.

Many of these donations collected in Europe are funneled through charities. According to the same Turkish intelligence report, donations meant for the PKK are regularly deposited to the accounts of the following charities:[29]

- Scandinavian Kurdish Peace Council.
- Council of Solidarity with the Kurdish People in France.
- London Kurdish Relationship Group.
- Kurdistan Human Rights Project (UK).
- Council of Say No to the War Against Kurdish People (Belgium).
- AKIN, a Kurdish information network (U.S.).
- Kurdistan Employers' Union or KARSAZ (Germany).
- Kurdish Foundation Trust.

In Australia recently, a series of raids began with an investigation into more than $200,000 of taxpayers' money that had been granted to the Kurdish Association of Victoria. The Australian government had reason to believe that the funds had been illegally transferred to the PKK.[30]

While the PKK is still believed to extort Kurdish-owned businesses and households today, former PKK members involved with the process in the past have confessed how this process worked in Europe in the 1990s. They approached families "for a small donation every month—sometimes in the form of a magazine subscription—and once a year, everyone was expected to make a big contribution. When necessary, threats were employed ...We would say, you work 12 months for yourself and one month, you should think of the struggle ... When that did not work ... the money was coerced."[31] The money collected from businesses was collected as a formal tax, and occasionally more sympathetic businesses were approached for larger one-time donations to cover budget deficits. It was estimated in the early 1990s that in the UK alone, the PKK was able to extort as much as 2.5 million pounds each year.[32] Sometimes these payments from Kurdish-owned businesses were euphemistically called "insurance fees."

---

28 As reported in *Today's Zaman*, "Intelligence report on PKK alarms Turkey," October 11, 2007.

29 *Today's Zaman*, "Intelligence report on PKK alarms Turkey," for the first seven charities. Kurdish Foundation Trust is mentioned by Nick Kochan, *The Washing Machine*, Thomson/South-Western, 2005, 93.

30 *Weekend Australian*, August 21, 2010.

31 Marcus, *Blood and Belief*, 231-2.

32 Roth and Sever, "The Kurdish Workers Party (PKK) as Criminal Syndicate," 910.

Recently Europol has been monitoring PKK/Kongra-Gel activities throughout the EU, and reports that the group continues its "organized extortion campaigns" within the expatriate Kurdish community. Although the group uses "labels like 'donations' and 'membership fees' [the money is] in fact extortion and illegal taxation."[33] A sting operation in Austria in February 2009 led to the confiscation of donation collection lists, notes on income, and donation receipt books.[34] According to a German publication the "organization usually demands that its supporters donate one month's wages per year, and those unwilling to cough up are expressly reminded that they have to pay this 'tax'."[35]

More troubling is when the threats lead to kidnapping and murder. There are from time to time reports in the Turkish press of Kurdish business owners who are allegedly shot dead by PKK militants for refusing to pay extortion money, or kidnapped for ransom.[36]

Narcotics

The PKK has been involved in drug trafficking since its beginning. At one time in the early 1990s, it was estimated to have controlled between 70-80 percent of the heroin trade in Europe.[37] Although heroin markets in Europe are far more competitive today with many different criminal organizations participating, Turkish Kurds are still believed to earn significant funding from the transit trade as drugs make their way across the Iranian border and on to Western markets. According to official reports, the organization raised approximately $75 million from the drug trade in 1993. Ten years later, annual revenues had fallen to an estimated $40 million, which is still a significant sum.[38] And according to Europol in its most recent report (2011), the PKK/Kongra-Gel is still very active in drug trafficking.[39]

In the 1990s, the Turkish National Police investigated hundreds of narcotics cases linked to the PKK. While most of the cases involved opiates, there were also cases in which cocaine, amphetamines, and precursor chemicals used to

33   Europol, *TE-SAT 2011: EU Terrorism Situation and Trend Report*, 22.
34   Europol, *TE-SAT 2010: EU Terrorism Situation and Trend Report*, 31.
35   *Spiegel* (July 11, 2008), as translated by the BBC Monitoring Service.
36   "PKK Terrorists kill two, kidnap three," *Today's Zaman*, August 10, 2011, and "PKK frees businessman kidnapped in southeastern Turkey," *Today's Zaman*, August 10, 2011.
37   German sources suggest 80 percent. Nick Kochan (*The Washing Machine*, Thomson/South-Western, 2005, 92) suggests as much as 70 percent of the UK drug trade.
38   Lyubov Mincheva and Ted Robert Gurr,"Unholy Alliances III: Communal Militants and Criminal Networks in the Middle East, with a Case Study of the Kurdistan Workers Party (PKK)," unpublished manuscript presented at the Annual ISA Meeting, San Francisco, March 28, 2008, 18.
39   Europol, *TE-SAT 2011*.

manufacture these drugs, were also confiscated.[40] There are also allegations that the group is growing cannabis in large quantities in Northern Iraq.[41]

The organization's role in drug trafficking was made explicit during the trial of Abdullah Ocalan. The defendant admitted that his brother and other PKK members charged a tax on traffickers who brought drugs across the Iranian-Turkish border.[42]

Because of Turkey's geographic location between the lucrative drug markets of Western Europe and the opium producing areas of the Golden Crescent, Turkey is an important transit route for opium. The mark-up from the time the opium is cultivated and processed in Afghanistan to the time it is sold at the wholesale level in Europe, is between 10 and 40 fold.[43] All along the Turkish-Iranian border, there are PKK "customs duty squads" that collect a "customs duty" of $65 for every kilo of heroin ($25 for every kilo of morphine base) coming across the border. One PKK defendant testified that as much as 40 metric tons of drugs had passed through his customs station every year. He knew of at least three other customs duty squads operated by the PKK, and knew of one squad that transferred $1.3 million to the organization in 2008. The traffickers, who typically transported the drugs by mule, were willing to pay the customs duties to guarantee safe passage across the border, where the drugs were loaded into motor vehicles for the journey to Istanbul and other further destinations.[44]

According to the U.S. Treasury Department and U.S. State Department, PKK/Kongra-Gel involvement in the drug trade continues to this day, but not all of the 60 to 120 tons of heroin transiting Turkey every year is controlled by the organization. There are a number of high-profile heroin traffickers of Turkish ethnicity, but who are not Kurdish, or who are not affiliated with the PKK.

Human Trafficking

While there is plenty of evidence of PKK involvement in human smuggling throughout the 1990s and possibly in the early 2000s, there is little recent evidence to suggest that these illegal networks are still thriving, although Europol claims that the PKK is involved in both "human trafficking, as well as illegal immigration inside and outside the EU."[45] In the past, the PKK would smuggle migrants to Italy via a variety of routes, sometimes along the same routes that the group would use to smuggle drugs into Europe. According to Interpol, the group would allegedly

---

40 Roth and Sever, "The Kurdish Workers Party (PKK) as Criminal Syndicate," 907.

41 Mincheva and Gurr, "Unholy Alliances III," 19.

42 Roth and Sever, "The Kurdish Workers Party (PKK) as Criminal Syndicate," 908.

43 Roth and Sever, "The Kurdish Workers Party (PKK) as Criminal Syndicate," 907.

44 Report from the Anatolia News Agency "The KCK Indictment," April 22, 2011, as translated by the BBC Worldwide Monitoring Service, May 20, 2011.

45 Europol, *TE-SAT 2011*, 22.

receive between 2,000 and 3,000 euros per migrant. According to a Romanian newspaper, migrants trafficked through Eastern Europe to Berlin, Paris and London by PKK operatives in 2005 were paying between 6,000 and 7,000 euros per person.[46]

Countermeasures

In 2006, the U.S. government appointed a special envoy to address the PKK issue with the governments of the U.S., Turkey and Iraq. This marked the start of much needed intelligence sharing between the three governments, including "imaging and communication intercepts to facilitate limited Turkish strikes against PKK targets."[47] But there is widespread consensus that success cannot be achieved without also depriving the organization of funds, what some have called "deresourcing."[48]

Countermeasures designed to intercept funding can be broken down into three categories: designations, asset freezes and sting operations leading to arrests.

Designations

In order for banks and other institutions to have the authority to track, freeze or seize particular funds, an organization or individual must first be designated as a terrorist entity. The PKK was designated as a terrorist organization by the EU in 2002 and by the U.S. in 1997 and 2001. The PJAK affiliate was designated in February of 2009. More recently, the U.S. government has been trying to make greater use of an additional tool: the Foreign Narcotics Kingpin Designation Act. This act has been around for more than 15 years, but only recently has it been used as an additional sanctions tool in international efforts to intercept terrorist funds. In May 2008, the PKK/Kongra-Gel was listed as a specially designated narco-trafficking group, and in October 2009, three leaders of the PKK (Karayilan, Altun, and Aydar) received "kingpin" designations. More recently in April 2011, five additional PKK leaders were designated under the Kingpin Act as "specially designated narcotics traffickers." (Bayik, Kalkan, Kartal, Ok, and Uzun) The rationale is that these designations will increase the likelihood that international banking institutions will cooperate in the search for their funds and transactions. Also, from a prosecutorial standpoint, it is much easier to get a conviction when the predicate money laundering crime (drug trafficking) is committed *before* the funds are moved. Landing a conviction for terrorism financing, which requires demonstrating that the funds are *intended* for use by a terrorist organization, is far more difficult.

---

46 Roth and Sever, "The Kurdish Workers Party (PKK) as Criminal Syndicate," 909.
47 Clark, "Reassessing U.S. National Security Strategy," 6.
48 Clark, "Reassessing U.S. National Security Strategy," 17.

Asset Freezes

The burden of proof for asset freezing is high in most countries. Often, the designated individual has enough warning to move money out of targeted accounts before the freeze occurs. If procedures are not followed to the letter, and the burden of proof is not met, then decisions can be reversed and costly to taxpayers. In one such case the Danish government in August 2010 froze $60,000 belonging to Roj TV (long believed to be a media wing of the PKK), but in October 2010 a higher court overturned the decision. In July 2011, an order went out to freeze the assets of two prominent PKK leaders (for drug trafficking crimes under the Kingpin Act), but it remains to be seen whether this leads to any intercepted funds. At least one of the individuals, Ali Reza Altun, goes by three different aliases. Moreover, it is also challenging to keep track of the number of charities acting on behalf of the PKK. And now there are new affiliates, such as TAK (Kurdistan Freedom Falcons) who are believed to be behind the more deadly terrorist attacks of recent years. Keeping one step ahead of individual aliases and organizations' capacity to rename and reinvent themselves remains an ongoing challenge.

Arrests

While there were many drug-trafficking related arrests in Europe—especially Germany—in the 1980s and 1990s, terrorism related arrests did not pick up until well after the post-9/11 designations went into effect. In 2005, German and Belgian authorities arrested three PKK members for running an extortion racket for the purpose of funding a terrorist organization. In 2006, two PKK members were arrested in France, and in 2007, 16 PKK members were arrested in France, including several prominent leaders, who later escaped while out on bail and awaiting their trial.[49]

In March 2010, a large, coordinated sting operation led to the arrests of suspected PKK members in Belgium, France, the Netherlands, and Turkey, with related investigations in Italy, Romania and Slovakia.[50] In Belgium alone, 18 members of the organization were arrested, and at least 25 sites were searched. In August 2010, the Australian government raided 17 homes and businesses in Sydney, Melbourne and Perth, arresting individuals accused of providing as much as $1 million to the PKK. And finally in November 2010, the Syrian government arrested roughly 1,000 people for "providing the PKK terrorist organization with logistical support" including the collection of "tribute money."[51]

With increased international cooperation and more widespread adoption of financial sanctions, the objective of cutting off funding to the PKK and other

---

49   Mincheva and Gurr, "Unholy Alliances III," 32.

50   Europol, *TE-SAT 2011*, 22.

51   "Turkey Reportedly Cooperating with Syria in Operations Against PKK," Anatolia News Agency, November 26, 2010; translated by the BBC Worldwide Monitoring Service, November 27, 2010.

terrorist groups shows promise. There will always be challenges, especially with counterfeit identification, front charities, and name changes of designated entities. But collectively, these efforts render the organization's continued existence much more difficult.

Chapter 6

Lashkar-e-Taiba (LeT)

Geoffrey Kambere, Puay Hock Goh, Pranav Kumar, and
Fulgence Msafiri

> Very few things worry me as much as the strength and ambition of LeT, a truly
> malign presence in South Asia.[1]
>
> Daniel Benjamin, Coordinator, Office of the Coordinator for Counterterrorism,
> Washington, D.C.

Since its formation in 1990, Lashkar-e-Taiba (LeT) has evolved from a local threat
focused against India to a global jihadist threat. While many experts have addressed
the operational facets of LeT, its finances have not received commensurate
attention. This chapter aims to redress that gap. It is divided into four major
parts. The first part provides a brief history about LeT, including its ideology,
organization, training, and operations. The second part focuses on LeT finances:
its primary funding sources, methods of moving money, and trends in spending.
The third part presents a brief case study of the 2008 Mumbai terror attacks; and
in the fourth section, we examine the countermeasures initiated by various actors,
weaknesses in the present response, recommendations, and conclusions.

Background

Origins

"In 1984, Zaki-ur Rehman Lakhvi organized a group of Ahl-e-Hadith Muslims
from Pakistan to wage jihad against the Soviets in Afghanistan."[2] A year later,
"Hafiz Saeed and Zafar Iqbal, two professors at Lahore University, formed the
Jamat-ud-Dawa (JuD) as a missionary group dedicated to the tenets of Ahl-e-
Hadith Islam. In 1986, Lakhvi merged his outfit with JuD to form the Markaz al-
Dawa-wal-Irshad (MDI)."[3] Abdullah Azzam, Osama bin Laden's mentor and the

---

    1   Daniel Benjamin, "The Obama Administration's Counterterrorism Policy at
One Year," Speech to the CATO Institute, January 13, 2010, http://www.cato.org/event.
php?eventid=6807 (accessed January 13, 2012).

    2   Stephen Tankel, *Lashkar-e-Taiba: Past Operations and Future Prospects*, New
America Foundation, National Security Studies Program Policy Paper (April 2011), 2,
http://newamerica.net/sites/newamerica.net/files/policydocs/Tankel_LeT_0.pdf.

    3   Tankel, *Lashkar-e-Taiba: Past Operations and Future Prospects*, 2-3.

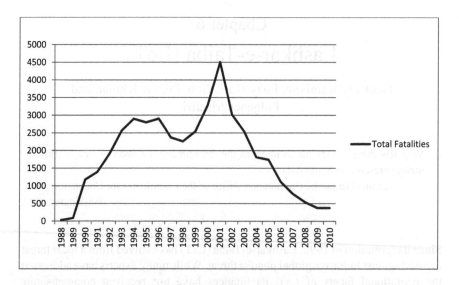

Figure 6.1   Overall Fatalities in Jammu and Kashmir

Source: "Fatalities in Terrorist Violence," from South Asia Terrorism Portal website, http://www.satp.org/satporgtp/countries/india/states/jandk/data_sheets/annual_casualties.htm (accessed May 4, 2011).

father of modern global jihad, was one of the cofounders of MDI. MDI enjoyed active support from both the Pakistani Intelligence Services (ISI) and the CIA for fighting alongside the mujahedeen.[4] After the Soviet withdrawal, Pakistan appropriated the assets created during the Afghan war to wage a proxy war against India in Jammu and Kashmir (J&K). In 1990, LeT was launched as a separate military wing of MDI.[5] Hence, LeT's commitment to global jihad, connections with Al Qaeda (AQ), and strong state support can be traced back to its very birth as an organization.

Violence erupted in J&K in 1989; however, the insurgency there started to wane in a few years. As a result, Pakistan brought in jihadi elements to resuscitate the Kashmir movement in the mid to late 1990s. It is estimated that the ISI spent over

----

4   C. Christine Fair, *Leader-Led Jihad in Pakistan: Lashkar-e-Taiba and the 2008 Mumbai Attack* (October 13, 2009), retrieved from *Social Science Research Network* website: http://ssrn.com/abstract=1753767 (accessed January 13, 2012); Bruce Riedel, "The Mumbai Massacre and its Implications for America and South Asia," *Journal of International Affairs*, 63:1 (Fall 2009), 115.

5   "Lashkar-e-Taiba Overview," Intelligence and Terrorism Information Center, December 21, 2008, http://www.terrorism-info.org.il/malam_multimedia/English/eng_n/html/gj_e002.htm (accessed January 13, 2012); and "The Rise of Lashkar-e-Tayyiba: A Magnet for American Jihadis," *The Investigative Project on Terrorism*, 2010, http://www.investigativeproject.org/documents/testimony/373.pdf, 5.

$50 million USD annually to support groups such as LeT, Hizb-ul-Mujahedeen, and Jaish-e-Mohammed (JeM). See Figure 6.1, which shows the peak of violence occurring after the slowdown in the early 1990s. Consequently, the conflict in J&K became less of a local insurgency and more of a campaign sponsored by Pakistan through its many proxies. The growing reputation of LeT as a jihadi force fighting to liberate Kashmir enhanced its ability to recruit and raise funds.[6]

Ideology

Jihad forms the cornerstone of LeT's ideology. In a publication titled "Why are We Waging Jihad," LeT leaders exhort Muslims to liberate themselves from persecution by the infidels and identify India, the United States, and Israel as the mortal enemies of Islam.[7] LeT's motivation toward the Kashmiri cause is not just territorial but ideological; the group argued that once J&K was liberated, it would serve as a base to restore Islamic norms in the Indian subcontinent.[8] MDI and LeT also aim at transforming Pakistan's entire society toward their radical interpretation of Islam through *dawa* (proselytizing) and *khidmat* (social service).[9]

LeT recruits from Pakistani followers of the Ahl-e-Hadith movement, which is Salafist in orientation, and believes that Muslims must return to a "pure form" of Islam. Because the Ahl-e-Hadith movement pales in comparison to the strength of Deobandi organizations in Pakistan, however, and because LeT also alienates many mainstream adherents to the Ahl-e-Hadith movement because of its calls for jihad, the LeT has generally been almost entirely dependent upon the ISI and on Saudi benefactors for its funding.[10]

Organization

Hafiz Saeed, one of the founders of JuD, was the *aamir* (chief) of both MDI and LeT. The MDI is functionally organized into separate departments for *dawa*, finance, external affairs, propaganda, and *khidmat*, whereas the LeT has a quasi-military structure organized by various geographic regions in J&K. By 2000, MDI and LeT had at least 70 district offices in Pakistan and a plethora of smaller ones totaling more than 2,000.[11] The organization had its headquarters in Muridke, near Lahore Pakistan, in a sprawling compound that houses numerous community

---

6   Tankel, *Lashkar-e-Taiba: Past Operations and Future Prospects*, 5.

7   Husain Haqqani, "The Ideologies of South Asian Jihadi Groups," in *Current Trends in Islamist Ideology* (Washington, D.C.: Hudson Institute, 2005).

8   Tankel, *Lashkar-e-Taiba: Past Operations and Future Prospects*, 3.

9   Qandeel Siddique, *What is Lashkar-e-Taiba* (Oslo: Norwegian Defence Research Establishment, 2008).

10   Tankel, *Lashkar-e-Taiba: Past Operations and Future Prospects*, 5, 9.

11   Tankel, *Lashkar-e-Taiba: Past Operations and Future Prospects*, 7.

services.[12] Subsequent to the 9/11 terrorist attacks, LeT is reported to have moved its headquarters to Muzaffarabad in Pakistan Occupied Kashmir (POK).[13]

LeT is reported to have several thousand members, of which 750 cadres are said to be operating in Kashmir.[14] A sociological profile of 100 LeT cadres found their backgrounds were similar to those of low-ranking officers of the Pakistan Army hailing from Punjab and the North West Frontier Province (NWFP). Interestingly, the cadres were better educated compared to other terrorist groups in the region, as its leaders emphasize the need for education to be able to wage a modern jihad.[15]

The cadres are equipped with weapons ranging from small arms such as AK-47s to heavier weapons such as rocket-propelled grenades, and also force multipliers such as night-vision devices, global positioning systems (GPS), and satellite phones. LeT is known for its proficiency in employing improvised explosive devices in Kashmir and Afghanistan.[16]

LeT's training is divided into three parts: *Daure-e-Aama* (basic training), *Daure-e-Suffa* (religious training and proselytizing), and *Daura-e-Khasa* (specialized training for guerrilla warfare). In addition to the three basic stages, selected cadres may receive special training for specific skills related to espionage, subversion, sabotage, and maritime operations.[17]

Operations

An overview of the operations conducted by LeT presents a vivid picture of how the terrorist organization has evolved from a local to a global threat. During the 1990s, most of LeT's operations were conducted in J&K, where the organization was known for targeting civilians, and *fidayeen* attacks (LeT's term for suicide attacks) against security forces. The December 2000 *fidayeen* attack against the Delhi Red Fort was one of the first terrorist attacks by LeT outside J&K.[18] In December 2001, Jaish-e-Mohammed (JeM) and LeT attacks on the Indian Parliament steered Pakistan and India to the verge of a conventional war. In response to international pressure, Pakistan's then-President Pervez Musharraf banned the MDI and LeT; however, the actions by the state remained cosmetic with no effect on LeT's capabilities or its financial resources in particular. The July 2006 bomb blasts against the Mumbai local rail network that killed more than 200 people was one of LeT's more recent acts displaying its intent.[19] Over the past decade, LeT has established sleeper cells

12 "The Rise of Lashkar-e-Tayyiba," 8.
13 Tankel, *Lashkar-e-Taiba: Past Operations and Future Prospects*, 40.
14 Fair, *Leader-Led Jihad in Pakistan*, 8.
15 "The Rise of Lashkar-e-Tayyiba," 9.
16 Tankel, *Lashkar-e-Taiba, Past Operation and Future Prospects*, 19.
17 "Lashkar-e-Taiba Overview," 48.
18 Tankel, *Lashkar-e-Taiba: Past Operations and Future Prospects*, 13.
19 "Lashkar-e-Taiba Overview," 31-2.

in India and nurtures radical groups such as Indian Mujahedeen (IM) and Students Islamist Movement of India (SIMI).[20]

In the aftermath of the U.S. invasion of Afghanistan in 2001, LeT provided active assistance to AQ in the form of safe havens, training, and acting as a gateway for aspiring jihadis to reach AQ.[21] Abu Zubayda was one of the most notable AQ members captured from a LeT safe house at Faisalabad.[22] The LeT followed a creative policy to allow its cadres leaves of absence during which they could fight with AQ as freelancers, which allowed for plausible deniability. British forces in Iraq captured at least two LeT operatives in 2004 and handed them over to the Americans.[23] Subsequent to this capture, Musharraf came down heavily on LeT, though this incident did not fracture the group's alliance with the state. It is noteworthy that even at the height of violence within Pakistan, LeT did not turn against the state.[24]

LeT's active involvement in Afghanistan can be traced to mid-2005 in the Kunar and Nuristan provinces.[25] An attack in July 2008 on a U.S. outpost at Wanat and the Indian embassy in Kabul, was attributed to LeT.[26] LeT also acts as a magnet to Western jihadis for training, funding, and even operational planning.[27] A wide array of American, Canadian, British, French, and Australian Muslims (including converts) has been trained in LeT camps.[28] The Virginia Paintball Group from the United States, Omar Khayyam from Britain, and Willie Brigitte from France were all trained in LeT camps in Pakistan and were later involved in providing material and operational support to the organization for its global operations.[29]

---

20   Fair, *Leader-Led Jihad in Pakistan*, 10.

21   Stephen Tankel, *Lashkar-e-Taiba: From 9/11 to Mumbai* (London: The International Center for the Study of Radicalisation and Political Violence, 2009).

22   Stephen Tankel, *Lashkar-e-Taiba in Perspective: An Evolving Threat*, New America Foundation, Counterterrorism Strategy Initiative Policy Paper (Washington, D.C.: 2010), http://www.carnegieendowment.org/files/Lashkar-e-Taiba_in_Perspective.pdf; Tankel, *Lashkar-e-Taiba: Past Operations and Future Prospects*, 12, 16, 18; "The Rise of Lashkar-e-Tayyiba," 10.

23   Tankel, *Lashkar-e-Taiba: From 9/11 to Mumbai*, 16.

24   Ashley Tellis, "Bad Company: Lashkar-e-Tayyiba and the Growing Ambition of Islamist Militancy in Pakistan," testimony to House Committee on Foreign Affairs, March 11, 2010, transcript retrieved from Carnegie Endowment for International Peace, http://carnegieendowment.org/2010/03/11/bad-company-lashkar-e-tayyiba-and-growing-ambition-of-islamist-militancy-in-pakistan/44h4 (accessed January 13, 2012), 4.

25   Ryan Clarke, *Lashkar-i-Taiba: The Fallacy of Subservient Proxies and the Future of Islamist Terrorism in India* (2010), Strategic Studies Institute, http://www.strategicstudiesinstitute.army.mil/pubs/display.cfm?pubid=973 (accessed January 13, 2012); Tankel, *Lashkar-e-Taiba in Perspective*, 2.; Tankel, *Lashkar-e-Taiba: Past Operations and Future Prospects*, 18.

26   Tankel, *Lashkar-e-Taiba: From 9/11 to Mumbai*, 20.

27   "The Rise of Lashkar-e-Tayyiba," 14.

28   Fair, *Leader-Led Jihad in Pakistan*, 8-9.

29   "The Rise of Lashkar-e-Tayyiba," 14; "Lashkar-e-Taiba Overview," 56.

LeT's role in global jihad is not limited to operations in Iraq, Afghanistan, or training would-be terrorists. It has been actively involved in various international terrorist attacks and is deeply enmeshed with global jihadi networks: LeT had varying degrees of involvement in the 2005 London train bombings, the failed plot by Richard Reid to blow up an airplane using a shoe bomb in 2002, and the thwarted attempt to detonate liquid bombs onboard a transatlantic aircraft in 2006.[30]

LeT Financing

This section covers LeT's sources of funds, means of transfer of finances, and how the group spends the funds. Sources of funds include state sponsorship, charities, and businesses. Money is transferred through banks, use of *hawala*, and by couriers. Finally, funds are utilized mainly for *dawa* (preaching), *khidmat* (provision of social services), and jihad (Islamic campaign against non-believers) through recruitment, training, and procurement of equipment and weapons.

State sponsorship

Most observers claim that the LeT is a terrorist group supported by the Pakistani state. Ashley Tellis believes "it is important to end the farce of treating these entities as if they are truly free agents, acting on their own accord, un-tethered to the state organs from which they derive protection, succor, and support."[31]

Likewise, Bill Roggio, a managing editor of *The Long War Journal*, attests that "LeT receives support from Pakistan's military and its intelligence service."[32] In addition, Tankel, writing for the New American Foundation, asserts that Pakistani financial and organizational support to LeT increased significantly during the 1990s.[33] Furthermore, Abubakar Siddique argues that LeT was able to expand quickly and launch jihad in the contested area of Himalayan Kashmir in the 1990s because it had been encouraged by Pakistan's army to do so.[34] As a final example

---

30   Tankel, *Lashkar-e-Taiba: Past Operations and Future Prospects*, 14; "The Rise of Lashkar-e-Tayyiba," 14; Clarke, *Lashkar-i-Taiba: The Fallacy of Subservient Proxies*, 16.

31   Ashley Tellis, "Bad Company."

32   Bill Roggio, "US Designates Lashkar-e-Taiba's Charitable Front as Terror Group," *The Long War Journal*, November 24, 2010, http://www.longwarjournal.org/archives/2010/11/us_treasury_designat.php (accessed May 10, 2011).

33   Stephen Tankel, "Lashkar-e-Taiba in Perspective: An Evolving Threat," New American Foundation, http://www.carnegieendowment.org/files/Lashkar-e-Taiba_in_Perspective.pdf.

34   Abubakar Siddique, "Charity Linked to Lashkar-e-Taiba Under the Spotlight," Radio Free Europe, Radio Free Liberty, http://www.rferl.org/content/article/1358669.html (accessed May 2, 2011).

of state sponsorship, Jyoti Trehan claims that the ISI gives both genuine and counterfeit money directly to LeT.[35]

Despite evidence of Pakistan's support to militant groups including LeT, Pakistan denies the allegations. After 9/11, Musharraf was forced to act against indigenous-based militants in Kashmir; however, his actions were questionable because LeT and JeM continued to operate beyond the "Line of Control (LoC)" in the contentious Kashmir area. As reported:

> Pakistan has refused to crack down on homegrown terror groups such as Jaish-e-Mohammed and Lashkar-e-Taiba, despite their covert and overt support for al-Qaeda, the Taliban, and other terror groups. Inside Pakistan's military and intelligence services, which are the real powers in Pakistan, groups like Jaish-e-Mohammed and Lashkar-e-Taiba are seen as "strategic" depth against India, and are used as instruments of foreign policy.[36]

However, Tankel claims that the Pakistan government's direct support to LeT via ISI started to diminish in 2002 following international pressure and the threat of war with India.[37]

Charities

LeT exploits JuD's social welfare organization with its more than 50,000 registered members to spread its influence and to raise funds.[38] Within Pakistan, donation boxes are placed in many JuD offices and shops spread out all over the country, and at public gatherings, where money is solicited for the continuation of LeT's ideology and to celebrate the martyrdom of fighters.[39]

For example, within Europe, Britain is a major center for fundraising for LeT because of its very large Pakistani immigrant population.[40] But some of the money raised for JuD charitable activities is used to finance LeT's operations; in fact, funding for the plot to use liquid bombs to detonate transatlantic aircraft in 2006 was funneled through the charities that raised funds in British mosques for earthquake victims in 2005.[41] Additionally, JuD officials often travel to Saudi Arabia seeking

---

35 Jyoti Trehan, "Terrorism and the Funding of Terrorism in Kashmir," *Journal of Financial Crime*; February 2002; 9:3, http://www.emeraldinsight.com/journals. htm7articles=1650632 (accessed May 9, 2011).

36 Roggio, "US Designates Lashkar—Taiba's Charitable Front as Terror Group."

37 Tankel, *Lashkar-e-Taiba: Past Operations and Future Prospects*, 14.

38 Tankel, *Lashkar-e-Taiba: From 9/11 to Mumbai*, 1-17.

39 Tankel, *Lashkar-e-Taiba: Past Operations and Future Prospects*, 10.

40 Clarke, *Lashkar-i-Taiba*, 25-6.

41 "Lashkar-e-Taiba Overview," 19.

donations for new schools at highly inflated costs that in turn are directed to fund LeT militant operations.[42]

LeT also receives charitable aid directly, especially from donors in Saudi Arabia and other Gulf states. According to Jonathan Fighel, Saudi Arabia covertly supports and promotes the "Saudi-Wahabbi political and religious influence in the Sunni Muslim world"[43] through its worldwide network of charities. LeT is one beneficiary.[44] In Kuwait, the Revival of Islamic Society has also provided direct support to al-Qaeda and LeT.[45]

Businesses

LeT controls many legitimate businesses, including fish farms, a hospital, a market, agricultural tracts, mobile clinics, and ambulance services.[46] The "farmers and labor wing" at JuD is responsible for the collection of *ushr*, an Islamic land tax, which requires farmers to contribute 10 percent of their total produce to charity for the provision of essential services, especially in areas where the government of Pakistan has failed to provide those social services.[47] Notably, the group collects hides of most of the animals slaughtered during the holy festivals of Eid al-Adha and sells them for a profit.[48] This practice has emerged as a big boost to the group's income as it is estimated that during each Eid festival at least 1.2 million animal hides are collected.[49]

Illegal Activities

LeT's illegal fundraising activities include false trade invoicing, counterfeiting, extortion, and involvement in the drug trade. With false trade invoicing, the LeT overcharges for its goods or services. For example, the group sometimes adds an extra "5 to 10 Pakistani rupees for the jihad to the bill especially when selling various Jihadi publications."[50] Conversely, under-invoicing occurs when Kashmiri

---

42   Declan Walsh, "WikiLeaks cables portray Saudi Arabia as a cash machine for terrorists," *The Guardian*, December 5, 2010, http://www.guardian.co.uk/world/2010/dec/05/wikileaks-cables-saudi-terrorist-funding (accessed January 13, 2012).

43   Jonathan Figel, "Pakistani-Jamal-ud-Da'wah: The Saudi Wahabbi Influence," http://www.islamdaily.org/wahabism/6987.Pakistanjamat-ud-awal-thesaudi-wahabbi-influence.htm/ (accessed May 13, 2011).

44   Figel, "Pakistani-Jamal-ud-Da'wah: The Saudi Wahabbi Influence."

45   Walsh, "WikiLeaks cables portray Saudi Arabia as a cash machine for terrorists."

46   "Lashkar-e-Toiba," South Asia Terrorism Portal, http://www.satp.org/satporgtp/countries/india/states/jandk/terrorist_outfits/lashkar_e_toiba.htm (accessed January 13, 2012); Tankel, *Lashkar-e-Taiba: Past Operations and Future Prospects*, 7.

47   Tankel, *Lashkar-e-Taiba: Past Operations and Future Prospects*, 10.

48   Tankel, *Lashkar-e-Taiba: Past Operations and Future Prospects*, 10.

49   Clarke, *Fallacy of Subservient Proxies*, 407.

50   Tankel, *Lashkar-e-Taiba: Past Operations*, 10.

carpet dealers reduce the value of their exports to Gulf countries, and the difference in the true value of the merchandise and the value shown on the invoice returns to India through the *hawala* channel.[51]

Counterfeiters have enabled LeT to raise money by integrating the genuine money being brought across the border into Kashmir with counterfeit money.[52] Extortion of money from the local population is also common with corrupt officials in the Jammu and Kashmir region.[53] There are limited reports of LeT direct involvement in drug trafficking. However, given LeT's geographic location, the group is almost certainly tempted to be involved in narcotic smuggling because of the huge profit potential, and because there are fewer restrictions than with money received through state sponsorship and donations.[54] Some sources say increasing trade in narcotics, in addition to state sponsorship, has enabled LeT to maintain its terrorism activities.[55] In 2002, there was a huge harvest of opium on the border between Afghanistan and Pakistan that was estimated to be 5,000 tons by international agencies.[56] This yield was refined into injectable heroin in laboratories and smuggled by ISI narcotic smugglers; the harvest's estimated worth of $2.5 billion USD is reportedly being used by Pakistan to support the Taliban and terrorism in J&K.[57]

Moving Money

LeT moves money through traditional banks, *hawala*, and cash couriers. Moving money through banks via the account number displayed on the group's website has proved to be the safest method for LeT. Money from over 400,000 Pakistanis living in Britain moves legally from British banks to Pakistani banks, particularly as funds raised for families in Pakistan or victims of catastrophic events, such as the devastating earthquake in 2005.[58] However, much of that legally transferred money may get funneled to terrorist organizations. Jayshree Bajoria notes that about $10 million USD was transferred to Pakistan in 2005 and more than half of that was channeled to LeT activities.[59] Also, Trehan, an inspector in the Indian police service, further notes that "Jammu and Kashmir banks have played a fairly

51 Trehan, "Terrorism and the Funding of Terrorism," 207.
52 Trehan, "Terrorism and the Funding of Terrorism," 207.
53 Trehan, "Terrorism and the Funding of Terrorism," 208.
54 Clarke, *Lashkar-i-Taiba*, 407.
55 Clarke, *Lashkar-i-Taiba*, 407.
56 Clarke, *Lashkar-i-Taiba*, 407.
57 Trehan, "Terrorism and the Funding of Terrorism," 208.
58 Jayshree Bajoria, "Lashkar-e-Taiba (Army of the Pure) (aka Lashkar e-Tayyiba, Lashkar e-Toiba; Lashkar-i-Taiba)," Council on Foreign Relations, http://www.cfr.org/pakistan/lashkar-e-taiba-army-pure-aka-lashkar-e-tayyiba-lashkar-e-toiba-lashkar--taiba/p17882#p2 (accessed January 14, 2010); "Lashkar-e-Taiba Overview," 19.
59 Bajoria, "Lashkar-e-Taiba."

dubious role in channeling terrorist funding in Jammu and Kashmir."[60] Harvard's Jessica Stern asserts that "LeT ... has acquired so much capital that they are actually planning to open their own bank."[61]

Hawala is an informal way of transferring value and is also a substitute remittance scheme, which operates differently from the established and regulated procedures of banks and other financial institutions.[62] Investigations by India's intelligence agencies after the Mumbai attacks in November 2008 revealed that LeT used *hawala* operatives and businessmen to move money from Gulf countries to LeT cells.[63] The *hawala* network has proved to be effective and cheap. *Hawala* channels were not only used to finance the Mumbai 2008 attacks but also for the Bangalore bombings in July 2008 and other terrorist attacks which have exposed *hawala* operators from Bangladesh and Oman.[64] These incidents imply that *hawala* is commonly used by LeT, which presents a challenge for Indian counterterrorism measures. If well-built cross-border relations between the *hawaladers* do exist, then curbing financing for terrorism inside India will be more difficult.[65] *Hawala* is built on trust and strong relationships among dealers so that even if one is arrested, investigators rarely get the desired domino effect; in fact, most *hawaladers* in transnational networks in South Asia are related.[66]

Trehan reports that the Pakistani ISI sometimes directly hands cash to terrorists, whereby the terrorists themselves can carry huge sums of money across the border into the Kashmir region.[67] This mechanism is good for the terrorists and the ISI as there are no electronic records in case of future investigations. In addition, preachers from JuD move freely while promoting jihad, returning to their bases with money they have collected, becoming, in essence, cash couriers.[68] At higher levels, money is moved to Kashmir by air transport from Pakistan through Nepal and Bangladesh to India because there are no constraints on moving money from Nepal to India, and this kind of money finds its way into the hands of the terrorist organization.[69] Additionally, Animesh Roul claims that "LeT has managed to build alternate routes through the porous borders of Nepal and Bangladesh while establishing bases in the Gulf countries."[70]

---

60   Trehan, "Terrorism and the Funding of Terrorism," 208.
61   Clarke, *Lashkar-i-Taiba*, 407.
62   Animesh Roul, "Lashkar-e-Taiba's Financial Network Targets India from the Gulf States," *Terrorism Monitor*, 7:19 (July 2, 2009), 8, The Jamestown Foundation, http://www.jamestown.org/programs/gta/single/?tx_ttnews[tt_news]=35221&tx_ttnews[backPid]=412&no_cache=1 (accessed January 13, 2012).
63   Roul, "Lashkar-e-Taiba's Financial Network," 6.
64   Roul, "Lashkar-e-Taiba's Financial Network," 6.
65   Clarke, *Lashkar-i-Taiba*, 406.
66   Clarke, *Lashkar-i-Taiba*, 406.
67   Trehan, "Terrorism and the Funding of Terrorism," 207.
68   Tankel, *Lashkar-e-Taiba: Past Operations and Future Prospects*, 11.
69   Trehan, "Terrorism and the Funding of Terrorism," 207.
70   Roul, "Lashkar-e-Taiba's Financial Network," 6.

How LeT spends

LeT spends funds in three major ways: *khidmat, dawa,* and military operations. In the effort to gain popular support, LeT's social warfare department called Idarah Khidmat-e-Khalq (IKK) plays a vital role by providing social services to the local populace.[71] On October 8, 2005, LeT is reported to have been the first to come to the aid of three million earthquake victims in Kashmir and Pakistan's Northwest Frontier Province when the Pakistani government was slow in taking immediate action.[72]

The group has utilized a good amount of money in its efforts to influence society through preaching and social welfare programs (*dawa*).[73] This has been done through recruiting and the spreading of ideology in J&K, often using funds donated for its social services work. Almost half of the external aid sent by Pakistani expatriates in the United Kingdom for the earthquake victims was funneled to the growth of the LeT.[74] Furthermore, "during the last decade, LeT purchased real estate throughout the country to open new offices and had more than 1,500 offices operating full time across Pakistan by the middle of the decade."[75] LeT is said to be investing some of the money it has raised in its legitimate businesses and enterprises in Islamic institutions and *dawa* model schools in Lahore and Muridke. These schools, in turn, have been sources of revenue to the terrorist organization through tuition payments.[76]

A hefty amount of LeT's money goes to its military operations. These operations are mostly efforts aimed at India and the widening of the U.S. footprint in India.[77] U.S. intelligence reveals that "in 2009, LeT's annual military operations budget ... totaled more than $5 million [USD] per year."[78]

As part of its operational requirements, LeT recruits "get a certain down payment on recruitment, a certain amount as monthly remuneration and a certain amount of incentives for big acts of terrorism and a certain amount as end of the tenure payment, which is roughly two years."[79] Furthermore, considering various estimations "on average Rs 3 lakhs is being spent on funding a Kashmiri terrorist and up to Rs 5 lakhs is being spent on funding a foreign terrorist."[80] It is estimated that the staggering amount of $33 million USD is being spent on

---

71   Roul, "Lashkar-e-Taiba's Financial Network," 12.
72   Jan McGirk, "Jihadis in Kashmir: The Politics of an Earthquake," *Qantara.de*, http://en.qantara.de/wcsite.php?wc_c=6175 (accessed October 27, 2005).
73   Tankel, *Lashkar-e-Taiba: Past Operations and Future Prospects*, 2.
74   Tankel, *Lashkar-e-Taiba: Past Operations and Future Prospects*, 2.
75   Tankel, *Lashkar-e-Taiba: Past Operations and Future Prospects*, 11.
76   Tankel, *Lashkar-e-Taiba: Past Operations and Future Prospects*, 7.
77   Tankel, *Lashkar-e-Taiba: Past Operations and Future Prospects*, 2.
78   Tankel, *Lashkar-e-Taiba: Past Operations and Future Prospects*, 10.
79   Trehan, "Terrorism and the Funding of Terrorism," 207.
80   Trehan, "Terrorism and the Funding of Terrorism," 207.

incentives for operatives and for their leaders, who reportedly get a much higher rate of remuneration. In addition, the terrorist group occasionally pays the families of operatives who are killed and those who take part in martyrdom actions, which also helps win local support.[81]

LeT also supports other terrorist groups and individuals. It is reported that LeT financially supported JeM in its attack on India's parliament in December 2001.[82] Other groups that have received LeT support include Indian and Western jihadist organizations. A French prosecutor asserted that LeT's representative in Paris served as a "compass" and provided logistical and financial support for Richard Reid, who attempted to detonate explosives hidden in his shoes while on board a flight bound for the United States from France in December 2001. And notable terrorist attacks against India, including the Mumbai 2008 attack, have been financed and supported by LeT cells in the Gulf.[83]

2008 Mumbai Terror Attacks

The 2008 Mumbai terror attacks should put to rest any doubts about LeT's threat to the international community.[84] The presumed reasons for the attacks were to derail the peace process between India and Pakistan and act as a provocation to push the two neighbors toward war. It was expected that punitive action by the Indian Army would impel Pakistan to move its forces from the Afghanistan-Pakistan region to the border with India. This would have relieved the pressure on the insurgents in the Afghanistan–Pakistan region who were under attack from the Pakistani military.[85]

Operational Details

Surveillance in preparation for the attacks was carried out beginning in 2006, and the perpetrators of the attack were trained over 18 months at four different locations in Pakistan.[86] The 10 terrorists departed Karachi on a small boat, transferred to a larger vessel, and eventually hijacked an Indian merchant vessel to sail them to India. Each terrorist had one AK-47, 200 bullets, eight grenades, a cellular phone, and other supplies. The group left a satellite phone behind in the boat, thus providing crucial evidence against LeT and the ISI.[87] On arrival at Mumbai,

---

81   Trehan, "Terrorism and the Funding of Terrorism," 207.

82   Tankel, *Lashkar-e-Taiba: Past Operations and Future Prospects*, 10.

83   Roul, "Lashkar-e-Taiba's Financial Network," 6.

84   Fair, *Leader-Led Jihad in Pakistan*, 6.

85   Tankel, *Lashkar-e-Taiba: From 9/11 to Mumbai*, 25.

86   Fair, *Leader-Led Jihad in Pakistan*, 16; "Lashkar-e-Taiba Overview," 66, 67.

87   Rohan Gunaratna, "Mumbai Investigation: The Operatives, Masterminds and the Enduring Threat," UNISCI Discussion Papers, 19 (January 2009), http://www.ucm.es/info/

the terrorists divided into groups of two men and attacked five main targets: two five-star hotels, a railway terminal, a café frequented by Westerners, and a Jewish community center. In all, 166 people were killed; the death toll included 30 non-Indians, including six Americans and six Jews.[88]

The operation was controlled in real time from Pakistan over cellphones.[89] The phone numbers used by the terrorists were linked to an account registered with Callphonex, a U.S. VOIP (Voice over Internet Protocol) provider. Payments for the phone account were made in two installments of approximately $200 to $250 USD each, through MoneyGram in Pakistan and Western Union in Italy. The e-mail account used to set up the service was traced to 10 different IP addresses in Pakistan, Chicago, Kuwait, and Moscow.[90]

Nine terrorists were killed, and one, Ajmal Kasab, was captured alive. Confessions extracted from this lone captive confirmed that all 10 terrorists were Pakistani LeT cadres. The evidence also pointed toward intimate ISI involvement in the attacks.[91] Under severe international pressure, Pakistan arrested Lakhvi for his role as the mastermind of the attacks; one of his visitors at the jail was the ISI chief. Hafiz Saeed was put under house arrest but released soon thereafter; JuD was banned but continues to operate under new identities.[92] The LeT considered the operation a grand success and is reported to have planned several attacks against Indian and American targets to mark the first anniversary of the operation in 2009.[93]

Costs of the Mumbai Attack

Trehan, a high ranking Indian police officer, has estimated the yearly cost of a Pakistani terrorist fighting in Kashmir to be approximately $12,500 USD; that figure includes training, monthly payments, awards for a spectacular act, and money to family members.[94] Similarly, we estimate the following costs in U.S. dollars for various material and activities for the Mumbai attacks as shown below:

- Personnel Costs ($12,500 per person) $125,000
- Surveillance (money paid to David Headley) $30,000
- Weapons and equipment ($1,500 each) $15,000

---

unisci/english/index.html (accessed January 13, 2012).

88   Tankel, *Lashkar-e-Taiba: Past Operations and Future Prospects*, 1, 16.

89   Tankel, *Lashkar-e-Taiba: Past Operations and Future Prospects*, 38, 67.

90   K.A. Kronstadt, *International Terrorism in South Asia* (Library of Congress, Washington, D.C.: Congressional Research Service), CRS Report for Congress, November 3, 2003, http://handle.dtic.mil/100.2/ADA444986 (accessed January 13, 2012).

91   Fair, *Leader-Led Jihad in Pakistan* 12, 1 3.

92   Tankel, *Lashkar-e-Taiba: From 9/11 to Mumbai*, 27, 28.

93   Tankel, *Lashkar-e-Taiba in Perspective*, 4, 6.

94   Trehan, "Terrorism and the Funding of Terrorism," 211.

- VOIP accounts $500
- Total $170,500

If we add in funds for incidental expenditures, one can estimate that the Mumbai terrorist attack may have cost the LeT around $200,000 USD. When compared with LeT's overall annual budget (probably in the $50 million or more range),[95] it is evident that terrorism remains a low-cost endeavor.

Countermeasures and Recommendations

We turn now to the actions that have been and should be taken to more effectively constrain this violent wing of LeT. We will first look at the actions that have been taken by international bodies and India, as well as the limitations of those actions. Thereafter, we will offer some recommendations about how the systems could be improved to better combat the financing instruments of LeT.

At this juncture, it is important to highlight that even though LeT has gone global with its aims, it never ceases to use India as a target for two key reasons. One, LeT continues to serve as a proxy for Pakistan, which allows it to be sheltered by Pakistan; and two, its distorted form of Ahl-e-Hadith ideology declares India a mortal enemy. Therefore, it is necessary that we consider India's actions and its system to combat the financing of terrorists (CFT) in this segment as they form a critical part of the whole repertoire of measures that need to be taken against LeT.

International Response against LeT

The main actions taken by international actors to counter or constrain the financing instruments of LeT were to freeze and seize the assets of LeT leaders. Suffice it to note that these actions were targeted mainly at the movement of money.[96] These measures against LeT and its front organizations such as JuD were carried out either directly by the United Nations and the United States or indirectly through pressure applied to Pakistan. Below are some examples of the measures taken:

---

95   Trehan, "Terrorism and the Funding of Terrorism," 210

96   S.K. Saini, "Problems and Prospects of Combating Terrorist Financing in India," *Strategic Analysis* 33:1 (January 2009): 87; Chiranjeeb Das, "Organized Crime—Changing the Face of the World," *Business Crime Bureau*, http://www.bcbegypt.com/english/Articles. htm, 5-6 (accessed May 10, 2011). The only regional body that is relevant to this fight against LeT is the South Asian Association for Regional Cooperation (SAARC). While SAARC adopted a "Consensus on Terror Protocol" in 2004 as a holistic regional measure to fight terrorism, this protocol has not been efficacious due to deep mistrust between the parties in the body. The countries in SAARC are Afghanistan, Bangladesh, Bhutan, India, Maldives, Nepal, Pakistan, and Sri Lanka. For this reason, this article has excluded the discussion of the regional measures.

- In 2002, Pakistan banned LeT, and the United States labeled it a foreign terrorist organization.[97]
- At the request of India, the United States labeled Dawood Ibrahim an international terrorist in October 2003.[98] The U.S. government seized his assets found in the U.S. and pressured Pakistan to arrest him.
- In 2008, the United Nations declared JuD a front organization for LeT. Because of this, the government of Pakistan was pressured into taking action. Assets of nine LeT leaders were seized. The main instruments applied were U.N. Resolution 1390 and 1373.[99]
- Most recently, as noted earlier, the United States in 2010 exacted an executive order against the Falah-i Insaniat Foundation (FIF), essentially the renamed JuD, and named it a terrorist organization.

India's Responses against LeT

Similar to international agencies such as the United Nations and the Financial Action Task Force (FATF), India has come to regard terrorist financing as a key enabler of terrorist operations in and against India. It has likewise taken steps to address these terrorist-financing concerns. Below are some of the actions that India has taken to combat LeT's financing sources:

- LeT was banned in India in 2001.[100]
- As noted in the earlier section, through a bilateral arrangement with the United States, India was able to declare Dawood Ibrahim an international terrorist.
- India banned *hawala* as the government knows most terrorist financing in India is done informally rather than through the formal financial system.[101]
- One of the more recent measures taken was to join the FATF as a full member in 2009.[102] By doing so, India demonstrated its commitment

---

97   Kronstadt, *International Terrorism in South Asia*, 2.

98   Animesh Roul, "Dawood Ibrahim: India's Elusive Most Wanted Man," *Militant Leadership Monitor*, 1:6 (June 30, 2010), 9.

99   Siddique, *What is Lashkar-e-Taiba?* 4.

100   Siddique, *What is Lashkar-e-Taiba?* 3.

101   Saini, "Problems and Prospects," 92. Nevertheless, this move seemed to be controversial as many critics questioned its value. By doing so, India is pushing the *hawala* system further underground, making it even harder to regulate and monitor. Rather, a more effective way could have been to make it official so that the system can be better regulated.

102   Financial Action Task Force, *Anti-Money Laundering and Combating the Financing of Terrorism: India* (Paris: FATF Secretariat, June 2010). India joined FATF as a full member in 2009. Since then, India has taken steps to bring its Anti-Money Laundering (AML)/Combating the Financing of Terrorism (CFT) system in line with the FATF's standards. Some actions taken: (1) amendment of Unlawful Activities (Prevention) Act, 1967 (UAPA), in 2008; and (2) amendment of Prevention of Money Laundering

to strengthening its legislative and regulatory system toward money laundering and terrorist financing. It is making those moves with the hope of constricting funding sources not only to LeT, but also to several other terrorist groups operating in India.

Limitations

Even though both international agencies and India have taken substantial steps against LeT, these measures have not been effective. This is demonstrated by the fact that LeT is still getting its funding not only from the government of Pakistan but also other overseas sources to support its operations. The key limitation in the international anti-money laundering (AML)/CFT system lies in the fact that its measures and recommendations are, by and large, nonbinding in nature, including both U.N. and FATF resolutions. For example, in applying U.N. Resolution 1373, India can do nothing against members of LeT residing in Pakistan. As India has no jurisdiction over LeT, it can only hope to prosecute LeT with Pakistan's cooperation.[103]

Unfortunately, Pakistan is not fully cooperative when it comes to fighting LeT, and its actions are often little more than cosmetic in nature. As already mentioned, the reasons for this response are three-fold. First, the LeT serves a strategic purpose for the government of Pakistan. LeT's goals are aligned with those of the Pakistani government; it has been reported that the Pakistani government considers LeT the most reliable terrorism asset it can wield against India.[104] Second, there are many ties between LeT and the ISI and Pakistan Army, which makes it hard for the latter to act against LeT. This is because the ISI, the Pakistan Army, and LeT all recruit their members from the Punjab and northwest regions of Pakistan, resulting in the members of all the groups having familial ties with one another.[105] Third, there could be severe blowback on the government of Pakistan from two main sources if it acts against LeT. The first potential source of trouble is the population that receives social services from LeT/JuD. As LeT/JuD continues to provide crucial social services to the Pakistani populace, any actions the government takes against the former will mean disruption of these services. The second potential source of blowback is from LeT itself. LeT has thus far not turned against the Pakistani government because of the impunity it enjoys in Pakistan. If the situation were to change, it is not hard to see that LeT might well join the rest of its counterparts (other terrorist groups in Pakistan) in fighting against the Pakistani government.

Act, 2002 (PMLA) in 2009. These amendments are meant to align India's system with the "requirements of the United Nations Convention for the Suppression of the Financing of Terrorism (FT Convention)." However, the FATF report also noted that there were numerous gaps in India's AML/CFT system that needed to be addressed.

103   Saini, "Problems and Prospects," 88.
104   Tankel, *Lashkar-E-Taiba: Past Operations and Future Prospects*, 5-6.
105   Tankel, *Lashkar-E-Taiba: Past Operations and Future Prospects*, 9.

Within India, India's CFT system is fragmented and uncoordinated and has not evolved to the point where it can be used as an effective tool. According to Saini:

> Terrorist financing-related information at present is not a priority for the central or state intelligence agencies. ... As a result, intelligence reporting on the issue lacks overall coordinated direction and is incident driven. Moreover, responsibility for the problem is diffused amongst a plethora of agencies, each working in watertight compartments, resulting in lack of accountability.[106]

In addition to using the anti-money laundering mechanisms, the entire CFT system is merely an enhancement to India's old methods for combating insurgencies in the past. As a result, terrorist groups such as LeT and its affiliates in India continue to be able to finance their operations in India not only through the formal but also the informal financial system.[107] These deficiencies in India's CFT system are reported in a FATF evaluation undertaken in 2010.[108]

Recommendations

The following are some recommendations that will, hopefully, help to mitigate these limitations. In the international arena, regional and global organizations need to continue to pressure Pakistan by making Pakistan more accountable for the actions of LeT, as well as its support organization and structures. Resolving the issue of Kashmir, clearly a difficult task, would also undermine support for LeT. This would reduce funding from Pakistan's expatriates supporting the J&K cause, and give the Pakistani government more freedom of action against LeT, which should lead to more effective countermeasures.

Internationally, organizations and states need to strengthen the AML/CFT system by adopting a more comprehensive monitoring and tracking system for charities; by making some measures more binding with the help of concrete evidence; by addressing the sources of funding from the Gulf region to LeT; and by putting more pressure on those states from which these sources are flowing, such as Dubai.

India, for its part, should strengthen diplomatic measures since most of India's terrorism problems are funded by external sources. It should continue to seek assistance from agencies like the FATF and the UN to act against supporters of

---

106   Saini, "Problems and Prospects," 93.

107   Saini, "Problems and Prospects," 93-4.

108   For more information on the weaknesses of India's CFT system, see Financial Action Task Force, *Anti-Money Laundering*. For the purpose of illustration, some examples of these weaknesses are (1) India's ineffective judiciary system toward AML/CFT (2) poor control of money movement across borders taking into consideration the large volume of human traffic flow as well as India's cash-based economy, and (3) a weak Suspicion Transaction Reporting (STR) mechanism.

LeT and affiliated groups operating in India. Also, bilateral arrangements with the U.S. will help in pressuring Pakistan. India should also aim to work more cooperatively with Pakistan to resolve the LeT issue.

Internally, India should set up a "whole of government" approach toward CFT, which crosses many domains, and should create an inter-government agency to coordinate and synergize efforts. India should also: bring the CFT system more in line with FATF standards; regulate NGOs and charities in India, including *hawala* (and perhaps consider lifting the ban on *hawala* so that it is not driven underground); give the intelligence and law enforcement agencies a more active role in CFT; build up dedicated resources to counter terrorism funding not only at the central government and state levels, but also at grassroots levels (e.g. police forces); enforce stronger border control, particularly with Nepal and Bangladesh; increase public awareness about the ills and concomitant effects of terrorist financing to create an environment conducive to building public trust in government policies; and leverage its population's skills in Internet technology, especially as terrorist financing is moving into the cyber domain.[109]

Conclusion

Today, LeT has global aims. LeT's funding sources have also diversified significantly and are no longer dependent solely on the government of Pakistan. The fact that LeT is still functioning and continuing to receive substantial financial support from various overseas sources means that the international CFT measures in place are not sufficiently effective. India's ineffectual system in constraining LeT's support to its affiliate groups in India further illuminates the gaps in the CFT measures against LeT. Cumulatively, all of this means more needs to be done. To this end, this chapter has attempted to provide some recommendations for how international and Indian CFT systems could be enhanced to constrict this lifeblood for LeT. More importantly, regardless of what strategy the international bodies and India are to employ, Pakistan must be included as part of the formula because Pakistan is still a strategic shelter for LeT. Without Pakistan's cooperation and active participation, LeT may never be eliminated.

---

109   Saini, "Problems and Prospects," 91-6.

Chapter 7
Financing the Taliban

Justin Y. Reese

The Taliban offers a useful case study of an organization that has exploited weak and ungoverned spaces for financial benefit. A brief history of the Taliban will be provided, followed by an examination of the unofficial economies of Afghanistan and Pakistan. This chapter will then explore how this economic environment was used by the Taliban to both raise and transfer funds. Finally, this chapter will discuss existing countermeasures, analyze their effectiveness, and recommend alternative options.

Background

The Taliban is a religious movement led by mullahs and derives its name and strength from the *talib* (Islamic students).[1] The beginnings of the Taliban are traced to a purported 30 members in the Pashtun village of Singesar, Afghanistan, whose first act was an armed intervention on behalf of the weak and poor in the spring of 1994.[2] This original group rapidly expanded to a force of 30,000-35,000, eventually claiming governance of Afghanistan within two years.[3] Many welcomed the consolidation of power the Taliban provided after the fall of Kabul and President Najibullah in 1992.[4] Taliban governance satisfied both a war weary constituency with a promise of peace and investors looking to broker development plans for the region. The Taliban's stated goals were to "restore peace, disarm the population, enforce Sharia law, and defend the integrity and Islamic character of

---

1 Ahmed Rashid emphasizes the importance of choosing *talib*, "one who seeks knowledge," versus mullah, "one who gives knowledge," in order to distance the fledgling movement from, "the party politics of the Mujaheddin," in Ahmed Rashid, *Taliban* (New Haven, CT: Yale University Press, 2000), 22-3.

2 "The most credible story, told repeatedly, is that in the spring of 1994 Singesar neighbors came to tell him that a commander had abducted two teenage girls, their heads had been shaved and they had been taken to a military camp and repeatedly raped. Omar enlisted some 30 Talibs who had only 16 rifles between them and attacked the base, freeing the girls and hanging the commander from the barrel of a tank," "Rashid, *Taliban*, 25.

3 Abdulkader Sinno, "Explaining the Taliban's Ability to Mobilize the Pashtuns," in *The Taliban and the Crisis of Afghanistan*, Robert D. Crews and Amin Tarzi, eds (Cambridge, MA: Harvard University Press, 2008), 59-89, 69-70.

4 Rashid, *Taliban*, 21.

Afghanistan."[5] The Taliban pursued these goals through a strategy designed to impose their interpretation of what village life should be and how a village should subsist, even as the majority of Taliban had no experience in rural Afghanistan.[6] The Taliban offered only a military solution to Afghanistan, and suffered from an inability to connect ideologically with the Afghan majority. The Taliban believed Allah would provide for the population thereby cleansing themselves of the responsibilities of governance.[7]

Even as the Taliban consolidated governance in Afghanistan, few members of the international community supported or endorsed their claim to sovereignty. Saudi Arabia, the UAE, and Pakistan were the only members to offer the Taliban political legitimacy. The highly visible and deplorable conduct of the Taliban—such as public executions through detestable methods compounded by other human rights violations—proved an insurmountable obstacle for international membership. Isolated and with a fragile grip on power, the Taliban regime was easily defeated by United States and allied forces in 2001. The Taliban forces that survived retreated and disappeared into the indigenous population of Afghanistan.

The Taliban continue to demonstrate resiliency as a result of sanctuary, sustainable lines of communication, and the ever present availability of funds.[8] The Taliban have established a strongpoint in the Federally Administered Tribal Areas (FATA) and North-West Frontier Province (NWFP) of Pakistan. According to the National Counterterrorism Center annual report on terrorism for 2007, attacks have risen in both Afghanistan and Pakistan, but especially in the NWFP and FATA.[9] Taliban influence in FATA is best reflected by the existence of sharia courts, local constabulary forces, tax collectors, and public offices held by appointed officials.[10] This aggressive social agenda compounded by the incapacity

---

5   Rashid, *Taliban*, 22.

6   "It is not the values of the village, but the values of the village as interpreted by refugee camp dwellers or madrassa students most of whom have never known ordinary village life," Robert D. Crews and Amin Tarzi, "Introduction," *The Taliban and the Crisis of Afghanistan*, edited by Robert D. Crews and Amin Tarzi (Cambridge, MA: Harvard University Press, 2008), 41.

7   Rashid, *Taliban*, 127.

8   Arabinda Acharya, Syed Adnan Ali Shah Bukhari, and Sadia Sulaiman, "Making Money in the Mayhem: Funding Taliban Insurrection in the Tribal Areas of Pakistan," *Studies in Conflict & Terrorism*, 32:2 (2009), 96.

9   Terror attacks in 2007 increased by 137 percent in Pakistan over 2006 attacks. Although the government signed a peace agreement in September 2006 with pro-Taliban tribes in North-West Frontier Province (NWFP) and Federally Administered Tribal Areas (FATA), the region accounted for 54 percent of the total attacks, up from 23 percent the previous year. Afghanistan registered a 16 percent increase in the number of attacks in 2007 as compared with the previous year. National Counter Terrorism Center, *2007 Report on Terrorism* (Washington, D.C.: NCTC, April 2008), 17-19.

10   Robert Canfield, "Fraternity, Power, and Time in Central Asia," in *The Taliban and the Crisis of Afghanistan*, edited by Robert D. Crews and Amin Tarzi, 59-89 (Cambridge,

	2002-03	2003-04	2004-05	2005-06	2006-07	2007-08	2008-09	2009-10
GDP ($US billions)	4.0	4.4	5.4	6.5	7.7	9.7	11.8	14.5
Population (millions)	28.3	29.1	29.9	30.8	31.6	32.5	33.4	34.4
Per capita GDP ($US)	141	151	181	211	244	298	353	422

Figure 7.1   Afghan Official Economy

Source: Adapted from Ian Livingston and Michael O'Hanlon, Afghanistan Index: Tracking Variables of Reconstruction & Security in Post 9/11 Afghanistan, Brookings Institute http://www.brookings.edu/~/media/Files/Programs/FP/afghanistan%20index/index20110731.pdf and World Bank, World Development Indicators, http://data.worldbank.org/indicator/SP.POP.TOTL.

of the Pakistani government to govern the NWFP and FATA allowed the Taliban in the tribal areas to serve as "a parallel administration with all the functions of the state."[11]

Economic Environment

Just as ungoverned spaces of the FATA and NWFP are enabling environments for the Taliban, so too is the weakly-regulated and opaque economy of Afghanistan. The total size of the official economy in Afghanistan for 2011 was roughly 17 billion USD. Figure 7.1 portrays the positive growth trends for both total GDP and per capita for Afghanistan.

In addition to the legal economy, the black economy in Afghanistan accounted for approximately $5.3 billion in 2009, with most of the activity revolving around opium and corruption.[12]

MA: Harvard University Press, 2008), 231.

   11   Canfield, "Fraternity, Power, and Time in Central Asia," 231.

   12   United Nations Office on Drugs and Crime, *Corruption in Afghanistan*, 2010, http://www.unodc.org/documents/data-and-analysis/Afghanistan/Afghanistan-corruption-survey2010-Eng.pdf; United Nations Office on Drugs and Crime, *Afghanistan Opium Survey 2009,* December 2009, http://www.unodc.org/documents/crop-monitoring/Afghanistan/Afgh-opiumsurvey2009_web.pdf.

Expenditures

Typically, labor costs comprise a large portion of a terrorist organization's budget. Originally (in the 1990s), however, the Taliban relied heavily on their ideological supporters to essentially gain cheap labor. According to Mullah Wakil, the aide to Mullah Omar, "the Sharia does not allow politics or political parties. That is why we give no salaries to officials or soldiers, just food, clothes, shoes, and weapons."[13] Additionally, where ideology did not provide the proper motivation for service the Taliban practiced forced conscription.[14] Over time, the rapid growth experienced by the Taliban slowed as they began to consolidate power in areas they controlled.[15] With their ideological mission accomplished, very few later members joined for purely idealistic reasons; instead, many joined the ranks of the Taliban for a wage.[16] "Taliban were offering daily wages twice what a sharecropper cultivating opium might earn."[17] Another estimate supports this shift in the Taliban's incentive-based recruiting program stating, "only 10 percent of the Taliban fighters were motivated by a strong desire to restore Taliban to power, while 60 to 70 percent had joined for a wage."[18] One Taliban account from February 2006 asserts that members received, "a signing bonus of $300 and $150 a month in salary" plus additional accruements such as, "new clothes, shoes, a motorbike, and Kalashnikov rifle."[19]

The annual expenditures of the Taliban after 2001 consisted mainly of operational costs, maintaining or creating organizational infrastructure, growth and recruiting initiatives, and savings.[20] Operational costs are those associated with offensive militant operations such as raids, attacks, and bombings. The organizational infrastructure costs represent the day-to-day cost of running the Taliban organization. This includes administrative functions, provisions, transportation, fuel, etc. The organizational infrastructure is also the area projected to consume the majority of funds. Growth and recruiting initiatives represent the propaganda and cost associated with physically spreading the message of the Taliban in order to expand the scope of their operations and influence within the constraints of their limited resources. The savings funds are monies the Taliban set aside to serve as resources for future discretionary use by management. The Taliban rely on a variety of fiscal inputs in order to meet these expenditure requirements.

---

13   Rashid, *Taliban*, 43.
14   Rashid, *Taliban*, 103.
15   Rashid, *Taliban*, 60.
16   Atiq Sarwari and Robert D. Crews, "Epilogue: Afghanistan and the Pax Americana," in *The Taliban and the Crisis of Afghanistan*, edited by Robert D. Crews and Amin Tarzi, 59-89 (Cambridge, MA: Harvard University Press, 2008), 345.
17   Sarwari and Crews, "Epilogue," 345.
18   Sarwari and Crews, "Epilogue," 345.
19   Sarwari and Crews, "Epilogue," 345.
20   Acharya et al., "Making Money in the Mayhem," 95.

These fiscal inputs include state support and sponsorship, the opium economy, kidnapping, the unofficial economy, popular support, and involuntary support.

State Support for the Taliban

Historically, the Taliban received support from state sponsors such as Pakistan and Saudi Arabia, especially during the mid to late 1990s when it rose to power and ruled Afghanistan. Prior to 9/11, Pakistan provided the Taliban official political recognition and became the main contributor of people, guns, and money. The Taliban emerged from the Jamiat Ulema-e-Islami run religious education system in Pakistan.[21] Pakistan provided the Taliban exclusive access to this madrassa system for recruits during their formative years. These recruits numbered in the thousands and made significant contributions on the battlefield in the form of reinforcements for a Taliban force suffering from battle fatigue in the late 1990s. The impact was extremely acute in the immediate aftermath of the Taliban setbacks around Kabul and Mazar in 1997 when calls for help from Mullah Omar to Samiul Haq resulted in the closing of Pakistani madrassas and entire student bodies consisting of 5,000 males were sent to join the ranks of the Taliban.[22] Pakistan then gave the Taliban the location of a depot providing the Taliban with, "18,000 kalashnikovs, dozens of artillery pieces, large quantities of ammunition, and many vehicles."[23] Pakistani military and technical advisers also played a critical role in transforming the Taliban into a formidable force, capable of pursuing organized offensive action and demonstrating the ability to project power throughout Afghanistan.[24] The Pakistani army achieved this through organizing the Taliban into brigades and divisions, with rapid mobility augmented by modern communications.[25] The government of Pakistan found a way to provide for the Taliban even as Pakistan's economy struggled during the late 1990s. Pakistan provided the Taliban $30 million in aid from 1997-1998 with $6 million earmarked to pay for the salaries of the Taliban leadership.[26] The level of Pakistani involvement is illustrated best by the "fact that Afghan cities under Taliban rule could be reached by dialing Pakistani telephone prefixes."[27]

---

21   Daniel L. Byman, *The Changing Nature of State Sponsorship of Terrorism* (Washington, D.C.: The Saban Center for Middle East Policy at The Brookings Institution, May 2008), 8.

22   Rashid, *Taliban*, 59, 91.

23   Rashid, *Taliban*, 28.

24   Crews and Tarzi, "Introduction," 29.

25   Crews and Tarzi, "Introduction," 29.

26   This aid appeared in the form of hard currency, food, fuel, arms, ammunition, maintenance, spare parts, and infrastructure development. Rashid, *Taliban*, 183-4.

27   Crews and Tarzi, "Introduction," 29.

Saudi Arabia also contributed to the Taliban's rise to power in Afghanistan. Saudi support to the Taliban arrived in the form of fuel, money, and hundreds of new vehicles flown into Kandahar airport from the Gulf port city of Dubai during the Afghan Civil War.[28] The Taliban also enjoyed monetary support from the Saudi community during the late 1990s through various unofficial channels reinforced by ties of shared ideology in regards to Deobandism and Wahhabism. Saudi Arabia also officially recognized the Taliban regime as the government of Afghanistan.[29] Official government support for the Taliban (both financial and political) dried up for the most part in 1998, coinciding with the Taliban refusal to hand over bin Laden to Saudi authorities.[30]

The U.S. even recognized the Taliban as the de facto authority in Afghanistan, thereby allowing dialog between U.S. corporate and government representatives for mutual gain.[31] "Until 1999, U.S. taxpayers paid the entire annual salary of every single Taliban government official."[32] U.S. policy began to shift with the emerging stories about the lack of women's rights and with the arrival of Osama bin Laden in 1996.[33] Diplomacy was used in an attempt to reduce the growing friction between the Taliban and the international community. In April 1998, Bill Richardson, America's chief delegate to the United Nations, traveled to Kabul with the prospects of possible recognition of the Taliban government in exchange for genuine progress towards peace.[34] In 2001, Colin Powell awarded the Taliban government for reducing opium production with a $43 million grant.[35]

After the 9/11 attacks and the overthrow of the Taliban regime, these official and *de facto* state sponsors withdrew or changed the profile of their support. As an insurgent group, rather than a ruling party in government, the Taliban receives some aid from Pakistan, although Pakistan denies the existence of any fiscal relationship. The conduit for state sponsorship now appears more passive than

---

28   Crews and Tarzi, "Introduction," 45.

29   Eben Kaplan and Greg Bruno, *The Taliban in Afghanistan*, Council on Foreign Relations, 2008, http://www.cfr.org/publication/10551/ (accessed August 6, 2008).

30   Sinno, "Explaining the Taliban's Ability to Mobilize the Pashtuns," 71.

31   This dynamic is best highlighted through the story of UNOCAL's relationship with the Taliban. The basic story line centers on U.S. involvement in the Centgas Project for a natural gas pipeline which by design would utilize Afghanistan as transit space. The Taliban enjoyed financial support during the course of UNOCAL's bid to acquire contractual relations with the Taliban.

32   Loretta Napoleoni, *Terror Incorporated: Tracing the Dollars Behind the Terror Networks* (New York: Seven Stories Press, 2005), 196.

33   Ahmed Rashid, *Descent into Chaos: The United States and the Failure of Nation Building in Pakistan, Afghanistan, and Central Asia* (New York, NY: The Penguin Group, 2008), 15.

34   The Economist, "Those Not Very Nice People in Afghanistan," April 23, 1998.

35   Ted Galen Carpenter, *How Washington Funded the Taliban*, CATO Institute, August 2, 2002, http://www.cato.org/pub_display.php?pub_id=3556 (accessed January 13, 2012).

active, and coordinated by key social actors and independent bureaucracies rather than central government entities.[36] The most visible form of passive sponsorship today is the ability to use the FATA and the NWFP portions of Pakistan as safe havens. General James Jones, as NATO Supreme Commander, testified before the U.S. Senate Foreign Relations Committee in September 2006 asserting that the Taliban headquarters was based in Quetta, Pakistan.[37] One estimate is that Pakistanis comprise one quarter of the Taliban's forces.[38] There are also allegations of cooperation between Pakistani Intelligence and the Taliban leadership.[39]

The relationship between Iran and the post-2001 Taliban is also a matter of much speculation and debate among governments, policy makers, academics, and media. Though the opinions vary as to the extent of enabling support Iran provides the Taliban, there is a growing chorus of agreement that a mutually beneficial relationship does in fact exist between the Taliban and Iran, and this relationship is damaging U.S. efforts to stabilize Afghanistan. U.S. Secretary of Defense Robert Gates in June 2007 offered insight to the U.S. position stating, "there's a fairly substantial flow of weapons ... given the quantities that we're seeing, it is difficult to believe that it's associated with smuggling or the drug business or that it's taking place without the knowledge of the Iranian government."[40] The U.S. Treasury Department, in October 2007, claimed that Iran's "Qods Force provides weapons and financial support to the Taliban to support anti-U.S. and anti-Coalition activity in Afghanistan,"[41] and that, "since at least 2006, Iran has arranged frequent shipments of small arms and associated ammunition, rocket propelled grenades, mortar rounds, 107mm rockets, plastic explosives, and probably man-portable defense systems to the Taliban."[42]

State sponsorship offers both challenges and opportunities for the Taliban. They gain access to funds, weapons and safe havens that they otherwise would not have. On the other hand, the Taliban become vulnerable to interference from Jamiat Ulema-e-Islami, members of Pakistan Intelligence, and Iran, and must strive to balance the perception of being either an autonomous authority or a puppet/proxy of outside sponsors.

---

36 Byman, *The Changing Nature of State Sponsorship of Terrorism* 7-11.

37 Rubin R. Barnett, "Saving Afghanistan," *Foreign Affairs*, 86:1, January/February, 2007.

38 Byman, *The Changing Nature of State Sponsorship of Terrorism*, 8.

39 Byman, *The Changing Nature of State Sponsorship of Terrorism*, 8.

40 United State Department of Defense, Media Interview with Robert Gates, June 13, 2007, http://www.defenselink.mil/transcripts/transcript.aspx?transcriptid=3987 (accessed January 13, 2012).

41 U.S. Department of Treasury, "Designation of Iranian Entities and Individuals for Proliferation Activities and Support for Terrorism," October 25, 2007, http://merln.ndu.edu/archivepdf/iran/State/94193.pdf.

42 Department of Treasury, *Fact Sheet*

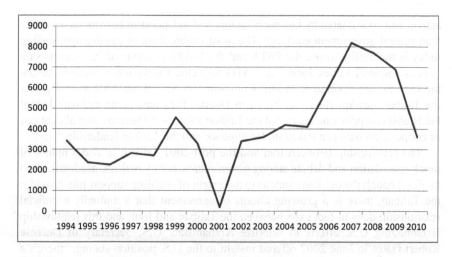

Figure 7.2   Afghanistan Opium Production 1994-2010 (metric tons)

Source: Adapted from United Nations Office on Drugs and Crime, Afghanistan Opium Survey 2010, September 2010, http://www.unodc.org/documents/crop-monitoring/Afghanistan/Afg_opium_survey_2010_exsum_web.pdf.

Sources of Financing: Opium Economy

One portion of the Taliban portfolio, which demonstrated tremendous growth since 2001, is the income generated from the opium economy of Afghanistan. The United Nations Office of Drug and Crime (UNODC) estimated the total export value of the 2007 opium harvest to be approximately $4 billion, accounting for 93 percent of global opium production.[43] The Taliban earnings from this opium economy are derived from a 10 percent tax on farmers producing an estimated $100 million for 2007.[44] When these earnings are augmented by peripheral services provided by the Taliban such as laboratory protection and convoy escort/security for product transit the figure grows to something in the vicinity of $200-$400 million.[45]

Figure 7.2 displays the long term trend in opium production. The sharp decline in 2000-2001 is due to a successful ban on opium production brought about by the Taliban regime, demonstrating both the reach of their authoritarian rule and the malleability of the opium economy. However, it should be noted that the

---

43   United Nations, *2008 World Drug Report* (United Nations Office on Drugs and Crime, 2008), 37, http://www.unodc.org/documents/wdr/WDR_2008/WDR_2008_eng_web.pdf.

44   Muhammad Tahir, "Fueling the Taliban: Poppies, Guns and Insurgents," *Terrorism Monitor*, VI, 14, The Jamestown Foundation, July 2008, 5.

45   Tahir, "Fueling the Taliban," 5.

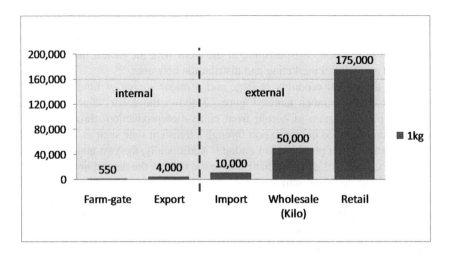

Figure 7.3   Cost of Heroin through Production–Distribution Cycle in 2000

Source: Adapted from Peter Reuter, "Can Production and Trafficking of Illicit Drugs be Reduced or Merely Shifted?" The World Bank Development Research Group, Macroeconomics and Growth Team, March 2008, http://www-wds.worldbank.org/external/default/WDSContentServer/IW3P/IB/2008/03/18/000158349_20080318133751/Rendered/PDF/wps4564.pdf.

ban was mostly done for economic reasons. At the time, there was a surplus of opium, decreasing its value. By temporarily banning the growing of poppies (but importantly not the ownership of stores of opium), the value of the remaining stock of opium would increase.

As an insurgent group, the Taliban encouraged opium production. In 2007, more than 80 percent of the total opium production was generated from locales with a permanent Taliban presence, as "poppy production has soared in provinces where the Taliban is most active."[46] The presence of the Taliban, "helps smugglers and farmers protect their laboratories, trade opium up to the border and fight back against anti-drug campaigners."[47] The relationship between opium and the Taliban persisted despite the introduction of U.S.-led coalition forces into Afghanistan in 2001 and in the face of an ever increasingly capable state security apparatus.

Geographically, 70 percent of Afghanistan's 2007 poppy production was generated from, "five relatively higher-income agriculturally rich provinces along the Pakistan border with Helmand Province alone accounting for 50 percent."[48] There exists a corresponding decline in 2007 of poppy cultivation in the more

---

46   U.S. Department of State, *International Narcotics Control Strategy Report: Volume I Drug and Chemical Control*, Bureau for International Narcotics and law Enforcement Affairs, March 2008, 235. Tahir, "Fueling the Taliban," 4.

47   Tahir, "Fueling the Taliban," 4.

48   U.S. Department of State, *International Narcotics Control Strategy Report*, 235.

impoverished, yet more secure, provinces in northern and western Afghanistan.[49] The geographic distribution of opium production is significant in demonstrating that opium production "is flourishing in the areas with the richest land and best developed agricultural marketing and distribution networks."[50]

While the opium economy is large and a major source of funding for the Taliban, it could be much larger. Figure 7.3 shows the dollar value associated with one pure kilogram of heroin from cultivation/production, through export from Afghanistan, and import/export through a transient state such as Turkey, and finally to an end user purchase in London.[51] Additionally, the vast majority of the profits are earned outside of Afghanistan (to the right of the dashed line).

The Taliban could tap into these higher profits by expanding into the external opium market. There is some evidence that this has occurred: for instance, in July 2008, Korean police arrested two Afghans, three Pakistanis, and four Korean citizens who were attempting to ship 12 tons of acetic anhydride to southern Afghanistan disguised as motor oil.[52]

Sources of Financing: Kidnapping

Kidnapping is another method used by the Taliban to generate income, retrieve captured members, and maintain international notoriety. The National Counterterrorism Center states in their annual report for 2007 that, "kidnapping by the Taliban continued to rise; the number of kidnappings in 2007 nearly doubled those reported in 2006."[53] Corresponding to these figures was the increased targeting of foreign nationals in 2007 and then subsequently using these hostages to negotiate prisoner exchanges and other concessions with the government of the hostages.[54] For example, the Italian government was able to secure reporter Daniele Mastrogiacomo only after Kabul released five Taliban prisoners in a structured prisoner for journalist swap at the request of the Italian government.[55] This prisoner release had further repercussions in the counterinsurgency efforts

49   U.S. Department of State, *International Narcotics Control Strategy Report*, 235.

50   U.S.Department of State, *International Narcotics Control Strategy Report*, 235.

51   Peter Reuter, "Can Production and Trafficking of Illicit Drugs be Reduced or Merely Shifted?" *Policy Research Working Papers Series*, World Bank, Development Research Group Macroeconomics and Growth Team, March 2008, 10-11, http://www-wds.worldbank.org/external/default/WDSContentServer/IW3P/IB/2008/03/18/000158349_200 80318133751/Rendered/PDF/wps4564.pdf.

52   Agence France Presse, "SKorean Police Bust 'Taliban Linked' Drug Ring," July 3 2008, http://afp.google.com/article/ALeqM5giJDG3ZlXNkBZEjgLIdStVqGySlw (accessed January 13, 2012).

53   National Counter Terrorism Center, *2007 Report on Terrorism*, 19.

54   National Counter Terrorism Center, *2007 Report on Terrorism*, 19.

55   Phil Stewart, "Italy Opens Pandora's Box with Taliban Hostage Swap," *Reuters*, March 23, 2007, available from The International Institute for Strategic Studies, http://

of Afghanistan when Mullah Mansur Dadullah, who was one of the prisoners released in this exchange announced he had assumed his slain brother's role in coordinating Taliban operations.[56] On another occasion, the Taliban was able to structure concessions and a possible ransom from the South Korean government after the kidnapping of 23 South Korean missionaries in 2007.[57] South Korea conceded to not allow any more missionary groups to travel to Afghanistan and allegedly paid $20 million to the Taliban for the release of the 19 surviving hostages.[58] Finally, one of the most politically embarrassing incidents occurred when Tariq Azizuddin, Pakistan's ambassador to Afghanistan was kidnapped in February 2008.[59] The Pakistan government is said to have released 55 Taliban operatives and made payment of several hundred thousand dollars to broker the release of the ambassador.[60] The Taliban practice of kidnapping foreigners has proven fruitful in a variety of ways, besides as a way of raising funds. The targeting of foreigners serves to attract international media attention during the incident, while simultaneously demonstrating state incapacity through the perception of insecurity. Also, humanitarian and non-governmental organizations (NGOs) withdraw from areas prone to kidnappings and attacks.

Source of Financing: Unofficial Economy

The unofficial economy of Afghanistan is the largest source of funds available for the Taliban. The opium economy is a subset of the unofficial economy, but due to its size and separate treatment in policy it is treated as a stand-alone source of financing for the Taliban. The unofficial economy is comprised of unofficial imports, exports, and domestic smuggling occurring beyond the reach of state control and legitimate institutional regulation.

The current form of the unofficial economy in Afghanistan has emerged from past attempts to regulate cross border trade with regional partnerships. For example, the Afghanistan Transit Trade Agreement (ATTA) is a tri-lateral trade agreement signed by Afghanistan, Pakistan, and Iran aimed at providing Afghanistan access to the Persian Gulf and Indian Ocean.[61] Operating under the

---

www.iiss.org/whats-new/iiss-in-the-press/press-coverage-2007/march-2007/italy-opens-pandoras-box-with-hostage-swap/ (accessed January 13, 2012).

56   Sarwari and Crews, "Epilogue," 354.

57   Choe Sang-Hun, "Freed by Taliban, 19 South Korean Hostages Will Face Relief and Anger Back Home," *The New York Times*, September 2, 2007.

58   Sang-Hun, "Freed by Taliban."

59   Bill Roggio, "Pakistan Frees Formers Guantanamo Prisoner, Afghan Taliban Commander," *The Long War Journal*, May 20, 2008, http://www.longwarjournal.org/archives/2008/05/pakistan_frees_forme.php (accessed January 13, 2012).

60   Roggio, "Pakistan Frees Formers Guantanamo Prisoner."

61   Neamatollah Nojumi, "The Rise and Fall of the Taliban," in *The Taliban and the Crisis of Afghanistan*, edited by Robert D. Crews and Amin Tarzi (Cambridge, MA:

auspice of this trade arrangement, goods are brought into Afghanistan without any associated customs fee. Once in Afghanistan the goods are smuggled into neighboring states such as Pakistan and sold at a price undercutting the regulated domestic market price. This enterprise—once subsidized by the state—became privatized during the Afghanistan Civil War when the Taliban was able to secure transit of goods for a fee. Unofficial exports from Afghanistan to Pakistan were valued at $1 billion with the Taliban receiving between $36 and $75 million as a participant in this enterprise during 1999 alone.[62] In the early 2000s, the size of this unofficial economy attracted the interest of major manufacturers such as Sony who sent representatives to markets in Afghanistan and Pakistan in order to identify which television sets were popular and to disseminate information of upcoming models for distribution.[63]

The Taliban rely upon the unofficial economy for much the same reason the organization relies upon ungoverned territory. Specifically, the Taliban is able to pursue financial practices beyond the reach of enforceable state regulation and without being subjected to any sort of tax or other state induced cost incurrence.

Sources of Financing: Popular Support

Popular support is the most challenging source of finance to quantify in dollar amounts. Much of the benefits reaped by the Taliban from popular support occur as non-denominated values in the form of passive support, tolerant cooperation, and safe haven/passage.[64] For example, it is widely believed the madrassa school system is a significant contributor of funds to further the Taliban due to their historical association with the movement. Madrassa leaders such as Maulana Sami ul-Haq defiantly make clear, "we are not bound by the government to audit our funding system because they do not give us any money."[65] Additionally, "in the absence of a functioning formal economy to provide employment and income for Afghans, the black economy has become dominant as the only generator of reliable and well-paid employment for a significant percentage of the population," furthering the association between the average Afghan and the Taliban for mutual

---

Harvard University Press, 2008), 59-89, 103-4.

62   Napoleoni, *Terror Incorporated*, 177.

63   Daniel Pearl, "Taliban Profits," *Worldview Magazine Online*, 15:3, 2002, http://www.worldviewmagazine.com/issues/article.cfm?id=95&issue=23 (accessed on August 3, 2008, site discontinued).

64   Non-denominated value defined as not having dollar value, yet retaining economic value.

65   Imtiaz Ali, "The Father of the Taliban: An Interview with Maulana Sami ul-Haq," *Spotlight on Terror*, 4:2, The Jamestown Foundation, May 23, 2007, http://www.jamestown.org/terrorism/news/article.php?articleid=2373418 (site discontinued).

subsistence.[66] For example, 366,000 households with an estimated 2.38 million people, or 10.3 percent of the total population for Afghanistan participate in the opium economy in Afghanistan.[67] This is a significant demographic which may provide popular support for the Taliban.[68]

Popular support serves as a cost saving mechanism across all line items of expenditure. For example, the Taliban may rely on the popular support for overt surveillance capabilities minimizing both Taliban exposure and risk. This saves the Taliban tremendous capital by freeing up funds which would be required to train, equip, and deploy their own forces to achieve similar capability. Another significant feature of the popular support enjoyed by the Taliban is the ethnic alignment of support across state boundaries provides a conduit for maneuver corridors and smuggling routes. While all these advantages serve the financial inputs of the Taliban well, the risks of over-reliance on popular support may prove challenging for the Taliban should conditions on the ground change. The level of popular support ebbs and flows and may drop in the face of increasing state stability.

Sources of Financing: Extortion

The Taliban derives income through coercion, illegitimate taxation, extortion, local seizure of assets, and forced conscription. These methods are used mostly in the southern and eastern regions of Afghanistan and the FATA of Pakistan where the state is weak. The Taliban establishes illegitimate 'customs points' at the border or 'toll collection points' along a stretch of road whose purpose is to charge each person and each car crossing. These customs points may also collect tax on smuggled items. In addition to this, the Taliban collects fuel from fuel stations, wheat as Ushr from farmers, and impose a fixed tax on traders.[69] Acharya et al. in 2009 illustrate the level of Taliban revenue development from taxation in the FATA of Pakistan. These authors claim that the Taliban pursuit of revenue consisting of centralized control, tax schedules, and audits is "very systemic and

---

66   Jane's, *Economy: Afghanistan*, Sentinel Security Assessments South Asia, July, 2008.

67   United Nations, *Afghanistan Opium Survey 2008*, United Nations Office on Drugs and Crime, August 2008, viii, available at: http://www.unodc.org/documents/publications/Afghanistan_Opium_Survey_2008.pdf.

68   United Nations, *Afghanistan Opium Survey 2008*, 13.

69   "This refers to the ten percent (in some cases five percent) of agricultural produce payable by a Muslim as a part of his religious obligation, like Zakat mainly for the benefit of the poor and the needy," "A Short Dictionary of Islamic Economic Terms," Soundvision. com, http://www.soundvision.com/Info/money/islamiceconomicterms.asp (accessed January 13, 2012). Iqbal Khattak, "Taliban Collecting Taxes to Raise Funds for 'jihad,' *Daily Times*, August 15, 2008, http://www.dailytimes.com.pk/default.asp?page=2008%5C08%5C15%5C story_15-8-2008_pg7_11 (accessed January 13, 2012).

even more efficient than the government system."[70] The ability of the Taliban to generate income from coerced support is a tangible example of state weakness. However, the Taliban must manage this practice carefully so as not to isolate or alienate themselves from their constituency. The Taliban learned the challenges associated with coerced support during the early years when the implementation of forced conscription upon a populace was not well received and led to significant blowback. Coerced support as a major source of income for the Taliban remains productive, but will always be limited by the inherent socio-economic condition of the indigenous population.

Movement of Finance

The Taliban has relied on informal methods—such as couriers, commodities, and *hawala*—to move funds into, out of, and around Afghanistan. For example, "during the invasion of Afghanistan in 2001, it was widely reported that the Taliban smuggled their money out of the country via Pakistan using couriers that handled bars of gold."[71] Additionally, the "Taliban have publicly announced various "rewards" offered in gold for acts of terror carried out by jihadists, further suggesting a reliance on commodities."[72] This has relieved the organization of some foreign government oversight, but introduces the difficulties related to transportation, storage, and liquidity inherent to commodities.

In addition to commodities, there is strong and growing evidence the Taliban has utilized the informal money transfer system commonly known as *hawala*.[73] According to the United Nations, $200 billion circulates annually through the *hawala* industry.[74] In this system, money is transferred between two intermediaries; one representing the person wishing to transmit funds and one representing the party wishing to receive funds. There is little to no paperwork kept by the intermediaries and, until very recently, no governmental oversight. As a result, 'there is no way the government can detect and interdict the money using classic AML/CFT (anti-money laundering and countering the financing of terrorism) tools.'[75]

---

70   Acharya et al, "Making Money in the Mayhem," 98.

71   Financial Action Task Force, *Terrorist Financing*, February 2008, 24, http://www.fatf-gafi.org/dataoecd/28/43/40285899.pdf.

72   U.S. Department of State, *International Narcotics Control Strategy Report: Volume II Money Laundering and Financial Crimes*, Bureau for International Narcotics and Law Enforcement Affairs, March 2008, 6.

73   Napoleoni, *Terror Incorporated*, 127-31,

74   Napoleoni, *Terror Incorporated*, 128

75   Acharya et al., "Making Money in the Mayhem," 104.

Countermeasures

Financial dimensions could be a critical vulnerability to exploit in order to bring about the demise of the Taliban.[76] Countermeasures have been taken to address each of the sources of funding as well as the movement of funds. To counter the state sponsorship coming from Pakistan, the U.S. has sought to strengthen bilateral relations to encourage Pakistan to work with the U.S. instead of the Taliban. After 9/11, the U.S. lifted all sanctions, forgave $3 billion of debt, and coordinated the quick disbursement of loans from the U.S. and the World Bank.[77] This initial measure of bilateral cooperation between the U.S. and Pakistan soon diminished, however, as allegations of Pakistan support for the Taliban continued to surface and further strain the relationship. The U.S. has continued to treat Pakistan as an ally in the Afghanistan project in spite of the noted passive sponsorship of the Taliban. Aid continued to pour into Pakistan on the scale of $10 billion between 2002 and 2006; much of it earmarked for the Pakistan military for directed use in operations suited to serve U.S. policy aims in the region.[78]

To counter the Taliban's ability to profit from the drug trade, the government of Afghanistan has pursued initiatives aimed at reducing the opium economy within Afghanistan. The National Drug Control Strategy (NDCS) of Afghanistan promotes an overall policy goal, "to secure a sustainable decrease in cultivation, production, trafficking, and consumption of illicit drugs with a view to complete and sustainable elimination."[79] In addition to developing an over-arching strategy to focus national efforts, the Afghan government, with assistance from the U.S. Drug Enforcement Agency (DEA), created the Sensitive Investigative Unit (SIU) and Technical Investigative Unit (TIU) as the investigative arms of the National Interdiction Unit (NIU).[80] The law enforcement arm is being further strengthened by the judicial maturing of Afghanistan's formal legal processes and prosecutorial capability of the Criminal Justice Task Force (CJTF).[81] Crop eradication strategies have also been implemented. This has produced limited to negligible gains with 19,047 hectares eradicated in 2007 followed by 5,480 hectares in 2008. The UNODC Afghanistan Opium Survey for 2008 suggests a major challenge

76   Acharya et al., "Making Money in the Mayhem," 97.
77   Rashid, *Descent into Chaos*, 31.
78   "Between 2002-2006 Pakistan received $10 billion in U.S. aid, of which more than half, $5.5 billion—the Pakistani Army received directly as Coalition Support Funds, or compensation for helping U.S. military operations in Afghanistan—or about $80-$100 million a month for services rendered." Rashid, *Descent into Chaos*, 370-1.
79   William A. Byrd, "Responding to Afghanistan's Opium Economy Challenge: Lessons and Policy Implications from a Development Perspective," *Policy Research Working Paper Series*, World Bank: South Asia Region, 2008, 16, http://www-wds.worldbank.org/external/default/WDSContentServer/IW3P/IB/2008/03/04/000158349_200 80304082230/Rendered/PDF/wps4545.pdf.
80   U.S. Department of State, *International Narcotics Control Strategy Report*, 238.
81   U.S. Department of State, *International Narcotics Control Strategy Report*, 238.

to eradication is the physical presence of the insurgency, especially in the south and south-west regions.[82] Crop substitution (often wheat) is another initiative being pursued to reduce the economic incentive for growing poppy. Quantifiable progress has been made in this area as the gross income ratio of opium to wheat (per hectare) improving to 3:1 in 2008 from 10:1 in 2007.[83] The government of Afghanistan is demonstrating awareness and initiative in confronting the opium problem, but is constrained by the institutional capacity to combat the depth of the problem and the ability to reduce the intrinsic relationship between opium and Afghan society.

To address the illegal economy, the government of Afghanistan has taken some steps in order to introduce regulation, transparency, and trade controls at the border. Government agencies such as the Afghanistan Investment Support Agency (AISA) work to reduce the opaque nature of the economic environment in Afghanistan to generate foreign direct investment rather than aid and debt.[84] Afghanistan is also working with the World Bank and regional neighbors to reform customs administration and continue to reduce infrastructure constraints such as the road network in Afghanistan.[85] To counter smuggling, more work needs to be done to ease restrictions on the use of foreign trucks and to reduce both the cost and time for processing containers into and out of Afghanistan.[86]

The government of Afghanistan, along with U.S. and coalition partners, has tried to undermine the Taliban's popular support. Humanitarian aid, reconstruction, security, development, and political inclusion are all areas that must receive sustained focus in order to reduce the influence of the Taliban among the population and reduce the level of popular support offered to them.

To counter the movement of Taliban funds, the United Nations has passed a series of resolutions beginning in 1999 specifically aimed at freezing the financial assets and economic resources of the Taliban.[87] These resolutions have also imposed travel restrictions on designated individuals to limit their freedom of movement. The United States has used Executive Order 13129 to block property and prohibit transactions with the Taliban, and implemented Executive Order

82   United Nations, *Afghanistan Opium Survey 2008*.

83   United Nations, *Afghanistan Opium Survey 2008*, viii.

84   The World Bank, "Afghanistan: Trade Brief," *World Trade Indicators 2008*, available at: http://info.worldbank.org/etools/wti/docs/wti2008/brief1.pdf.

85   Jane's, *Economy: Afghanistan*.

86   The cost and time for processing containers into and out of Afghanistan is currently at $2100 and 71 days per container for import and $2500 and 67 days per container for export; The World Bank, "Afghanistan: Trade at a Glance," *World Trade Indicators 2008*, http://info.worldbank.org/etools/wti/docs/wti2008/taag1.pdf.

87   1999-UN Resolution 1267, 2000-UN Resolution 1333, 2002-UN Resolution 1390, 2003-UN Resolution 1455, 2004-UN Resolution 1526, 2005-UN Resolution 1617, 2006-UN Resolution 1735, 2008-UN Resolution 1822 cover individuals and entities associated with al-Qaida, Osama bin Laden, and/or the Taliban wherever located, http://www.un.org/sc/committees/1267/index.shtml (accessed January 13, 2012).

13224 which, "expands the United States' power to target the support structure of terrorist organizations, freeze the U.S. assets and block the U.S. transactions of terrorists and those that support them, and increases our ability to block U.S. assets of, and deny access to U.S. markets to, foreign banks who refuse to cooperate with U.S. authorities to identify and freeze terrorist assets abroad."[88]

Conclusion

This chapter has examined the critical sources of financing and the methods employed by the Taliban to move these finances. The enabling environment of Central Asia, more specifically the unofficial economic environments and ungoverned territories of Afghanistan and Pakistan are key enablers in the Taliban's ability to generate income. A broad strategy focused on the fundamentals of state building may produce pressure on the sources of financing for the Taliban, but must be conducted along with regional and international anti-terror financing strategies. An increasing capacity for governance in both Pakistan and Afghanistan inherently undermines the current fiscal practices associated with the Taliban. Enforceable policies aimed at the unofficial economy, opium economy, and other criminal activity will not move the Taliban towards extinction, but reduce the organization to a level much more manageable by the state.

---

88   United States Department of Treasury, *Terrorism Sanctions,* Office of Terrorism and Financial Intelligence, http://www.ustreas.gov/offices/enforcement/ofac/programs/terror/terror.shtml (accessed September 1, 2008, site discontinued).

Chapter 8

The Liberation Tigers of Tamil Eelam (LTTE)

Christopher L. Corley

The Liberation Tigers of Tamil Eelam (LTTE) brutally waged a 33-year-long guerrilla war against the government of Sri Lanka, seeking to fulfill their objective of creating an independent Tamil homeland in the northern and eastern portions of Sri Lanka. Nevertheless, following the government's successful counter-insurgency campaign of 2008-2009, this terrorist group has all but been defeated with its key leadership either captured or killed, its conventional military force wiped out, and its base of operations destroyed. The longevity of this group would not have been possible without a well-diversified fundraising strategy. Successfully employing a multi-faceted approach comprised of legal, semi-legal, and illegal means, the LTTE was arguably one of the wealthiest and best equipped terrorist organizations in the world. Tapping heavily into the extensive Tamil diaspora located across the globe, the LTTE used both voluntary and coercive methods to line its pockets. The group used its legitimate shipping interests to traffic arms, narcotics, and human cargo. Although the LTTE primarily used its funds to build its military capacity, it was also heavily invested in the legal defenses of its operatives as well as in unsuccessful efforts to lobby Western governments for removal from foreign terrorist designation lists. Extensive military campaigns along with successful Western law enforcement crackdowns weakened the LTTE post-9/11, yet this group managed to maintain its resiliency until its apparent defeat in 2009. As such, it offers an excellent framework for understanding governmental challenges that must be overcome in order to address the key center of gravity that this group's extensive fundraising capability provided. Only by attacking the LTTE problem with a multi-faceted approach was Sri Lanka seemingly successful at stifling the LTTE's extensive fundraising capability. Now, with the conventional arm of the LTTE defeated, only time will tell if this group's extensive fundraising capacity will fully collapse or instead be transformed into a purely for-profit criminal enterprise.

Conflict Background

Located off of the southeastern coast of India, the Democratic Socialist Republic of Sri Lanka, formerly known as Ceylon, is comprised of a mixed ethnic population

estimated to be approaching 21 million.[1] The native Sinhalese hold a decisive
majority, making up approximately 74 percent of the total population.[2] The Tamils
are the second largest ethnic group at about 17 percent.[3] An internal division exists
between the Ceylon Tamils (12 percent), who were originally of Indian descent,
but whose ancestors have lived on the island for hundreds of years, and the Indian
Tamils (5 percent) who were brought to Sri Lanka from India by the British to
work the tea plantations in the 19th Century.[4] Finally, a mixed minority group
consisting of Muslims, Moors, and Malays makes up another seven percent, while
a diverse mix of other immigrant groups makes up the last two percent of the total.[5]

Sri Lanka was colonized by the Portuguese (1505-1658), the Dutch (1658-
1796), and the British (1796-1948) and finally gained its independence from
colonial rule in 1948.[6] Although the violence between the predominantly Buddhist
Sinhalese and Hindu Tamils did not manifest itself fully until after independence,
the seeds of the modern conflict were planted during colonial rule through policies
encouraging religious intolerance, educational and employment discrimination,
and racism.[7] Although all of Sri Lanka's early colonizers practiced some forms
of discrimination, perhaps the most damaging was the British belief that "race—
particularly as linked to language—is the primary determinant of social identity
and of a civilization's worth."[8] Originally, the Sinhalese were the benefactors of
this British policy. They benefited from the British colonial system and culture
but never became fully accepted as equal partners in British society.[9] Meanwhile,
the Tamils attempted to better their own livelihood by learning the English
language, ultimately allowing them to acquire a "disproportionate share of public

1   U.S. Department of State, "Background Note: Sri Lanka," http://www.state.gov/r/
pa/ei/bgn/5249.htm (accessed September 5, 2007); Central Intelligence Agency, "The
World Factbook: Sri Lanka," https://www.cia.gov/library/publications/the-world-factbook/
geos/ce.html (accessed November 12,2007); and The Library of Congress, "A Country
Study: Sri Lanka," http://lcweb2.loc.gov/cgi-bin/query/r?frd/cstdy:@field(DOCID=lk005)
(accessed November 12, 2007).

2   U.S. Department of State, "Background Note: Sri Lanka," and Carin Zissis, "The
Sri Lankan Conflict," September 11, 2006, http://www.cfr.org/publication/11407/sri_
lankan_conflict.html (accessed September 5, 2007).

3   U.S. Department of State, "Background Note: Sri Lanka," and Zissis, "The Sri
Lankan Conflict."

4   U.S. Department of State, "Background Note: Sri Lanka," and Zissis, "The Sri
Lankan Conflict."

5   U.S. Department of State, "Background Note: Sri Lanka," and Zissis, "The Sri
Lankan Conflict."

6   David Little, *Sri Lanka: The Invention of Enmity* (Washington D.C.: United States
Institute of Peace Press, 1994), 3, 11-12, and U.S. Department of State, "Background Note:
Sri Lanka."

7   Little, *Sri Lanka: The Invention of Enmity*, 11-17.

8   Little, *Sri Lanka: The Invention of Enmity*, 15.

9   Little, *Sri Lanka: The Invention of Enmity*, 16-17.

employment in the British-run colonial administration."[10] British establishment of a quota system in the government and universities further solidified minority rights in Ceylon, ultimately becoming a significant matter of contention with the majority Sinhalese.

After peaceful independence from colonial rule, the first major outbreak of violence occurred in 1958, when the Sinhalese-dominated government instituted several policies, such as the Sinhala Only Act, advocating the primacy of the Sinhala language, culture, and religion, which alienated the Tamil minority.[11] Worsening economic conditions in 1971 further alienated the Tamils when the Sinhalese government passed legislation that made it increasingly more difficult for Tamils to "seek professional education and find employment in the public sector."[12] These controversial policies, coupled with a new constitution in 1972 that made Sinhala the official language of Sri Lanka and Buddhism the official religion, further alienated the predominantly Hindu Tamils.[13] Against this background, the origins of the ideas of modern Tamil secession were born.

In an attempt to pursue a diplomatic solution to their growing alienation and quickly eroding benefits, in 1972 the Tamils formed the Tamil United Liberation Front (TULF) political party. However, disillusioned and frustrated with the TULF's slow progress against the Sinhalese-dominated government, younger Tamils began to explore the use of violence as an alternative to failing diplomacy.[14] In late 1972, radical young members of the TULF split off to form a militant group known as the Tamil New Tigers, the precursor to the Liberation Tigers of Tamil Eelam (LTTE), which was formally established in 1976.[15] Fearing a civil war as a result of the growing unrest, the Sri Lankan government enacted a series of stringent emergency measures, including the Prevention of Terrorism Act of 1979, which eventually became the platform for the government's aggressive campaign against the Tamils in the northern province of Jaffna.[16] Perceiving the government's actions as a direct threat to Tamil sovereignty, the LTTE began targeting the Sri Lankan military in 1979.[17] An LTTE ambush on a Sri Lankan military patrol in early 1983 killed 13 soldiers and created the spark for the modern

---

10   Chelvadurai Manogaran, *Ethnic Conflict and Reconciliation in Sri Lanka* (Honolulu, HI: University of Hawaii Press, 1987): 4.

11   Little, *Sri Lanka: The Invention of Enmity*, 4, and Manogaran, *Ethnic Conflict and Reconciliation in Sri Lanka*, 11-12.

12   Little, *Sri Lanka: The Invention of Enmity*, 5.

13   Little, *Sri Lanka: The Invention of Enmity*, 5 and Zissis, "The Sri Lankan Conflict."

14   Little, *Sri Lanka: The Invention of Enmity*, 6.

15   The Library of Congress, "A Country Study: Sri Lanka," and MIPT Terrorism Knowledge Base, "Group Profile: Liberation Tigers of Tamil Eelam (LTTE)," http://www.tkb.org/Group.jsp?groupID=3623 (accessed September 5, 2007).

16   Little, *Sri Lanka: The Invention of Enmity*, 6.

17   MIPT Terrorism Knowledge Base, "Group Profile: Liberation Tigers of Tamil Eelam (LTTE)."

civil war.[18] Subsequently, throughout the summer of 1983, governmental security forces sought revenge on those responsible for the LTTE ambush by provoking Tamils nationwide.[19] Their heavy-handed tactics started a series of riots, killing an estimated 2,500 Tamils, leaving tens of thousands homeless, and causing more than 200,000 to flee the country.[20] The north and eastern provinces quickly became hotspots for the growing insurgency as government authorities attempted to suppress the growing power of the LTTE.

Violence between the LTTE and Sri Lankan government continued throughout the 1990s, until the government and LTTE agreed to a ceasefire in late December 2001.[21] In early 2002, both parties agreed to sign a memorandum of understanding, cementing a fragile truce that was partially mediated through the unprecedented efforts of five Nordic countries including Norway, Sweden, Denmark, Finland, and Iceland.[22] Although ongoing acts of violence by both sides threatened the truce, it was not until the December 2004 tsunami disaster that large-scale violence erupted again. Unable to agree on the distribution of $3 billion in international aid for tsunami relief, increasing tensions led to a series of attacks, assassinations, and suicide bombings by the LTTE.[23] Both sides reaffirmed their commitment to the cease-fire, but the continuation of violence throughout 2006 and 2007 illustrated the difficulty of a lasting peace process. In 2006 and 2007, the Sri Lankan military launched a series of attacks against LTTE bases and resources, attempting to gain the upper hand. In January 2007, the Sri Lankan government announced that it had captured a LTTE stronghold located in the town of Vakarai on the east coast, forcing an LTTE retreat further inland and severing several vital supply networks.[24] Nevertheless, following its traditional pattern of attacks, ambushes, and assassinations, the LTTE continued its campaign of terror until late 2008, early 2009, when the group suffered a series of significant military defeats at the hands of the Sri Lankan Army (SLA).[25] By January 2009, the SLA had made significant progress against the group, using rapid maneuvering to capture

---

18   MIPT Terrorism Knowledge Base, "Group Profile: Liberation Tigers of Tamil Eelam (LTTE)."

19   Little, *Sri Lanka: The Invention of Enmity*, 6-7 and Stanley Jeyaraja Tambiah, *Sri Lanka: Ethnic Fratricide and the Dismantling of Democracy* (Chicago, IL: The University of Chicago Press, 1986), 19-33.

20   Zissis, "The Sri Lankan Conflict," and U.S. Department of State, "Background Note: Sri Lanka."

21   *Jane's World of Insurgency and Terrorism*, "Liberation Tigers of Tamil Eelam (LTTE)," http://jwit.janes.com/public/jwit/index.shtml (accessed September 5, 2007).

22   Zissis, "The Sri Lankan Conflict."

23   U.S. Department of State, "Background Note: Sri Lanka."

24   *Jane's World of Insurgency and Terrorism*, "Liberation Tigers of Tamil Eelam (LTTE)."

25   *Jane's World of Insurgency and Terrorism*, "Liberation Tigers of Tamil Eelam (LTTE)."

strategic terrain in Pooneryn, Kilinochchi, Elephant Pass, and Mullaitivu.[26] By May 2009, the SLA had the last remnants of the LTTE surrounded in a small, four-square kilometer stronghold located in the heavily forested Mullaitivu district.[27] Desperate to preserve its cause but unable to continue combat operations, the LTTE unsuccessfully attempted to broker a unilateral ceasefire agreement. Unfettered, the SLA continued to apply steady pressure on the LTTE until finally, on May 18, 2009, the government announced that LTTE leader Velupillai Prabhakaran had been killed and that the SLA had captured all remaining LTTE controlled areas, effectively ending combat operations.[28] To date, "international security and intelligence organizations consider the LTTE to have been one of the most ruthless terrorist organizations in the world."[29] The LTTE's survivability and boldness to engage the more modern and better-equipped Sri Lankan and Indian militaries is a testament to its considerable operational capabilities. This would not have been possible without the substantial financial capital, which the group acquired through a diverse system of legal, semi-legal, and illegal fundraising methods.

Annual Income Estimates

LTTE annual income estimates vary extensively depending on the source; however, even the most conservative estimates indicate that this organization was probably one of the wealthiest terrorist organizations in the world.[30] The Rand Corporation's conservative estimate places LTTE annual income at a round figure of $82 million (U.S.)[31] *Jane's Intelligence Review* and the Associated Press suggest a much higher estimate of between $200-$300 million,[32] while the most

---

26   *Jane's World of Insurgency and Terrorism*, "Liberation Tigers of Tamil Eelam (LTTE)."

27   *Jane's World of Insurgency and Terrorism*, "Liberation Tigers of Tamil Eelam (LTTE)."

28   *Jane's World of Insurgency and Terrorism*, "Liberation Tigers of Tamil Eelam (LTTE)."

29   *Jane's World of Insurgency and Terrorism*, "Liberation Tigers of Tamil Eelam (LTTE)."

30   Zissis, "The Sri Lankan Conflict."

31   C. Christine Fair, "Urban Battlefields of South Asia: Lessons Learned from Sri Lanka, India, and Pakistan," RAND, 2004, 30.

32   *Jane's Intelligence Review*, "Feeding the Tiger—How Sri Lankan Insurgents Fund Their War," http://jir.janes.com/public/jir/index.shtml (accessed September 5, 2007; The Associated Press, "AP Impact: An Investigation into Fundraising and Weapons Smuggling by Sri Lanka's Tamil Tigers," *The International Herald Tribune: Asia-Pacific*, Monday, November 5, 2007, http://www.iht.com/articles/ap/2007/11/06/asia/AS-FEA-GEN-Sri-Lanka-Tiger-Inc.php (accessed November 8, 2007; "LTTE Arms-Buying Goes Global," *South Asian Media Net*, Tuesday, November 6, 2007, http://www.southasianmedia.net/index_story.cfm?id=440311&category=Frontend&Country=SRI% (accessed November

generous estimate comes from Strategic Foresight, which estimates LTTE annual income to have been somewhere between $175 and $385 million.[33] These low, medium, and high estimates, all provided by credible sources, suggest that we still have much to learn about the true nature and extent of the LTTE's diverse revenue streams. Nevertheless, income appears to exceed expenses, and according to Strategic Foresight sources, the LTTE "spends a minimum [of its annual finances] on its cadres and the maximum on sustaining a war economy and its support base internationally."[34] LTTE budgetary expenditures are difficult to assess; however, Jane's Terrorism and Insurgency Centre estimates that the LTTE averaged approximately $8 million per year in annual operating costs.[35] Although the exact amounts are arguable, these sources agree that the majority of the LTTE's income came from a combination of legitimate and illegitimate means—mostly from the Tamil Diaspora residing in Western countries. Estimates place up to 90 percent of the LTTE's funding as originating from overseas sources.[36]

Early State Sponsorship

In the early 1980s, the Tamils began receiving direct material support from a sympathetic Indian government. India launched an air-dropping campaign to mitigate what it perceived to be harsh treatment and forced starvation of the Tamils by an aggressive Sinhalese-dominated regime.[37] The Research and Analysis Wing (RAW), India's foreign intelligence agency, began providing official support to the LTTE as early as 1981.[38] Establishing a network of thirty training bases and equipping the LTTE with modern weaponry, the RAW even went so far as to place several members of the LTTE's leadership on its payroll.[39] However, in July 1987 India formed a pact with Sri Lanka (The Indo-Sri Lankan Accord),

8, 2007); and Peter Apps, "Sri Lanka Tigers Run Multi-Million Dollar Empire-Report," *Reuter's India*, Monday, July 23, 2007, http://in.reuters.com/article/topNews/idINdia-28618620070723?sp=true (accessed November 8,2007).

33   Excerpt from "Cost of Conflict in Sri Lanka, 2006," http://www.strategicforesight.com/ccinsrilanka.htm (accessed January 13, 2012).

34   Excerpt from "Cost of Conflict in Sri Lanka, 2006."

35   *Jane's Intelligence Review*, "Feeding the Tiger—How Sri Lankan Insurgents Fund Their War."

36   Peter Chalk, "Liberation Tigers of Tamil Eelam's (LTTE) International Organization and Operations: A Preliminary Analysis," Commentary No. 77, A Canadian Security Intelligence Service Publication, March 17, 2000, http://www.fas.org/irp/world/para/docs/com77e.htm (accessed May 9, 2007).

37   U.S. Department of State, "Background Note: Sri Lanka."

38   FAS Intelligence Resource Program, "Research and Analysis Wing (RAW)," http://www.fas.org/irp/world/india/raw/index.html (accessed September 5, 2007).

39   FAS Intelligence Resource Program, "Research and Analysis Wing (RAW)," and Zissis, "The Sri Lankan Conflict."

effectively ending its material support to the Tamil insurgents. As a result of the pact, India agreed to deploy an Indian Peace-Keeping Force (IPKF) to the north and east provinces, after securing Sri Lanka's promise to grant several key Tamil demands, including official status for the their language.[40] Unsatisfied, the LTTE refused to disarm and before long, the IPKF found itself conducting a bloody counter-insurgency campaign against the rebels. After approximately three years of unsuccessful counter-insurgency operations, the IPKF withdrew in 1990 in response to heavy casualties and escalating violence at the hands of the LTTE.[41]

Popular and Coercive Fundraising Methods

More than two and a half decades of civil war in Sri Lanka claimed the lives of an estimated 100,000 Tamils and displaced hundreds of thousands more.[42] Almost one quarter of the worldwide Tamil population lives outside of Sri Lanka, with estimates placing the Diaspora between 800,000 to 1.6 million, before the heavy fighting in 2008-2009.[43] Subsequently, the resulting waves of Tamil immigration have created significant expatriate populations in Canada (200,000-250,000); India (150,000); the UK (110,000); Germany (50,000); and an additional 30,000 spread across Switzerland, France, and Australia.[44] Lesser numbers of Tamils have relocated to other places such as the United States, Southeast Asia, the Middle East, and even Africa.[45] It is among these émigrés that the LTTE conducted a significant portion of its fundraising efforts, using a mixed approach of soliciting voluntary contributions, coercion, and siphoning from legitimate charities and government programs.

---

40   U.S. Department of State, "Background Note: Sri Lanka."

41   Zissis, "The Sri Lankan Conflict."

42   The Mackenzie Institute, "What Next for the Tamil Tigers?" http://www. mackenzieinstitute.com/2009/tigers-050109.htm (accessed July 3, 2009): Zissis, "The Sri Lankan Conflict," K. Alan Kronstadt, "Sri Lanka: Background and U.S. Relations," Congressional Research Service: The Library of Congress, Updated August 1, 2006, and Audrey Kurth Cronin, "Foreign Terrorist Organizations," Congressional Research Service: The Library of Congress, February 6, 2004, http://www.fas/org/irp/crs/RL32223.pdf.

43   Jayshree Bajoria, Council on Foreign Relations, "The Sri Lankan Conflict," http;//www.cfr.org/publication/114007/sri_lankan_conflict.html (accessed July 3, 2009); Zissis, "The Sri Lankan Conflict," K. Alan Kronstadt, "Sri Lanka: Background and U.S. Relations," and Audrey Kurth Cronin, "Foreign Terrorist Organizations."

44   *Jane's Intelligence Review*, "Feeding the Tiger—How Sri Lankan Insurgents Fund Their War," and "AP Impact: An Investigation into Fundraising and Weapons Smuggling by Sri Lanka's Tamil Tigers," *The International Herald Tribune*.

45   *Jane's Intelligence Review*, "Feeding the Tiger—How Sri Lankan Insurgents Fund Their War," and "AP Impact: An Investigation into Fundraising and Weapons Smuggling by Sri Lanka's Tamil Tigers," *The International Herald Tribune*.

Using its once extensive propaganda capability, the LTTE ran a sophisticated international fundraising campaign aimed at voluntary contributions from professionals, affluent businessmen, and older, more established Tamils.[46] The Tigers preferred to acquire their donations voluntarily; however, they were quick to resort to intimidation and coercion should their solicitations fail to produce the desired voluntary support.[47] Boldly petitioning wealthy Tamils for large amounts of funds, the LTTE was extremely successful in its overt collection efforts. One prominent Californian physician contributed as much as $4 million in the last decade, pledging up to $100,000 at a time, depending on the purpose of the request.[48] Similarly, the Associated Press reports that authorities recently investigated a Wall Street financier suspected of donating millions to the rebel cause.[49] Unlike other countries with significant Tamil Diasporas, within the United States, more of the LTTE's financial success came from "a small number of wealthy individuals than from the expatriate community at large."[50]

The LTTE was also particularly astute at petitioning the Tamil Diaspora for "special war causes," aimed to appeal primarily to Tamil sympathy for a separate Tamil state. Also known as "urgent war funds, war taxes, or special contributions,"[51] these collections were traditionally taken during periods of particularly heavy fighting against government security forces. For example, in early 2000 the LTTE petitioned Tamil expatriates in the UK, Canada, and Australia for $1,000 per family to support its military efforts to retain control of its crucial supply routes along highway A9, which were under threat at the time by the Sri Lankan military.[52] Interestingly, RAND reports that these "special war cause" donations would rise and fall, depending on LTTE's successes or failures

---

46   Chalk, "Liberation Tigers of Tamil Eelam's (LTTE) International Organization and Operations."

47   Daniel Byman, Peter Chalk, Bruce Hoffman, William Rosenau, and David Brannan, "Trends in Outside Support for Insurgent Movements," RAND, 2001, 50.

48   Chalk, "Liberation Tigers of Tamil Eelam's (LTTE) International Organization and Operations,"Fair, "Urban Battlefields of South Asia: Lessons Learned from Sri Lanka, India, and Pakistan," 32, and Byman, Chalk, Hoffman, Rosenau, and Brannan, "Trends in Outside Support for Insurgent Movements," 51.

49   "AP Impact: An Investigation into Fundraising and Weapons Smuggling by Sri Lanka's Tamil Tigers," *The International Herald Tribune.*

50   Byman, Chalk, Hoffman, Rosenau, and Brannan, "Trends in Outside Support for Insurgent Movements," 51.

51   The Mackenzie Institute, "Other People's Wars: A Review of Overseas Terrorism in Canada," (2002), http://www.mackenzieinstitute.com/2003/other_peoples_wars5.htm (site discontinued), and The MacKenzie Institute, "What Next for the Tamil Tigers?"

52   The Mackenzie Institute, "Other People's Wars: A Review of Overseas Terrorism in Canada," and Chalk, "Liberation Tigers of Tamil Eelam's (LTTE) International Organization and Operations."

on the battlefield.[53] For example, as Wanigasekera notes, "following an airport attack in 2001, that destroyed many aircraft belonging to the government without a single civilian casualty, [the LTTE experienced] a series of successful fund-raising events in Europe."[54] This suggests that propaganda may have been a potential source of gravity that security forces could exploit, especially during times of heavy conflict, when the LTTE was losing.

One reason for the LTTE's success at petitioning for these "special war causes" was the group's extensive follow-up apparatus that ensured collection of voluntary and involuntary donations. Using political, cultural, and social gatherings to collect information on expatriates, "the LTTE maintained systematic records of all Diaspora community members, including addresses, telephone numbers, email addresses, and even bank account numbers."[55] For example, in London, British Tamils who attended an informational meeting held by the Eelam Solidarity Campaign, an LTTE front organization, were encouraged to leave their names and contact information for follow-up.[56] Shortly thereafter, the LTTE began its follow-up campaign, and once contacted regularly, these Tamils gradually accepted their responsibility to donate a monthly stipend for the Tiger's Cause.[57] To facilitate its monthly collections, the LTTE established a "fixed contribution" system based on family income. These "fixed contributions" varied from $50-$500 a month depending on income and location.[58] According to Wanigasekera, "those who failed to make their regular contribution got a polite call from the LTTE two days after the deadline, a follow-up reminder in a week's time, and finally, a visit to their homes after two weeks."[59] Now known as the "British template," this system was later used in other countries and was supported by a "comprehensive, recording, accounting, and compliance process."[60] So successful was the LTTE's

---

53 Byman, Chalk, Hoffman, Rosenau, and Brannan, "Trends in Outside Support for Insurgent Movements," 50-1.

54 Vipula Wanigasekera, "Management of the Tamil Diaspora—LTTE's Primary Function Abroad," III-59, paper presented at the Institute for Defense Analyses, "Building a CATR Research Agenda, Proceedings of the Third Bi-Annual International Symposium of the Center for Asian Terrorism Research (CATR)," March 1-3, 2006, Columbo, Sri Lanka, http://stinet.dtic.mil/oai/oai?verb=getRecord&metadataPrefix=html&identifier=A DA464068 (accessed November 8, 2007).

55 Wanigasekera, "Management of the Tamil Diaspora," III-56-7.

56 The Mackenzie Institute, "Other People's Wars: A Review of Overseas Terrorism in Canada," and Chalk, "Liberation Tigers of Tamil Eelam's (LTTE) International Organization and Operations."

57 The Mackenzie Institute, "Other People's Wars: A Review of Overseas Terrorism in Canada," and Chalk, "Liberation Tigers of Tamil Eelam's (LTTE) International Organization and Operations."

58 Wanigasekera, "Management of the Tamil Diaspora," III-64.

59 Wanigasekera, "Management of the Tamil Diaspora," III-64.

60 The Mackenzie Institute, "Other People's Wars: A Review of Overseas Terrorism in Canada," and Chalk, "Liberation Tigers of Tamil Eelam's (LTTE) International

organization of its expatriate community, that estimates placed its revenues at well over $10 million per month from these expatriate communities.[61]

Although the LTTE was successful at using voluntary and semi-voluntary collection methods, it was probably best known for its coercive methodology. Fear drove the LTTE's taxation system, so by relying heavily on extortion, kidnapping, shakedowns, taxes, physical abuse, and violence, the LTTE was able to capitalize on its ruthless reputation and collect from unwilling donors. French Tamils were often victims of LTTE involuntary fundraising efforts. One source records that the LTTE demanded Tamil families in France pay "EUR 2,000 per year and businesses EUR 6,000 per year in revolutionary taxes."[62] Particularly innovative was the group's practice of outsourcing its collection efforts to street gangs, to whom it paid a 20 percent commission for their service.[63] Tamils who refused to contribute were subjected to abductions, beatings, and torture until their families agreed to pay their ransoms.[64] Allegedly, the LTTE maintained a farmhouse outside Paris for abusing its more stubborn contributors.[65] Similarly, Tamils in Germany's Ruhr region were expected to pay between $30-$60 dollars a month depending on individual wealth, with those refusing to pay subjected to violence directed at them, or their families still residing in Sri Lanka.[66] Likewise, according to the McKenzie Institute, "on April 10th, 1994, Swiss police arrested 15 members of the LTTE for intimidating Tamils [in Switzerland], beating and confining those who refused to donate around $60 a month to the cause."[67] Tamil refugees in Canada also were also victimized by the LTTE's involuntary collection system. "Those who refused to comply with the demand for $30 a month sometimes found it necessary to move to avoid visits from enforcers. However, if they contacted family members back in Sri Lanka, especially if their families were living in LTTE controlled areas, it became clear that the Tigers were monitoring them as well and would demand a cut if money was sent home. Moreover, the family would be pressured into revealing the new address of their

---

Organization and Operations."

61   Wanigasekera, "Management of the Tamil Diaspora," III-53-4.

62   *Jane's Intelligence Review*, "Feeding the Tiger—How Sri Lankan Insurgents Fund Their War."

63   *Jane's Intelligence Review*, "Feeding the Tiger—How Sri Lankan Insurgents Fund Their War." See also Shanaka Jayasekara, "LTTE Fundraising & Money Transfer Operations," paper presented at the International Conference on Countering Terrorism, Colombo, Sri Lanka, October 18-20, 2007, http://www.sinhalaya.com/news/english/wmprint.php?ArtID=14195 (accessed November 8, 2007).

64   *Jane's Intelligence Review*, "Feeding the Tiger—How Sri Lankan Insurgents Fund Their War."

65   *Jane's Intelligence Review*, "Feeding the Tiger—How Sri Lankan Insurgents Fund Their War."

66   The Mackenzie Institute, "Other People's Wars: A Review of Overseas Terrorism in Canada."

67   The Mackenzie Institute, "Other People's Wars: A Review of Overseas Terrorism in Canada."

reluctant relative in Canada ... ."[68] Allegedly, the LTTE even sold operating licenses to Tamil convenience stores owners in the greater Toronto area in an attempt to diversify its taxation methods, although Canadian authorities have not been able to confirm these reports.[69]

The Roles of Charities, NGOs and Social Welfare

Savvy to popular and involuntary collection methods, the Tigers were also astute at siphoning off money from non-governmental organizations (NGOs), charities, and even the social service and the welfare systems of Western countries.[70] According to G.H. Peiris at the University of Peradeniya, these non-profit organizations may have been providing up to $2 million a month to the LTTE cause.[71] The benefit of using non-profits is multi-fold: First, it is exceedingly difficult for authorities to prove that funds raised for charity or humanitarian purposes are being diverted to terrorism.[72] Second, these organizations offer excellent cover under the guise of legitimate fundraising organizations, which are cleverly "shrouded in a veil of legitimacy,"[73] "enjoying the public trust, and having access to considerable sources of funds, all while maintaining a tax exempt status."[74] Third, these organizations "maintain a global presence, [as they are located] within or near areas exposed to terrorist activity, are subject to little or no [governmental regulation] requirements, and have few obstacles to their creation."[75] Fourth, plugging into the generous social welfare systems of Western countries offers yet another source of revenue, means

---

68   The Mackenzie Institute, "Other People's Wars: A Review of Overseas Terrorism in Canada."

69   The Mackenzie Institute, "Other People's Wars: A Review of Overseas Terrorism in Canada."

70   Chalk, "Liberation Tigers of Tamil Eelam's (LTTE) International Organization and Operations."

71   *Jane's Intelligence Review*, "Feeding the Tiger: How Sri Lankan Insurgents Fund Their War."

72   Chalk, "Liberation Tigers of Tamil Eelam's (LTTE) International Organization and Operations."

73   Matthew A. Levitt, "Stemming the Flow of Terrorist Financing: Practical and Conceptual Challenges," Lecture Given at Program Sponsored by U.S. Embassy Vienna, Austria, January 20-23, 2003, http://www.usembassy.at/en/embassy/photo/lev_lecture.htm (accessed September 11, 2007).

74   Financial Action Task Force on Money Laundering, "Report on Money Laundering and Terrorist Financing Typologies 2003-2004," https://www.hsdl.org/homesec/docs/dhs/nps03-043004-01.pdf&code=29aa0e0847ae68a4403873e79610c05a (accessed September 11, 2007).

75   Financial Action Task Force on Money Laundering, "Report on Money Laundering and Terrorist Financing Typologies 2003-2004."

for legitimacy, and a target for extortion, ironically, at the government's expense.[76] Often, the charitable links were three or four times removed, making it difficult for authorities to connect them to the LTTE. For example, as Jayasekara notes:

> The International Medical Health Organization (IMHO), formerly known as the Tamil Health Organization—USA, provides financial and material support to a partner organization known as the Centre for Health Care (CHC) in Kilinochchi. Based on documentation provided by the Norwegian Tamil Health Organization (NTHO), the organization structure of the CHC supports 15 Thilleepan Medical Centres (with an additional three under construction) and four Moblile Thilleepan Medical Centres. The head of the LTTE Medical Unit, Arun, on 3 June 2004, declared that all Thilleepan Medical Centres were part of the LTTE.[77]

Beginning in the early 1980s, the LTTE established cells and offices throughout the world, staffing their charities and front companies with professional cadres of financial and procurement experts.[78] Several well-known LTTE charitable fronts included the Australasian Federation of Tamil Associations, the Swiss Federation of Tamil Associations, the French Federation of Tamil Associations, the Illankai Tamil Sangam, the Tamil Coordinating Committee in Norway, the International Federation of Tamils in the UK, the Federation of Associations of Canadian Tamils (FACT), Tamils Rehabilitation Organization (Canada), Tamil Eelam Association of British Columbia, Tamil Eelam Society of Canada, Tamil Relief Organization, World Tamil Coordinating Committee, and World Tamil Movement.[79] Although exact numbers are unkown, the Tamils Rehabilitation Organization (Canada) was reported to have sent more than $300,000 a year back to northeastern Sri Lanka.[80] Similarly, the Tamil Relief Organization (British Branch) allegedly sent millions of pounds directly to the LTTE.[81]

The lines are sometimes blurry between the LTTE front charities and those organizations that tap into governmental social programs and federal grants. The

---

76 The Mackenzie Institute, "Other People's Wars: A Review of Overseas Terrorism in Canada."

77 Jayasekara, "LTTE Fundraising & Money Transfer Operations."

78 *Jane's World Insurgency and Terrorism*, "Liberation Tigers of Tamil Eelam (LTTE);" and *Jane's Intelligence Review*, "Feeding the Tiger: How Sri Lankan Insurgents Fund Their War."

79 Chalk, "Liberation Tigers of Tamil Eelam's (LTTE) International Organization and Operations: A Preliminary Analysis;" and The Mackenzie Institute, "Other People's Wars: A Review of Overseas Terrorism in Canada.,"

80 Chalk, "Liberation Tigers of Tamil Eelam's (LTTE) International Organization and Operations: A Preliminary Analysis;" and The Mackenzie Institute, "Other People's Wars: A Review of Overseas Terrorism in Canada."

81 Chalk, "Liberation Tigers of Tamil Eelam's (LTTE) International Organization and Operations: A Preliminary Analysis;" and The Mackenzie Institute, "Other People's Wars: A Review of Overseas Terrorism in Canada."

Mackenzie Institute records that "in the 20 years since supporters and organizers for the LTTE started to arrive in Canada, they have created numerous organizations to add credibility to their cause and strengthen their hold on the Sri Lankan Tamil community there."[82] It appears that the reach of the LTTE was so extensive that it effectively took over many of the services designed to assist Tamils attempting to integrate into Western society. From 1990-1993, Tamil Cooperative Homes Incorporated successfully received construction-funding grants from the Ontario Ministry of Municipal Affairs and Affordable Housing for subsidized government housing projects at a cost of almost $5 million.[83] Subsequently, government subsidies to this same organization amounted to approximately $84,000 in FY 2000.[84] Canadian authorities speculate that socialized housing programs offered by these LTTE controlled organizations were provided mainly to people of value to the World Tamil Movement.[85] Similarly, according to the Mackenzie Institute, "the Tamil Eelam Society of Canada received millions in federal, provincial, and municipal grants following its inception [in 1978.] Much of this money came for immigrant services (including language and resettlement programs), but also citizenship multicultural grants—which provided core funding and let the group run some of its other activities. In totality, the Tamil Eelam Society received about $2 million in federal funding in 1999-2000 and 2000-2001, and over $11 million since 1994."[86] Finally, LTTE fronts tapped into government funding grants for such causes as reducing gang violence among youth. For example, the Canadian Tamil Youth Development Centre, received $50,000 from the Canadian National Strategy on Community Safety and Crime prevention for producing a gang-related violence study in FY 2000.[87] According to the Mackenzie Institute, this organization also "received $90,000 for similar studies in 2002, with an additional $6,000 from the City of Toronto under their 'Breaking the Cycle of Violence grants program'."[88] Exactly how much of this funding for social programs went directly to the LTTE coffers is unknown.

---

82   The Mackenzie Institute, "Other People's Wars: A Review of Overseas Terrorism in Canada."
83   The Mackenzie Institute, "Other People's Wars: A Review of Overseas Terrorism in Canada."
84   The Mackenzie Institute, "Other People's Wars: A Review of Overseas Terrorism in Canada."
85   The Mackenzie Institute, "Other People's Wars: A Review of Overseas Terrorism in Canada."
86   The Mackenzie Institute, "Other People's Wars: A Review of Overseas Terrorism in Canada."
87   The Mackenzie Institute, "Other People's Wars: A Review of Overseas Terrorism in Canada."
88   The Mackenzie Institute, "Other People's Wars: A Review of Overseas Terrorism in Canada."

Human Trafficking and Smuggling

The LTTE's illegal immigration programs, human trafficking, and smuggling schemes helped ensure that a steady supply of Tamils arrived in immigration friendly countries. Charging $18,000-$32,000 per transaction, human smuggling was a lucrative moneymaker for the Tigers.[89] One estimate places their profits from this illicit trade at $180,000 to $226,000 per year.[90] Authorities believe that the LTTE actually "orchestrated the movement of Tamils into host countries with liberal refugee policies and generous welfare systems."[91] Once immigrants arrived at their destinations, the LTTE helped them with forged identity papers, jobs, and even access to social welfare programs and housing.[92] There may also have been a relationship between the wealth and status of potential immigrants and their countries of destination. According to *Jane's Intelligence Review*, "the middle and professional classes tended to migrate to the richer countries in the West, [while the poor] migrated to less developed countries" [where they were exploited by the LTTE for war taxes, smuggling or other illicit operations.][93] By using their extensive arms smuggling connections, the Tigers were able to recruit prospective immigrants from other countries, who they sometimes used to carry money for drugs or arms purchasing transactions.[94] The LTTE ran a complex human smuggling process where "[potential immigrants were shipped] to Thailand, Laos, Vietnam, and Cambodia, where Russian tourist visas were received. The "tourists" then flew to Moscow, crossed borders into Baltic States and the Ukraine, where they [were transported to locations where they could] illegally penetrate Western Europe."[95] While some immigrants found themselves in the countries of their choosing and were quickly assimilated into the Tiger's fundraising system, others were not so lucky. Some immigrants found themselves forced into involuntary servitude arrangements imposed by LTTE recruitment agents who required

89   See Byman, Chalk, Hoffman, Rosenau, and Brannan, "Trends in Outside Support for Insurgent Movements," 52.

90   "LTTE Finance Chief, Family, in Human Trafficking Racket," *Current Affairs: Sri Lanka*, 7 April 2000, http://www.priu.gov.lk/news_update/Current_Affairs/ca20004/2000407LTTE-chief-and-family.html (accessed November 8, 2007).

91   "LTTE Finance Chief, Family, in Human Trafficking Racket," *Current Affairs: Sri Lanka*.

92   Chalk, "Liberation Tigers of Tamil Eelam's (LTTE) International Organization and Operations."

93   *Jane's Intelligence Review*, "Feeding the Tiger: How Sri Lankan Insurgents Fund Their War."

94   STRATFOR, "Cooperation Increasing Among South Asian Rebels," (November 14, 2000), http://www.stratfor.com/products/premium/print.php?storyID=102254 (accessed September 5, 2007).

95   STRATFOR, "Cooperation Increasing Among South Asian Rebels."

exorbitant paybacks on pre-departure fees.[96] Children were especially vulnerable to exploitation, having been trafficked for commercial sexual purposes, forced labor, and even as child soldiers for the LTTE.[97]

Although human trafficking provided lucrative fundraising options for the LTTE, they were perhaps best known for their illicit arms trafficking and procurement efforts. Although it appears that the LTTE was primarily involved in the arms trade business for procurement purposes—to maintain its competitiveness with the Sri Lankan military—they also engaged in arms smuggling for profit.[98] Experts estimate that up to 30-40 percent of the LTTE's total arsenal came from overseas sources, and as such, they were able to maintain a particularly robust arms procurement capability.[99] So diverse was the LTTE's international arms procurement capability that Chalk categorized it into five geographic zones of operation:

1. Northeast and Southeast Asia, focusing particularly on China, North Korea, Cambodia, Thailand, Hong Kong, Vietnam, and Burma (Myanmar). 2. Southwest Asia, focusing particularly on Afghanistan and Pakistan (through the so-called "Afghan Pipeline."). 3. The former Soviet Union, focusing primarily on the Ukraine. 4. Southeastern Europe and the Middle East, focusing particularly on Lebanon, Cyprus, Greece, Bulgaria, and Turkey. 5. Africa, focusing particularly on Nigeria, Zimbabwe, and South Africa.[100]

Moreover, according to *Jane's World of Insurgency and Terrorism*, "in the past decade the LTTE transported consignments of weapons from Bulgaria (SA-14, LAW), Ukraine (50 tons of TNT and 10 tons of RDX), Cyprus (RPGs), Cambodia (small arms), Thailand (small arms), Myanmar (small arms), and Croatia (mortars). The amount of explosives and mortars transported by the LTTE remains the largest quantity of armaments ever transported by a non-state armed group."[101] Although sources and routes for the LTTE's procurement operations varied, the southern province of Tamil Nadu in India was a key center of gravity for the LTTE's arms smuggling operations.[102] Located just 22 miles

96   U.S. Department of State, "Trafficking in Persons Report," (June 12, 2007), Country Narratives—Countries Q through Z, Sri Lanka (Tier 2 Watch List), http://www.state.gov/g/tip/rls/tiprpt/2007/82807.htm (accessed September 5, 2007).

97   U.S. Department of State, "Trafficking in Persons Report."

98   *Jane's Intelligence Review*, "Feeding the Tiger: How Sri Lankan Insurgents Fund Their War."

99   *Jane's Intelligence Review*, "Feeding the Tiger: How Sri Lankan Insurgents Fund Their War."

100   Chalk, "Liberation Tigers of Tamil Eelam's (LTTE) International Organization and Operations: A Preliminary Analysis."

101   *Jane's World of Insurgency and Terrorism*, "Liberation Tigers of Tamil Eelam."

102   *Jane's Intelligence Review*, "Feeding the Tiger: How Sri Lankan Insurgents Fund Their War," and *Jane's World of Insurgency and Terrorism*, "Liberation Tigers of Tamil

from Sri Lanka (45 minutes by fast boat), the LTTE used its highly successful Sea Tigers to move shipments virtually unmolested by the Sri Lankan and Indian Navies until late in the conflict when a Joint patrolling agreement was successful at reducing arms shipments to the Tigers.[103] The support base at Tamil Nadu was an important trans-shipment point for the LTTE's other illicit operations including narcotics and contraband smuggling.[104]

The nature and extent of the Tiger's involvement in narcotics smuggling was and still is the source of much debate. The arms-smuggling routes that the LTTE used placed the group in close proximity to major drug production and transiting centers, making narcotics trafficking—and especially heroin trafficking—a tempting option for the Tigers, who were always looking for new ways to maximize their profits.[105] The Mackenzie Institute reports that the LTTE involvement in heroin trafficking "dates back to the late 1970s, with distribution networks in Canada, France, Italy, Poland, and Switzerland; with trans-shipments of heroin and opium to and from India, Myanmar, Pakistan, Thailand, and Sri Lanka itself."[106] Interestingly, it was the appearance of these narcotics trafficking networks "that first caught the attention of authorities as they were some of the first members of the Tamil Diaspora to appear."[107] Always efficient, the LTTE used its vast network of shipping resources primarily used for illegal arms trade, to extend its narcotics trafficking capability. According to *Jane's Intelligence Review*, "the Central Bureau of Investigation (CBI) of India claimed that LTTE ships engaged in narcotics trafficking. The CBI Superintendent of Police Thyagrajan said: 'To generate extra money [Kumaran Pathmanathan, head of LTTE shipping operations,] took to smuggling drugs in a big way and used his shipping company as a cover for drug and arms trans-shipments.' Although Tamil drug couriers with links to the LTTE have been arrested worldwide, it appears that no LTTE ships plying the narcotics routes have been searched."[108] Perhaps the best indication

Eelam."

103   *Jane's Intelligence Review*, "Feeding the Tiger: How Sri Lankan Insurgents Fund Their War;" *Jane's World of Insurgency and Terrorism*, "Liberation Tigers of Tamil Eelam;" and "Q&A: Sri Lanka Conflict," BBC News, Tuesday, May 19, 2009, http://news.bbc.co.uk/2/hi/south_asia/2405347.stm (accessed July 3, 2009).

104   *Jane's Intelligence Review*, "Feeding the Tiger: How Sri Lankan Insurgents Fund their War."

105   South Asian Terrorism Portal, "Liberation Tigers of Tamil Eelam (LTTE)," http://www.satp.org/satporgtp/countries/shrilanka/terroristoutfits/ltte.htm (accessed September 6, 2007); and Chalk, "Liberation Tigers of Tamil Eelam's (LTTE) International Organization and Operations: A Preliminary Analysis."

106   John C. Thompson, The Mackenzie Institute, "The Liberation Tigers of Tamil Eelam: Essential Points," http://www.mackenzieinstitute.com/2009/BN25-2009-apr%20The%20Liberation%20Tigers%20of%20Tamil%20Eelam.html (accessed July 3, 2009).

107   The Mackenzie Institute, "What Next for the Tamil Tigers?" http://www.mackenzieinstitute.com/2009/tigers-050109.htm (accessed July 3, 2009).

108   *Jane's World of Insurgency and Terrorism*, "Liberation Tigers of Tamil Eelam."

of the importance of the LTTE's ties to narcotics smuggling occurred in 1986 when the Tiger's international advisor, V. Manoharan, was arrested in Paris for smuggling heroin, along with seven other Tamils.[109] Manoharan would ultimately be imprisoned in France for his role in this operation.[110] Nevertheless, the LTTE leadership practiced some degree of separation with regard to its involvement in narcotics. For example, it is unlikely that the LTTE was ever directly involved in the street level distribution of heroin, choosing instead to outsource this activity through its affiliated street gangs. According to Jane's Terrorism and Insurgency Center, "the Royal Canadian Mounted Police (RCMP) claims that a portion of the $1 billion dollar drug market in Montreal was controlled by Sri Lankans connected to the LTTE."[111] Subsequently, the LTTE may have been profiting as much as $100-$200 million annually from its narcotics trafficking endeavors.[112]

Credit Card Fraud

Credit card fraud appears to be another commonly used tactic for revenue generation. The LTTE likely outsourced these somewhat sophisticated operations to technologically proficient individuals with the promise of commissions. Moreover, this tactic was used successfully by the LTTE in several different countries.[113] Recent cases illustrate the lucrative nature of these types of operations:

> In May 2006, a six-person Tamil team successfully stole $354,070 in cash from automatic teller machines, using blank cash cards, an encoder machine, and personal account information from UK card holders, before their efforts alerted Singapore authorities who raided their operation after only three days of successful activity. In May 2007, 16 LTTE operatives were caught in Norway, skimming $890,000 from bank accounts by using legitimate credit card data. Similar arrests have been made in similar bank fraud operations in Thailand, Kenya, and Sri Lanka.[114]

---

109 Current Affairs, "European Report Details LTTE/Tamil Militant Drug Smuggling," (March 13, 2000), http://www.priu.gov.lk/news_update/Current_Affairs/ca200003/20000313LTTE_in_drug_smuggling.html (accessed September 6, 2007).

110 Current Affairs, "European Report Details LTTE/Tamil Militant Drug Smuggling."

111 *Jane's Intelligence Review*, "Feeding the Tiger: How Sri Lankan Insurgents Fund Their War."

112 Excerpt from *Cost of Conflict in Sri Lanka*, http://www.strategicforesight.com/ccinsrilanka.htm (accessed October 9, 2007).

113 *Jane's Intelligence Review*, "Feeding the Tiger: How Sri Lankan Insurgents Fund Their War."

114 *Jane's Intelligence Review*, "Feeding the Tiger: How Sri Lankan Insurgents Fund Their War."

Indeed, the LTTE's bank card fraud activity illustrates its willingness to outsource its illicit activities to capable agents, highlighting yet another characteristic of its once highly diversified fundraising efforts.

Legitimate and Semi-Legitimate Businesses

The LTTE also maintained an extensive sea cargo transport and merchant shipping capability that operated throughout Southeast Asia. Partially legitimate, the LTTE's shipping interests were managed by shell companies for the purpose of transporting both legitimate and illegitimate cargo. According to Jane's Terrorism and Insurgency Center, "these ships flew flags of convenience from countries with lax registration requirements such as Panama, Honduras, or Liberia; and were used extensively in arms shipment operations, even going so far as to change names while at sea."[115] Using legitimate cargo transportation as cover for arms smuggling, these ships carried rice, flour, sugar, cement, fertilizer, and timber about 90 percent of the time.[116] These partially legitimate shipping interests provided the LTTE with an essential mechanism for moving funds, weapons, human beings, narcotics, and other commodities around the globe. Other legitimate business and commercial holdings owned by the LTTE included proxy-run "gold and jewelry trade, wholesale commodity freight and distribution, and the provision of local computer, telephone, and bus services."[117]

Remittance Channels

The Tiger's remittance channels were almost as diversified as their fundraising activities. Using a mixed methodology of legitimate and illegitimate means, the LTTE was mostly successful at hiding their funding streams from Sri Lankan authorities. Common LTTE remittance practices included: "tying collection activities to charities that were legally registered; remitting funds through individual personal accounts; and tying collections to business transactions—like over-invoicing for goods and services."[118] Interpol credits the LTTE with using *hawala* to hide and move funds outside of more formal banking channels.[119]

---

115 *Jane's Intelligence Review*, "Feeding the Tiger: How Sri Lankan Insurgents Fund Their War;" and *Jane's World of Insurgency and Terrorism*, "Liberation Tigers of Tamil Eelam."

116 *Jane's World of Insurgency and Terrorism*, "Liberation Tigers of Tamil Eelam."

117 Byman, Chalk, Hoffman, Rosenau, and Brannan, "Trends in Outside Support for Insurgent Movements," 54.

118 Wanigasekera, "Management of the Tamil Diaspora," III-65.

119 *Jane's Intelligence Review*, "Feeding the Tiger: How Sri Lankan Insurgents Fund Their War."

However, the Tigers do not seem to have been afraid to store money in the formal banking sector, and once had extensive holdings in the U.S., Canada, the UK, and Switzerland, as well as offshore accounts in such places as St. Croix and the Virgin Islands.[120] Similarly, the LTTE used its front charities and NGOs to move money around the world, taking advantage of their tax-free status as well as the international community's reluctance to delve deeply into their operations. Finally, the LTTE's shipping companies and seemingly legitimate holdings in telecommunications offered additional mechanisms for movement of funds worldwide.[121]

Expenditures

Using its extensive financial holdings and the capability to move funds worldwide, the LTTE invested the bulk of its profits back into the National Defense Fund, used primarily for arms purchases.[122] This was because the LTTE desired to address the strategic imbalance it once faced against the Sri Lankan military, an imbalance which grew with the government's expanded defense spending in 2008 and 2009.[123] For example, the seemingly unchallenged air dominance of the Sri Lankan Air Force, flying Israeli-made Kfir fighter jets, fueled the Tiger's desire to obtain increasingly more sophisticated surface-to-air missile (SAM) capability to address this important strategic imbalance.[124] In August 2006, four LTTE operatives from Canada traveled to Long Island, New York. The two LTTE agents attempted to broker a deal where an initial shipment of ten SA-18 SAMs, 500 AK-47s, and associated SAM employment training would be purchased for $900,000 to $937,000, with a follow-up purchase of 50-100 more SA-18s, depending on how well the weapons performed under battlefield conditions.[125] As a result of this investigation, law enforcement officials

---

120　*Jane's Intelligence Review*, "Feeding the Tiger: How Sri Lankan Insurgents Fund Their War."

121　*Jane's Intelligence Review*, "Feeding the Tiger: How Sri Lankan Insurgents Fund Their War."

122　Chalk, "Liberation Tigers of Tamil Eelam's (LTTE) International Organization and Operations: A Preliminary Analysis."

123　The Mackenzie Institute, "The Tigers Die Hard," The Mackenzie Institute, "The Liberation Tigers of Tamil Eelam: Essential Points;" and Jane's Terrorism and Insurgency Centre, "Sri Lankan Defense Spending Set to Reach Record Levels," http://home.janes.com/info/jtic/ (accessed August 20, 2009).

124　*Jane's Intelligence Review*, "Feeding the Tiger: How Sri Lankan Insurgents Fund Their War," and The U.S. Department of Justice, "Four Defendants Are Caught in an Undercover Sting Operation, Attempting to Purchase a Large Number of Surface-to-Air Missiles, Missile Launchers, and Hundreds of AK-47 Automatic Rifles," http://www.fas.org/asmp/campaigns/MANPADS/2006/dojpr21aug06.htm (accessed September 5, 2007).

125　*Jane's Intelligence Review*, "Feeding the Tiger: How Sri Lankan Insurgents Fund Their War," and The U.S. Department of Justice, "Four Defendants Are Caught in

uncovered evidence of LTTE efforts to procure "other military arms, unmanned aerial vehicles for jamming radio transmissions and radar, submarine design software, flight lessons, cell towers, radio controller equipment, global positioning system equipment, shortwave radio equipment, radio and satellite equipment, air traffic control equipment, cameras, computers, and other items to be used by the LTTE."[126] The boldness of this attempt to procure these items in the United States suggests the seriousness of the LTTE's desire to address its strategic imbalance with the Sri Lankan military.

The LTTE was also willing to expend exorbitant sums of money to lobby its removal from the State Department's Foreign Terrorist Organization list. According to a U.S. government source, "beginning in 2004 and continuing over a period of several months, [LTTE operatives] met with a confidential informant and two purported State Department officials [to discuss] the financial terms of a bribe, including a $1 million dollar up-front payment, [for helping facilitate the removal of the LTTE from the State Department list.]"[127] The riskiness of this effort to directly solicit its removal from the list may indicate that the group's designation as a foreign terrorist organization in 1997 resulted in significant setbacks to the LTTE's fundraising efforts and lobbying capability in the United States.[128] Allegedly, the LTTE even "hired the prestigious U.S. law firm run by Ramsey Clark, former Attorney General under the Lyndon Johnson Administration, to pursue legal mechanisms for removal of the State Department designation. Although the effort failed, it nevertheless indicates the LTTE's ability to access the very highest echelons of the U.S. legal establishment."[129]

A final pattern emerges with regard to how the LTTE once spent its funds. On several occasions, the group spent large sums on the expensive and protracted legal defenses for its high-level operatives. Perhaps the best-known example of this was the 1995 arrest and prosecution of Manikavasagam Suresh, the LTTE representative to Canada.[130] Attempting to secure his release, the organization initiated a mass mail-out campaign, organized demonstrations, and hired two highly-paid lawyers to provide legal representation.[131] To date, the LTTE's effort

---

an Undercover Sting Operation, Attempting to Purchase a Large Number of Surface-to-Air Missiles, Missile Launchers, and Hundreds of AK-47 Automatic Rifles," http://www.fas. org/asmp/campaigns/MANPADS/2006/dojpr21aug06.htm (accessed September 5,2007).

126   U.S. Department of Justice, "Four Defendants Are Caught in an Undercover Sting Operation."

127   U.S. Department of Justice, "Four Defendants Are Caught in an Undercover Sting Operation."

128   *Jane's World of Insurgency and Terrorism*, "Liberation Tigers of Tamil Eelam."

129   Chalk, "Liberation Tigers of Tamil Eelam's (LTTE) International Organization and Operations."

130   Chalk, "Liberation Tigers of Tamil Eelam's (LTTE) International Organization and Operations."

131   Chalk, "Liberation Tigers of Tamil Eelam's (LTTE) International Organization and Operations."

to secure his release represents one of the most highly contested trials in Canadian history.[132] Also notable was the LTTE's willingness to pay V. Manoharan's family his salary while he was imprisoned in France for two years serving out his sentence on narcotics charges.[133] Clearly, the LTTE's loyalty to its senior operatives was indicative of its dedication to its cause.

Governmental Counters

Sri Lanka's efforts to counter the LTTE's extensive financial capability are multi-faceted. Although more successful in some areas than others, it appears that the governmental counters followed a methodical approach in an attempt to counter the LTTE's most successful centers of gravity. As noted previously, the backbone of the LTTE's overseas fundraising came from its popular and coerced contributions from the Tamil Diaspora in North America, Europe, and Asia. As such, the government cooperated with law enforcement authorities in other countries, at times providing key intelligence information necessary for Western law enforcement agencies to round up LTTE operatives attempting to raise funds and acquire military weaponry and dual use technology for wartime use. Examples include the April 2006 RCMP raid on the World Tamil Movement offices in Montreal; the April 2006 arrests of LTTE operatives who attempted to bribe U.S. State Department officials; the September 2006 unsuccessful arms purchase attempt in Long Island, New York; the September 2006 arms procurement arrests in Baltimore and Guam; the April 2007 French police raids on LTTE-related entities and operatives in Paris; and the 2006-2007 credit card fraud arrests in Singapore, Norway, Thailand, Kenya, and Sri Lanka.[134] Although these examples of international cooperation are obvious successes, perhaps the greatest success from these operations has been the increased understanding authorities have gained of the LTTE's global financial network and procurement structure.[135] According to *Jane's Intelligence Review*, when "taken in total, the investigations show that the LTTE had a shared methodology that it followed irrespective of location. The pattern was for the LTTE to create, staff, and project its influence through front organizations and outsourced Tamil gangs to raise money from

---

132   Chalk, "Liberation Tigers of Tamil Eelam's (LTTE) International Organization and Operations."

133   Chalk, "Liberation Tigers of Tamil Eelam's (LTTE) International Organization and Operations."

134   *Jane's Intelligence Review*, "Feeding the Tiger: How Sri Lankan Insurgents Fund Their War."

135   *Jane's Intelligence Review*, "Feeding the Tiger: How Sri Lankan Insurgents Fund Their War."

Tamil communities and ultimately, convert the gains into arms."[136] This enhanced understanding of the LTTE's fundraising methodology should be helpful to future governmental efforts to curtail the group's activities.

Western law enforcement crackdowns would not have been possible without the formal terrorist designations given the LTTE by India (1992), the U.S. (1997), the U.K. (2001), Canada (2006), and the E.U. (2006).[137] The Sri Lankan Ministry of Defense successfully lobbied countries with large Tamil Diasporas in an attempt to further disrupt this group's activities. As recent as June 2007, the ministry suggested that Australia was preparing to formally designate the group as a terrorist organization.[138] However, *Jane's Intelligence Review* suggests that the most likely impact these formal terrorist designations had was "restricting the group's key leadership's ability to travel in areas where they desired to seek funding."[139] While formal designations are an excellent first step, they may not be enough, as many countries still lacked the legal infrastructure to really crack down on the LTTE's fundraising operations. Subsequently, until its defeat, it was surmised that the LTTE would continue to concentrate its fundraising efforts in countries with weaker statutory provisions such as Norway, Sweden, and Australia, or by attempts at bypassing them in counties like the U.S., Canada, or the U.K. through the continued use of fronts or by changing the names of their organizations to further disrupt governmental crackdowns.[140]

The Sri Lankan government also cooperated with the U.S. in an attempt to find and track the Tiger's financial resources. Although no formal assets were identified for freezing or seizure, the United States did provide training for the Sri Lankan government and banking sector.[141] Similarly, other Sri Lankan efforts to disrupt LTTE assets were also mostly unsuccessful. Although the Sri Lankan government was able to freeze $707,000 from the Tamil Rehabilitation Organization in May, 2006, the LTTE turned this setback into a propaganda tool by accusing the government of targeting assets slated for tsunami and war affected Tamil populations.[142] Furthermore, the government's inability to levy any formal charges against the Tamil Rehabilitation Organization, following over a year's

---

136   *Jane's Intelligence Review*, "Feeding the Tiger: How Sri Lankan Insurgents Fund Their War."

137   *Jane's Intelligence Review*, "Feeding the Tiger: How Sri Lankan Insurgents Fund Their War."

138   *Jane's Intelligence Review*, "Feeding the Tiger: How Sri Lankan Insurgents Fund Their War."

139   *Jane's World of Insurgency and Terrorism*, "Liberation Tigers of Tamil Eelam."

140   Chalk, "Liberation Tigers of Tamil Eelam's (LTTE) International Organization and Operations."

141   U.S. Department of State, "Country Reports on Terrorism: Sri Lanka," April 30, 2007, http://www.state.gov/s/ct/rls/crt/2006/82734.htm (accessed September 5, 2007).

142   TamilNet, "Account Freeze by Sri Lanka Violates UN Declaration-TRO," http://www.tamilnet.com/art.html?catid=13&artid=23189 (accessed September 5, 2007).

worth of investigations, seemed to give credence to the LTTE's claims.[143] This example is a testament to the LTTE's once-extensive propaganda generation capability, and illustrates the potential pitfalls faced by a government attempting to disrupt the financial streams of an organization that is clearly using its financial resources to wage a bloody civil war.

Attempting to disrupt the LTTE's arms procurement and trafficking capability, Sri Lanka also pursued such initiatives as the Container Security Initiative and the Megaports program at the Port of Columbo.[144] These initiatives were important as they "enhanced the physical security of port facilities, increased patrols of waterways, ports, and coastal facilities, container security, and protection against explosives and the creation of databases to track ships and seamen--all imperative measures to mitigate the threat."[145] These measures appear to have achieved some promising results, as it appears that the LTTE's arms procurement capability became increasingly diminished. Likewise, according to *Jane's World of Insurgency and Terrorism*, "following the 11 September 2001 attacks on the U.S., there were increased efforts to curtail the flow of funds and arms to the LTTE from foreign sources. Second, the terms of the government-LTTE Memorandum of Understanding of February 2002, and the substantially strengthened coastal surveillance by the government security forces, also had a restrictive effect on the LTTE's arms procurement."[146] Nevertheless, Sri Lanka's maritime interdiction efforts may be for naught if international agreements and cooperation cannot be achieved. For example, for many years, the lack of a comprehensive defense pact with India frustrated naval cooperation efforts to interdict LTTE arms procurement by leaving the 22-mile-long maritime smuggling route between Sri Lanka and the southern Indian province of Tamil Nadu virtually unprotected.[147] Although unsupported by hard data, it is estimated that the Sri Lankan Navy was intercepting only a fraction of the LTTE's incoming arms shipments.[148] Fortunately, increased cooperation in the form of joint patrolling between the Sri Lankan and Indian navies helped to close this important arms smuggling route, helping the government achieve the upper hand militarily.[149]

Also promising were the successful military offenses of 2006-2007 and 2008-2009, which weakened the LTTE's hold on key terrain in the north and eastern provinces. In August 2006, the Sri Lankan government launched a major offensive

---

143   TamilNet, "Account Freeze by Sri Lanka Violates UN Declaration-TRO."

144   U.S. Department of State, "Country Reports on Terrorism: Sri Lanka."

145   Ophir Falk and Yaron Schwartz, "Terror at Sea: The Maritime Threat," http://www. ict.org.il/index.php?sid=119&lang=en&act=page&id=5218&str=LTTE (accessed September 5, 2007).

146   *Jane's World of Insurgency and Terrorism*, "Liberation Tigers of Tamil Eelam," see also Fair, "Urban Battlefields of South Asia," 65-6.

147   *Jane's World of Insurgency and Terrorism*, "Liberation Tigers of Tamil Eelam."

148   *Jane's World of Insurgency and Terrorism*, "Liberation Tigers of Tamil Eelam."

149   "Q&A: Sri Lanka Conflict," BBC News.

against LTTE strongholds located in the eastern province.[150] Government forces launched aerial strikes and ground attacks on Tiger base camps, sinking twelve LTTE boats in a sea battle off the northern coast in early September.[151] They also took control of Sampur, "a key town near the northeastern port of Trincomalee, from where the LTTE rebels had launched artillery strikes on the port."[152] In early 2007, the military captured the LTTE stronghold at Vakara, just northeast of Columbo, a significant psychological blow to the rebels after several weeks of intense fighting against government forces.[153] Subsequently, in the spring of 2007 the Sri Lankan Air Force conducted a successful bombing campaign in the northeast provinces, destroying a key LTTE naval base located there.[154] The military victories of 2007 seemed to reinforce the government's commitment to gain military superiority over the LTTE, prompting a plan to spend approximately $70 million on military equipment purchases in the second half of 2007.[155] The high priority military equipment acquisition plan included the purchases of four F-7GS fighter aircraft, four MiG-29SM, one MiG29UB fighter, two PT-6 aircraft, Blue Horizon II unmanned aerial vehicles, two JY-11 mobile radars, spare parts for the Mi-24 and Mi24/35 helicopters, heads-up displays for five Mi-24 helicopters, cameras for Beech King aircraft, new/updated aircraft repair facilities, two Beech King aircraft fitted with maritime surveillance radars and cameras, two AN-32B transports, three MI24/35 helicopters, and two K-8 aircraft.[156] The Sri Lankan military was initially promised $900,000 in U.S. Foreign Military Financing funds to purchase uniform items, night vision, radios, body armor, and communications equipment and $540,000 in U.S. International Military Education and Training funds to "build military competencies, teach respect for human rights, and increase operability of the officers and non-commissioned officer (NCO) cadres." However, this promise of foreign military aid was later withdrawn by the U.S., due to human rights violations, prompting a late 2007 pledge of $50,000,000 from Pakistan.[157] Heavy fighting in late 2007 and throughout most of 2008 would prompt the Sri Lankan government to increase its own military defense budget, setting record levels for both 2008 and 2009. By 2008, defense budgetary allocations had reached

150 *Jane's World of Insurgency and Terrorism*, "Liberation Tigers of Tamil Eelam."
151 *Jane's World of Insurgency and Terrorism*, "Liberation Tigers of Tamil Eelam."
152 *Jane's World of Insurgency and Terrorism*, "Liberation Tigers of Tamil Eelam."
153 *Jane's World of Insurgency and Terrorism*, "Liberation Tigers of Tamil Eelam."
154 *Jane's World of Insurgency and Terrorism*, "Liberation Tigers of Tamil Eelam."
155 Robert Karnoil, "Sri Lanka Looks to Boost Forces Against Northern Rebels," *Jane's Defense Weekly*, August 1, 2007, http://jdw.janes.com/public/jdw/index.shtml (accessed August 20, 2009).
156 Karnoil, "Sri Lanka Looks to Boost Forces Against Northern Rebels."
157 U.S. Department of State, "Sri Lanka: Security Assistance," http://www.state.gov/t/pm/64481.htm (accessed September 5, 2007 and August 30, 2009); Bajoria, "The Sri Lankan Conflict;" and Jon Grevatt, "Pakistan Offers Funds to Tackle Sri Lankan Insurgency," *Jane's Defense Industry*, January 1, 2008, http://jdin.janes.com/public/jdin/index.shtml (accessed August 20, 2009).

a record high of $1,500,000,000, as the government stepped up its spending to put increased pressure on the rebels.[158] For 2009, the government would approve an increase of an additional $98,000,000 with the majority of funds set to support the operational expenses of the Sri Lankan Army.[159]

Defeated or Merely Disrupted?

The events of May 2009 would appear to mark the end of the LTTE's 33-year-long separatist campaign against the governmental forces of Sri Lanka. These appear to have been fatal blows: the conventional military defeat of the group; seizure of all previously held territories; deaths of influential LTTE leadership including Vellupillai Prabhakaran and his son Charles Anthony; political chief Balasingham Mahendran; peace secretariat leader Seevaratnam Pulidevan; intelligence chief Pottu Amman; and senior military leader Ramesh as well as the August 2009 capture of LTTE financing chief and international spokesman Selvarasa 'Kumaran' Pathmanathan.[160] Nevertheless, these key events have significant implications for the LTTE's still-intact financial networks.

The Sri Lankan government needs to continue to disrupt the LTTE's financial and procurement network—both key centers of gravity directly related to the Tiger's ability to fight successfully in this protracted insurgency. The government needs to continue to win its military campaigns in Tiger-held territories in the north and east, especially if it hopes to stop the flow of arms and equipment. Moreover, any future re-emergence of the LTTE will depend on the group's ability to acquire its finances and weaponry from abroad.[161] The military campaigns and successes in 2006 and 2007 and later in 2008 and 2009 have crushed the conventional military capability of the LTTE, overrun its long-held sanctuaries, and resulted in the killing or capturing of its key leadership. Following the government's announcement of victory on May 19, 2009, there have been no new terrorist attacks by the LTTE (as of this update in late October). The peaceful summer and fall of 2009 would seem to suggest that the government's expenditures and military campaigns were ultimately successful. Nevertheless, the U.S. State Department continues to warn travelers that "although hostilities have concluded remnants of the insurgency group remain [and therefore] the possibility remains that the organization may

---

158   Athas, "Sri Lankan Defense Spending Set to Reach Record Levels."

159   Athas, "Sri Lankan Defense Spending Set to Reach Record Levels."

160   "Sri Lanka Declares Victory as LTTE Chief is Killed," *Jane's Country Risk Daily Report*, May 18, 2009, http://www.janes.com/products/janes/security/news/country-risk-daily.aspx (accessed August 20,2009); and "Last Prominent LTTE Leader Captured," *Jane's Intelligence Weekly*, August 7, 2009, http://jiwk.janes.com/MicroSites/index.jsp?site=jiwk&pageindex=section_frontpage (accessed August 20, 2009).

161   *Jane's Intelligence Review*, "Feeding the Tiger: How Sri Lankan Insurgents Fund Their War."

continue to carry out attacks."[162] Jane's Terrorism and Insurgency Centre notes "a legacy as powerful as that of the LTTE will not fade easily and it is highly likely that splinter sleeper suicide cells will continue to carry out assassinations which means some form of Tamil separatism will continue."[163] Subsequently, the obvious question at this juncture is will the group re-emerge and attempt to continue hostilities? Only time will tell. However, the government's actions and behavior in the present may very well affect the ultimate outcome of this conflict and influence whether or not it will return to open hostilities.

The military's attempts to invest in modern military hardware are important, but attempts to professionalize the NCO and officer cadres may be the most influential. The key campaign battles of 2008 and 2009 required a degree of technological sophistication as well as tactical competence, key skill sets that the Sri Lankan military successfully recognized as necessary to win victory against this formidable foe. Perhaps most promising though was the government's efforts to address previous human rights violations through proper training. Members of the government's security forces have committed abuses in the past including torture, rape, the use of heavy-handed tactics, violence as well as infringements on privacy rights, illegal detentions, and other forms of abuse.[164] As conflict escalated throughout 2008 and 2009, accusations of governmental abuse also intensified. Global Security.org reports:

> The government's respect for human rights declined as armed conflict escalated. The overwhelming majority of victims of human rights violations, such as killings and disappearances, were young male Tamils. Credible reports cited unlawful killings by paramilitaries and others believed to be working with the awareness of the government, assassinations by unknown perpetrators, politically motivated killings, the continuing use of child soldiers by a paramilitary force associated with the government, disappearances, arbitrary arrests and detention, poor prison conditions, denial of fair public trial, government corruption and lack of transparency, infringement of freedom of movement, and discrimination against minorities.[165]

---

162   U.S. Department of State, "Travel Warning Sri Lanka," http://travel.state.gov/travel/cis_pa_tw/tw/tw_3011.html (accessed September 4, 2009).

163   *Jane's Country Risk Daily Report*, "Sri Lanka Declares Victory as LTTE Chief is Killed."

164   U.S. Department of State, "Country Reports on Human Rights Practices—2002, March 31, 2003, http://www.state.gov/g/drl/rls/hrrpt/2002/18315.htm (accessed October 12, 2007).

165   Global Security.org, "Liberation Tigers of Tamil Eelam (LTTE), World Tamil Association (WTA), World Tamil Movement (WTM), Federation of Associations of Canadian Tamils (FACT) Ellalan Force," www.globalsecurity.org/military/worldpara/ltte.htm (accessed July 3, 2009).

During the final few months of the conflict when the government pushed the LTTE back to a tiny strip of land on the coastline of northeastern Sri Lanka, "the Tigers pulled an estimated 70,000 (Army estimate) and 200,000 (LTTE estimate) Tamil civilians into their enclave with them, using them as human shields, a forced labor pool, and a last source of compelled conscripts and child soldiers."[166] Subsequently, in order to root out the last remaining rebel stronghold, despite its claims of innocence, the government likely used artillery and other heavy weapons to attack rebels hiding in the no-fire zone, resulting in an unknown number of civilian casualties.[167] Following cessation of hostilities, the government's efforts to prevent outside investigations by human rights organizations and denial of access to the affected area by political leaders, international aid agencies, medical relief organizations, and journalists, does little to substantiate their claims of innocence.[168] Moreover, in an effort to root out the remaining remnants of the LTTE, the government has set up internment camps and is holding an estimated 250,000 to 300,000 Tamils in an effort to screen out the remaining rebels that the government believes are hiding among these civilians.[169] The government's behavior in the last days of the conflict has done little to substantiate its claims of innocence and care for the well-being of Sri Lankan Tamils. If this poor treatment and abuse continues, the government itself may be exclusively responsible for resurgence of this conflict. Although some human rights improvements have been made over the last couple of years, to win the hearts and minds of the Tamil minorities in the north and east provinces the government will need to do better with its efforts to build its social capital. Internment camps are not a step in the right direction.

Sri Lanka's announcement of plans to redevelop the war-torn land reclaimed from the LTTE in the Eastern Province is a positive step. In September 2007, the government announced a plan to spend almost $60 million on infrastructure

---

166   Thompson, "The Liberation Tigers of Tamil Eelam: Essential Points."

167   Ranga Sirilal, "Sri Lanka Says Final Standoff With Tigers Approaches," *Reuters*, March 26, 2009, www.reuters.com/article/asiaCrisis/idUSCOL84177 (accessed July 3, 2009); Steve Herman, "LTTE Leader Killed, Sri Lanka Claims Total Control of Island Nation," GlobalSecurity.org, www.globalsecurity.org/military/library/news/2009/05/mil-090518-voa03.htm (accessed July 3, 2009); Lydia Polgreen, "Tamils Now Languish in Sri Lanka Camps," *The New York Times*, July 12, 2009; BBC News, "Q&A: Sri Lanka Conflict," and Bajoria, "The Sri Lankan Conflict."

168   Bajoria, "The Sri Lankan Conflict," Herman, "LTTE Leader Killed, Sri Lanka Claims Total Control of Island Nation," and BBC News, "Q&A: Sri Lanka Conflict."

169   Polgreen, "Tamils Now Languish in Sri Lanka Camps;" Herman, "LTTE Leader Killed, Sri Lanka Claims Total Control of Island Nation;" "Sri Lanaka's Fragile Post-Prabhakaran Future," *Jane's Country Risk Daily Report*, 2, http://www.janes.com/products/janes/security/news/country-risk-daily.aspx (accessed August 20, 2009); and *Jane's Intelligence Weekly*, "Sri Lankan Post-War Poll Yields Mixed Results," http://www.jiwk.janes.com (accessed August 20, 2009).

development and administration in this province.[170] This type of governmental effort to reclaim territory previously held by the LTTE, properly secure it, and redevelop it, will likely go a long way towards building credibility and social capital it desperately needs among the Tamil minority that has historically been excluded. The government will need to look for other opportunities to take advantage of its successes in such a way that it can maximize their effect. Perhaps in the future the government could use seized LTTE funds to redevelop these long-neglected areas.

In order to prevent the reemergence of the LTTE, the Sri Lankan government will have to do a better job of suppressing the LTTE's once-highly effective propaganda machine. Money previously frozen from the Tamil Rehabilitation Organization shows that the government will have to be more strategic with its counter-financing efforts to ensure potential successes are not remarketed by the LTTE as governmental failures. Likewise, the Sri Lankan government will need to continue to work with its Western allies to prevent the flow of or disrupt LTTE propaganda headed to Diaspora populations. The LTTE made extensive use of the Internet, satellite phone links, faxes, etc. to further its cause in sophisticated detail.[171] Not only will the government need to interdict the group's DVDs, video, pamphlets, and calendar production capability before they can arrive in foreign countries, it will need to locate LTTE propaganda Web sites and communications capability to target it, disrupt it, or shut it down. Similarly, an effective counter-information operations campaign may be able to capitalize on the LTTE's strategic errors, such as its 2005 effort to prevent Tamils from voting for moderate political candidates in areas under its control; the extensive seizure of land, livestock, and taxes in areas under its control; human rights abuses and the use of child soldiers; and, finally, its battlefield losses.[172] One public opinion poll found that 84 percent of Sri Lankans believe peace can be achieved through talks and negotiations; 95 percent of the Tamil population believes the same.[173] Perhaps the government could take advantage of this belief by addressing some of the Tamil grievances, including unemployment and lack of representation. This would no doubt go a long way towards usurping the LTTE's once-vibrant support base.

Perhaps most importantly, in order effectively to stifle the LTTE's fundraising efforts, the Sri Lankan government will need to work harder at disrupting the popular and coerced diaspora funding methods, charitable fronts, and social welfare programs run by the LTTE both at home and abroad. In order to be

---

170 *Asia Tribune*, "Norway Arming and Financing LTTE Through Eriteria, Prabhakaran Offered Asylum in Eriteria," September 16, 2007, http://www.asiatribune. com/index.php?q=node/7396 (accessed October 9, 2007).

171 Chalk, "Liberation Tigers of Tamil Eelam's (LTTE) International Organization and Operations."

172 Zissis, "The Sri Lankan Conflict," and *Jane's World of Insurgency and Terrorism*, "Liberation Tigers of Tamil Eelam."

173 Kronstadt, "Sri Lanka: Background and U.S. Relations."

effective in both theaters, better human intelligence (HUMINT) is necessary to target LTTE fronts by tracking the money flow, and then shutting them down when the timing is right. This is likely to be a challenge for Sri Lankan and Western governments alike, as historically the Tamil population has been suspicious and fearful of the police, governmental authority, and the military, usually avoiding any unnecessary contact.[174] Also problematic is the fact that intelligence collection entities and police often lack the necessary language and cultural skills required to understand and process the raw intelligence collected—and this may be particularly difficult for law enforcement entities from Western countries attempting to cooperate with Sri Lankan authorities.[175] In the past, government's efforts to collect intelligence in Sri Lanka and abroad have suffered due to a lack of informants. Similarly, one of the main complaints of Western law enforcement organizations is the fact that Tamils are often afraid to come forward to tell them who is responsible for the extortion. Much of this is due to the LTTE's effective control of its overseas collection system as well as Tamil fears for relatives living in Sri Lanka, especially in areas previously under LTTE control.[176] As a result, security forces have either been unable to break up extortion rings or have been forced to use poor tactics such as cordon and search of residential neighborhoods and pickets and roadblocks, which have had the unwanted effect of humiliating Tamils and providing fuel to the LTTE cause.[177] In the future, Sri Lanka will need to develop a system of incentives to foster better information flow. Perhaps this could best be accomplished by offering special micro-loan programs, preference for governmental jobs, or even the relocation of high-level informants. In some cases it may be necessary to totally shut down Tamil extortion gangs and illegitimate or even suspicious charities. However, Sri Lanka will have to have some alternatives available to prevent this from becoming an LTTE propaganda victory. Perhaps this could be accomplished by working with and/or sponsoring Tamil groups counter to the LTTE cause, creating state-run charities, or by offering international charities and NGOs incentives to come to Sri Lanka. Potential incentives could include protection, transportation, and even some formal state-sponsorship. At a minimum, whatever Sri Lanka decides to do about these charities, it will need to ensure that charitable organizations maintain the transparency needed for legitimacy and that the funds go to the war-torn areas that actually need them.

Finally, in order to be successful at shutting down the LTTE's financing capability, the government will need to ensure that the LTTE's maritime procurement and trafficking structure is not able to recapitalize. Continued international cooperation is absolutely necessary. Sri Lanka will need to continue forming comprehensive

---

174 Fair, "Urban Battlefields of South Asia," 8, 13.

175 Fair, "Urban Battlefields of South Asia," 8, 13, 63.

176 The Mackenzie Institute, "Other People's Wars: A Review of Overseas Terrorism in Canada."

177 Fair, "Urban Battlefields of South Asia," 57-8.

defense agreements and conducting joint naval exercises with India to preclude the reemergence of the Tamil Nadu smuggling route. Sri Lanka's attempts to better its military technology and air interdiction capability and its strategic partner in the form of the Indian Navy were instrumental in putting pressure on the once heavily-armed Sea Tigers. These practices should continue and Sri Lanka should work to ensure a clear understanding of the rules of engagement as well as realize that responsibilities for patrol zones need to be improved. Sri Lanka also needs to stop allowing ships registered in countries with lax requirements (Panama, Honduras, and Liberia) to dock in Sri Lankan ports. Finally, stronger denial operations are a must. If Sri Lanka can lock down its ports, forcing future efforts to off-load arms and military equipment cargo into areas where its enemies are forced to transport through the dense jungle instead of docking in favorable locations, it will put a significant logistical burden on any remnants of the LTTE. This, coupled with denial of key terrain such as major highways and roadways, could effectively make the LTTE's future arms procurement efforts much more difficult. The more ways the Sri Lankan government can deny former centers of gravity to the LTTE, the better off it will be.

Conclusion

The LTTE's well-developed and multi-faceted fundraising capability is an important center of gravity that contributed to the longevity and sustainability of its three-decade-long campaign against the Sri Lankan government. The slowdown of Diaspora fundraising streams following 9/11, significant military losses over the last couple of years, and Western law enforcement crackdowns hurt the LTTE in the short-term, yet this group still managed to maintain its resiliency until the military defeat and subsequent deaths of its key leaders dealt it a crushing blow. In order to ensure this group does not re-emerge in the coming years, Sri Lanka will need to continue to foster international cooperation and partnerships. This is especially important because the LTTE once raised the bulk of its funds in foreign countries, using a variety of legal, semi-legal, and illegal means. These global fundraising networks and their overseas leadership have yet to be successfully dealt with. As such, Sri Lanka will need to find new ways to provide Western law enforcement agencies the necessary human intelligence (HUMINT) needed to crackdown on the LTTE's enforcement gangs, charitable fronts, and sanctuaries lest these former fundraising mechanisms be used by former guerillas purely for profit. Sri Lanka will also need to cooperate with its neighbors to continue crackdowns on the LTTE's once extensive shipping capability, key to its formerly highly successful human, narcotics, and gun smuggling activities. A good first step towards this goal was the formation of a comprehensive naval agreement pact with India, clearly defining patrol zones, responsibilities, and rules of engagement.

Sri Lanka also needs to take better advantage of key events and opportunities to foster better relations with the Tamil minority. For example, rather than being able to use the tsunami disaster of 2004 as an opportunity to build goodwill with Tamils, negotiations broke down when the distribution of international aid could not be agreed upon. In the future, Sri Lanka will need to look past its internal political squabbles and take advantage of opportunities to build political capital with its highly alienated Tamil population. This is key to a successful strategy because trust and relationships are necessary to foster the kind of HUMINT that Sri Lanka desperately needs to strike at the remnants of the LTTE both at home and abroad. By building trust, one hopes Sri Lanka can begin to get at the root causes of the Tamil grievances, as there is a price to be paid for continuing a policy of discrimination and alienation. Incentives will need to be created to foster cooperation, propaganda streams will need to be shut down, social capital will need to be built, alternative programs will need to be developed and fostered to address the economic and humanitarian needs in the north and east, and basic security and protection will need to be maintained if Sri Lanka desires truly to get at the root causes of this conflict. Finally, heavy-handed governmental crackdowns must stop. Although the $60 million the government has pledged to bolster infrastructure in the eastern province is a step in the right direction, it would seem that this meager sum is disproportionate to the amount of money Sri Lanka has previously funneled into bolstering its military capability. Now that the government no longer has to compete with the LTTE in a military arms race, perhaps it can concentrate more funding on this long-neglected region. A more balanced allocation of the country's limited financial resources may prove to be more effective, allowing the government to buy down the social and infrastructure problems in Tamil-controlled regions while still maintaining an acceptable level of military capability.

Although these recommendations are not all-inclusive, they provide the basic framework for what could be an effective strategy for attacking the remnants of the LTTE's fundraising capability at several levels. Most of these suggestions are a continuation or amplification of previously successful efforts that have worked well for Sri Lanka in the past. All are feasible; however, perhaps the greatest difficulty for Sri Lankans—both Sinhalese and Tamil—will be moving forward past the wrongs of history and discrimination to forge the types of alliances necessary to truly address the basis of the country's problems. In order to do this, both Sinhalese and Tamil will need to lay aside their centuries-old differences and work towards a common goal desired by both ethnic groups: peace. Perhaps government can take the first step towards forging a lasting peace by establishing some goodwill with the Tamils. This may prove to be much more difficult and costly for Sri Lanka than simple monetary expenditures on infrastructure and social programs. This will require communication, mutual understanding, and compromise, characteristics neither group has been particularly good at in the past. Although alliances and partnerships are important, only by undermining the political support base of the LTTE can the government ever hope to stop this once deep-pocketed terrorist group.

Chapter 9
Terrorist Financing in the Philippines

Wade A. Germann, Eric Hartunian, Richard A. Polen, and
Krishnamurti Mortela

This chapter will focus on the nature of terrorist financing in the Philippines. We will
begin with a brief history of the conflict between the Moros and the Christians, and
how that has brought about several of the terror groups discussed in this chapter.
Following the history, we will identify the terrorist groups and their origins. These
groups include the Moro National Liberation Front, the Moro Islamic Liberation
Front, the New People's Army, and the Abu Sayyaf Group. We have divided the
methods of Philippine terror funding into four categories: the sources by which
they gain funds, the methods by which they move and store their funds, their
expenditures, and the countermeasures that the Philippine Government is using in
an effort to combat terrorist financing.

Mindanao: History and Culture

The population of Mindanao is comprised of three groups: Moros or Bangasa Moro-
Muslims; Lumads who are indigenous, predominately non-Muslim people; and
Christian settlers. In 1946 the Philippines received its independence from the United
States and continued to exploit Mindanao's rich resources and available land to the
benefit of the north. While the numbers of Christian emigrates from central and
northern Philippines to Mindanao remained relatively small during the American
colonial period, it began to intensify following World War II.[1] By the 1970s, the
immigration of Christian Filipinos to Mindanao had created a social landscape where
Moros and Lumads had become the minorities with Muslims accounting for only one
quarter of Mindanao's population, down from about three quarters at the beginning
of the century.[2] The Philippine government also continued the policy of encouraging
plantation agriculture and deforestation on a large scale in Mindanao, allowing some

---

1   Susan D. Russell, et al., "The Mindanao Conflict and Prospects for Peace in the
Southern Philippines," excerpted from "Mindanao: A Perspective on Youth, Inter-Ethnic
Dialogue and Conflict Resolution In the Southern Philippines," Center for Southeast Asian
Studies and Office of International Training, Northern Illinois University, 2004, 3.

2   Sylvia Concepcion, Larry Digal, Rufa Guiam, Romulo de la Rosa, Mara
Stankovitch, "Breaking the links between economics and conflict in Mindanao," Presented
at the "Waging Peace" conference, Manila, December 2003, 7, http://ki-volunteer.org/index.

of the most productive lands to be occupied by transnational corporations.[3] Both Moros and Lumads felt that not only was the access to their ancestral lands and other productive resources being taken, but that their cultural identities were being overwhelmed by the Christian settlers.

Generations of instability and conflict have created many unresolved intertwined issues, including: the question of ancestral domain and agrarian rights; the plight of thousands of displaced and landless families who have witnessed the destruction of their property; social and cultural discrimination between people of different historical or religious traditions; widespread poverty; the exploitation of natural resources, described as 'development aggression;' and finally, the inability to develop a system of governance compatible with the values of the three different groups of people.[4]

The gap between the Muslims and Christians widened in the 1960s, manifesting itself in the form of economic disparity and a strong desire for a return to autonomy and smaller self-governed societies. It was during the 1970s that violent encounters between Moros, Lumads, and Christians become common in Mindanao over rights to ancestral land and political marginalization.[5] As competition for land intensified, both Christian and Muslim landowners established private armies to extend or defend their holdings.

From the earliest days of its establishment the Government of the Republic of the Philippines (GRP) marginalized Mindanao. National governments were generally aware of problems in Mindanao, but few presidents gave it much attention or any priority. Mindanao was seen as a resource rich area to be exploited by the rest of the Philippines.[6] The dictatorial regime of President Ferdinand Marcos (1965-1986) triggered a series of events in the late 1960s, including the killing of Muslims, which sparked the formation of an insurgency in Mindanao and the formation of the Moro National Liberation Front (MNLF). The government's response to the Moro rebellion in 1972 was a declaration of martial law by Marcos; years of fighting and military confrontations between the two groups ensued. By the mid-1970s, the war had reached a stalemate and under heavy pressure from the international community, both parties sat down for peace talks.[7]

The Tripoli Agreement was signed in Libya in 1976 between the MNLF and the Philippine government.[8] The agreement granted autonomy to 13 provinces

---

php?option=com_docman&task=doc_download&gid=2&Itemid=79 (accessed January 13, 2012).

3 Concepcion, et al., "Breaking the links between economics and conflict in Mindanao," 7.

4 Russell, et al., "The Mindanao Conflict," 6-7.

5 Russell, et al., "The Mindanao Conflict," 3.

6 Russell, et al., "The Mindanao Conflict," 3.

7 Concepcion, et al., "Breaking the links between economics and conflict in Mindanao," 10-17.

8 Russell, et al., "The Mindanao Conflict," 3.

in Mindanao, Sulu, and Pawan Islands and established a regional government with its own executive, legislative, and judicial branches, with an independent security force.[9] The agreement eventually unraveled in disputes over how it was implemented, and within a year war had resumed.

Corazon Aquino became President of the Philippines (1986-1992) after the overthrow of Ferdinand Marcos under the promise that her regime would be 'radically different' from the Marcos dictatorship. Civil-society actors were invited to participate in drawing up a new Philippine Constitution which was ratified in 1986. It included provisions for the creation of the Autonomous Region in Muslim Mindanao (ARMM), which provided a limited measure of self-rule. However, the autonomous government lacked the resources to tackle the problems of the poorest regions of the Philippines, and the devastation caused by years of war. In the views of many Muslims, the ARMM simply became another layer of bureaucracy, providing positions and opportunities for the already privileged few.[10]

Fidel V. Ramos, a former head of the armed forces, was elected to the Presidency in 1992 (1992-1998). Mindanao was a primary component in Ramos' overall development vision, and he was determined to forge a comprehensive and enduring peace settlement, starting with the MNLF. Ramos believed that peace was a prerequisite for successful economic development in Mindanao. In 1996 the Final Peace Agreement (FPA) was signed between the GRP and MNLF. It provided for new institutions, led by the MNLF and supported by the government, to oversee a major development effort in a Special Zone of Peace and Development (SZOPAD) covering the territory stipulated in the Tripoli Agreement. Problems in the implementation of the FPA began almost immediately as the government attempted to solve the massive socio-economic problems within the SZOPAD. However, it is regarded as a remarkable benchmark, given the MNLF's decision to scale down its demands from separatism to autonomy.[11]

The situation began to change once again for the worse when Joseph Ejercito Estrada was elected President in 1998 (1998-2001), bringing many opponents of the FPA into the government. Under Estrada's direction, the armed forces launched a military offensive against several of the MILF's camps in Abu Bakar, and subsequently declared victory over the MILF (a splinter group of the MNLF discussed later in this chapter). Estrada also alienated the MNLF by creating a Mindanao Coordinating Council to manage infrastructure projects in the ARMM, thus weakening the role of the institutions set up under the FPA. In 2001, Estrada's

---

9 Concepcion, et al., "Breaking the links between economics and conflict in Mindanao," 10.

10 Concepcion, et al., "Breaking the links between economics and conflict in Mindanao," 10-17.

11 Concepcion, et al., "Breaking the links between economics and conflict in Mindanao," 10-17.

Presidency came to an end when he was ousted from power for involvement in government corruption.[12]

Estrada was succeeded by his Vice President, Gloria Macapagal Arroyo (2001-present), who declared a policy of 'all-out peace.' Arroyo sent emissaries to talk to the MNLF and MILF and formed a presidential task force to take the lead in rehabilitating areas in Mindanao that had been devastated by years of war.[13] However, Arroyo suspended the formal peace talks with the MILF in 2002 under reports that the MILF was sheltering criminal gangs and conducting ceasefire violations, although closed negotiations reportedly continued.[14]

After the attacks of September 11, 2001, President Arroyo was one of the first Asian leaders to express support for the U.S. 'War on Terrorism.' Her pledged support included statements about continuing the war against 'local terrorists' that included Muslim armed groups in Mindanao. With the Abu Sayyaf Group (ASG) and New People's Army (NPA) (groups discussed later in this chapter) already listed on the U.S terrorist organizations list, U.S. forces were sent to train Philippine troops who were pursuing the Abu Sayyaf, and Arroyo obtained a $356 million package for counter-terrorism aid.[15] The MNLF and MILF were excluded from the list because they are widely regarded as revolutionary organizations fighting for independence. However, the Philippine Government and the United States strongly believe the MILF and MNLF have links to all of these groups including Jemaah Islamiyah (JI) and al-Qaeda (AQ), although the MILF claims to officially disavow terrorism.[16]

There is not just one conflict in Mindanao, but several, as the lines between identity, kinship, ideology, and a common enemy in the Philippine government, become interconnected among the insurgent and terrorist groups. Today's tangled web of rebel factions intertwined with foreign international terrorist organizations makes for confusing and often misunderstood conditions for both Philippine government forces and rebel groups alike, as terrorist and insurgent ideologies compete for power and land. In this context it is important to look at each of the distinct rebel groups in Mindanao separately in order to understand their unique objectives, but not forget that each of these groups are tied together through common historical struggles and a multitude of personal and religious links.[17]

---

12 Concepcion, et al., "Breaking the links between economics and conflict in Mindanao," 10-17.

13 Concepcion, et al., "Breaking the links between economics and conflict in Mindanao," 10-17.

14 Russell, et al., "The Mindanao Conflict," 5.

15 Concepcion, et al., "Breaking the links between economics and conflict in Mindanao,"15.

16 International Crisis Group, "Southern Philippines Backgrounder: Terrorism and the Peace Process," ICG Asia Report No. 80, 13, July 2004, 1.

17 For more information on insurgent vs terrorist groups in Mindanao see the International Crisis Group, "Southern Philippines Backgrounder."

Moro National Liberation Front (MNLF)

After decades of political, social, and economic deterioration for the Moros in Mindanao, sentiments for an independent Muslim community finally became strong enough to take root. The MNLF defines its struggle as one against the Philippine state, not against Mindanao Christians, and its ideology attempted to go beyond local concerns and gain control over social services, to benefit from economic development, and protect their ancestral lands from Christian settlers and government owned corporations. The MNLF's educated leadership promoted a Bangsa Moro identity above the various ethnic affiliations of Mindanao Muslims with the ultimate goal of an independent Bangsa Moro state.[18]

The MNLF was able to gain a large amount of support from the global Muslim community because they claimed to be a movement representing all Muslims in the Philippines. Throughout the 1970s the MNLF gained most of its funding from Libya, who supported the training of fighters within its borders, and from the Chief Minister of the state of Sabah in Malaysia, Tun Mustapha, a Tausug whose family originated from Sulu.[19]

In 1996, after years of fighting and failed peace agreements with the government, Nur Misuari, head of the MNLF, and President Ramos, reached a peace agreement in Libya. The agreement provided for the employment and repatriation of MNLF rebels and socio-economic development assistance. Nur Misuari was later appointed chairman of the Southern Philippines Council for Peace and Development (SPCPD) and elected governor of the ARMM. In 1998, after little economic improvement for Muslims had been achieved, Misuari was not re-elected governor and again continued to launch attacks with the MNLF against the Philippine National Army. He was later arrested in Malaysia and is currently awaiting trial in jail in Manila.[20] The MNLF still retains governmental recognition as a representative of the Moro people of Mindanao at the government level, although they have seen a diminished military capacity over the years as the MNLF has evolved into a more political role.

Moro Islamic Liberation Front (MILF)

In 1977 the resumption of hostilities between the Filipino government and the MNLF was accompanied by fragmentation within the MNLF, eventually leading to the formation of the Moro Islamic Liberation Front (MILF) in 1984.[21] The MILF had more of a religious ideology, and its primary support base is in Central

---

18   Russell, et al., "The Mindanao Conflict," 2.

19   Concepcion, et al., "Breaking the links between economics and conflict in Mindanao," 9.

20   Russell, et al., "The Mindanao Conflict," 4.

21   Russell, et al., "The Mindanao Conflict," 3. International Crisis Group, "Southern Philippines Backgrounder," 4.

Mindanao, in particular Maguindanao and Lanao del Sur, but it also has a presence in Muslim communities of North Cotabato, Sultan Kudarat, South Cotabato, Lanao del Norte and the Zamboanga peninsula.[22] Local rebel commanders dominate these enclaves with varying degrees of allegiance to the MILF central leadership because their power is rooted in clan and tribal loyalties. Between 1987 and 1990 the MILF claimed to have 122,000 trained supporters that could be mobilized to back the 10,000 to 15,000 armed regulars.[23] By the mid-1980s, the MILF had become the strongest group militarily in Mindanao.

After the Philippine army's attack on the MILF's camp headquarters at Abu Bakar in 2000, and the death of Hashim Salamat in 2003, the MILF forces have been dispersed into smaller autonomous units.[24] Hashim's successor, Al-Haj Murad Ebrahim, faces the challenge of keeping it from separating into its many segmented parts.[25]

New People's Army (NPA)

The New People's Army is the military wing of the Communist Party of the Philippines (CPP) and was formed in 1969 with the aim of overthrowing the Philippine government through a long protracted war. The NPA was founded by Jose Maria Sison (currently the CPP's Central Committee Chairman) as a communist group based on the teachings of Mao.[26] The NPA is primarily a rural guerrilla group, but does have a small active urban infrastructure available to support it. The NPA targets Philippine security forces, politicians, judges, and even rival splinter groups and criminals. It derives most of its funding from support-based contributions in the Philippines and Europe, from taxes extorted from local businesses and politicians, and is believed to have received support from China.[27] The NPA is known to operate under an umbrella organization known as the New Democratic Front (NDF) that represents 13 smaller communists groups in political talks. Although there have been several smaller groups that have broken away from the NPA, such as the Revolutionary Army of the People, Revolutionary Party of Workers in Mindanao (RPM-M), and Proletarian Revolutionary Army, none have the size and influence of the NPA. The NPA is reported to be slowly growing in

22   Concepcion, et al., "Breaking the links between economics and conflict in Mindanao," 10.

23   International Crisis Group, "Southern Philippines Backgrounder," 4-5.

24   International Crisis Group, "Southern Philippines Backgrounder," 4.

25   Astrid Tuminez, 'The Past is Always Present: The Moros of Mindanao and the Quest for Peace," working paper No. 99 for The Southeast Asia Research Center Management Committee, City University of Hong Kong, May 2008, 29-30.

26   FAS Intelligence Resource Program, New People's Army (NPA), http://www.fas. org (accessed July 22, 2008).

27   Armed Conflicts Report, Philippines-CPP/NPA, January 2008, http://www. ploughshares.ca.libraries (accessed July 22, 2008).

popularity and numbers after years of low memberships, has an estimated 10,000 members today.[28]

Abu Sayyaf Group (ASG)

The failure of the Tripoli Agreement, the fragmentation of the liberation movement, and the weakening of the MNLF's leadership contributed to the emergence of a more radical armed group, the Abu Sayyaf Group (ASG), based on the island of Basilan. Unlike the MNLF and MILF, the Abu Sayyaf Group is explicitly anti-Christian. The group appears to operate as a network of networks with an alliance of smaller groups or cells that compete or cooperate to maximize their individual needs.[29] They continue to be involved in various terrorist activities (to include ties with Jemaah Islamiya (JI) and al-Qaeda (AQ), kidnappings of foreign tourists and missionaries for ransom, bombing attacks, and arms smuggling. Its leaders continue to present justifications for their activities in crude political and religious messages. Contrary to some assertions that the group has lost its political strategy or focus, they have always tended to function more like an organized crime gang.[30] Abu Sayyaf membership is believed to number between 400 and 1,000 members.[31]

Sources of Funding

Just as any organization needs money in order to operate, so too do terrorists. However, a terrorist organization needs to be much more diversified in their methods to obtain their financial necessities. These methods can be divided into four broad categories: state sponsorship, illegal activities, legal activities, and popular support.[32] The primary terrorist groups operating in the Philippines all use one or more of these categories in order to fund their operations. The money raised (or liberated from others) is used for a variety of purposes ranging from the actual terror attack itself, to providing housing and subsistence for their members. This section will look at examples of how financial backing has been obtained by these various groups since the 1970s, and conclude with an estimate, based on both factual and anecdotal evidence, of how much money these terrorist organizations are able to raise through their varying means and methods.

---

28   FAS, New People's Army.
29   International Crisis Group, "Southern Philippines Backgrounder," 7.
30   Concepcion, et al., "Breaking the links between economics and conflict in Mindanao," 11.
31   Council on Foreign Relations, "Abu Sayyaf Group (Philippines, Islamist Separatists," June 25, 2008, http://www.cfr.org (accessed July 17, 2008).
32   Michael Freeman, "Lecture on Terrorist Financing" Monterey, CA; Naval Postgraduate School, July 2008.

The first category, state sponsorship, has largely faded away in the last 20 years. The early 1970s, however, was the heyday for state contributions to terrorist organizations in the Philippines. From 1972 to 1975, Libya contributed an estimate $35 million to the MNLF to support the training of their fighters.[33] The NPA, between 1972 and 1974 received contributions from China in the form of weapons.[34] And finally, in 1991, the ASG received an estimated $6 million from Libya. Additionally, the ASG received services from Libya in the form of brokering ransom money for hostages taken by the ASG. The reduction in state sponsored funding to these groups may be in response to the pressure that these state sponsors of terrorism have received by being identified with terrorist organizations. In fact, Libya was only recently taken off of the U.S. State Department's list of countries that support terrorist organizations.

Illegal activity by terrorist organizations in the Philippines accounts for a large percentage of the four groups combined total income. These activities include kidnapping for ransom, drug producing and trafficking, organized crime, and coerced support. Kidnapping for ransom is conducted primarily by the ASG. Their kidnapping spree began in March 2000 with the kidnapping of 55 school children, teachers, and a priest. In April 2000, ASG conducted a raid on a resort in Malaysia where 21 tourists were taken hostage. Three months later, in July, three French journalists who were covering the initial hostage event of March were also taken captive. The ASG received an estimated total of $15 to $30 million in ransom money for the release of these hostages.[35] The success of these kidnappings led the ASG to continue and in May 2001, they kidnapped another 30 tourists from a diving resort in southern Mindanao.

The illegal drug market appears to be a large source of income for the MILF and ASG. Some estimates believe that the drug industry may be worth an estimated $5 billion dollars for the entire Philippine region.[36] However, these numbers are reflective not only of the four terrorist organizations discussed here, but also of various criminal gangs to include the Pentagon Gang and the Kuratong Gang. One example of the links between the ASG and the marijuana trade was discovered when over $10 million worth of marijuana was destroyed in July 1999 by the Philippine police.[37] Additionally, links have materialized between the Philippine

33   Christopher Collier and Noel Morada, "The Philippines: State vs Society," in *Asian Security Practice: Material and Ideational Influence*, edited by Muthiah Alagappa Muthiah Alagappa Muthiah Alagappa (Stanford University Press, 1998), 549-78, 558.

34   Marco Garrido, "Southeast Asia: Philippines-Gun Crazy,"*Asia Times*, January 23, 2003.

35   Daniel Barlow and Aurel Croissant, "Following the Money Trail: Terrorist Financing and Government Responses in Southeast Asia," *Studies in Conflict & Terrorism*, no. 30, 2007, 135.

36   Sheila Coronel, "Criminals Inc." *Philippine Center for Investigative Journalism*, 2003, http://www.pcij.org/imag/PublicEye/criminals.html (accessed January 13, 2012).

37   Zachary Abuza, "Funding Terrorism in Southeast Asia: The Financial Network of Al Qaeda and Jamaah Islamiya." *NBR Analysis* 14:5, December 2003, 53.

terrorist groups and the Hong Kong Triad, a major drug ring located in Asia's Golden Triangle.[38] Organized crime is the third major component of the illegal activity category in which these four organizations gain income. One type of this criminal activity that is prevalent in Mindanao is the illegal logging industry which earns the MILF an estimated $74,000 per month. Other activities include the smuggling of goods, to include food products, material supplies, and weapon.

Coerced support, the final category of funding for a terrorist organization, includes items such as extortion or revolutionary taxes. One of the schemes that the NPA employs is the use of "Permit to Campaign Cards." These cards are essentially used to provide potential government officials clear and safe passage to campaign in certain regions of the Philippines. The revenue generated from these cards range from $96,000 for a governor to campaign, to $2,000 for a municipal vice mayor.[39] Similarly, the MILF was responsible for charging an estimated $1.7 million dollars over a three year period from a Canadian Mining Company in Mindanao.[40] The funds paid by the company were in exchange for protection and the continued ability to complete their project under safe conditions. The ever present threat of harm by these terrorist groups helps to ensure that a variance of companies, ranging from telecommunications to small business owners, helps to make extortion a fairly secure and reliable source of income.[41]

Legal activity, such as a legitimate business, also provides funding for these terrorist organizations. One of the largest ventures involved the use of pork barrel funds directed to the NPA. Government officials who were sympathizers with the leftist party, lobby for government contracts to be given to their districts in which the NPA would be the prime beneficiaries. Even in some government contracts, it is reported that funds are diverted to the communist movement. For example, in 2004, leftist lawmakers diverted about eleven million dollars in pork barrel funds to the NPA, or their front organizations.[42] It is estimated that in 2004, approximately $9 million dollars were funneled to the NPA in this fashion.[43] Other types of fronts may include international trading companies, travel companies, and employment services.[44] Manpower Services, a Filipino company, is a legitimate company who has suspected ties with the MILF. It is believed that a portion of the proceeds that their clients pay in order to secure jobs abroad is funneled to various terrorist

38   Federal Research Division, *A Global Overview of Narcotics-Funded Terrorist and Other Extremist Groups.* Washington D.C., Library of Congress, 2002.

39   M.S. Arguelles and L.S. Macatangay, "PIA Daily News Reader," *Philippine Information Agency*, February 16, 2007, http://www.pia.gov (accessed August 1, 2008).

40   Marilyn Berlin Snell, "The Cost of Doing Business," *Sierra Club*, http://www.sierraclub.org (accessed July 30, 2008).

41   Coronel, "Criminals Inc."

42   Gonzales Paolo Romero, "CPP-NPA raising funds for 2007 polls," *Philippine Star*, July 10, 2006.

43   *Sun Star*, "Sun Star Cebu: Gloria's adviser seeks inquiry on use of 'pork'," November 13, 2005, http://www.sunstar.com (accessed August 1, 2008).

44   Barlow and Croissant, "Following the Money Trail," 137.

organizations in the amount of approximately $4,000 per month per laborer. With over 1.5 million Filipino labors working in the Middle-East alone, the income earned from this source is substantial.

Popular support includes actions such as donations from private parties or aid rendered from a charitable organization. The International Islamic Relief Organization (IIRO) has been identified as the front-runner for giving aid to terrorists in the Philippine region. In the early 1990s, the Philippine branch was operated by Mohammed Jamal Khalifa, Osama bin Laden's brother-in-law. During his tenure, it was estimated that anywhere from 70 percent-90 percent of the total funds coming into the charity were diverted for terrorist causes.[45] Private sponsors are also a vital source of income for these terrorist organizations. Donations ranging from $20,000 to $47,000 have reportedly been given to support various terrorist organizations in the region.[46]

Combining these totals to make an estimate of a yearly income is difficult. However, assuming that these categories are fairly stable in their ability to generate revenue, it could be estimated that these groups earn anywhere from $75 to $100 million dollars annually. The majority of the funds are derived from the illegal activity, followed by popular support at around $20 million, and legal activity for $10 million. State sponsorship, a major contributor in the early seventies, has not been as great a factor in the past 20 years and provides little to zero income for the Filipino terrorist organizations today.

Movement of Funds

Terrorist groups in the Philippines move the money earned from various sources through a variety of formal and informal ways in order to store or distribute the funds where they are needed. These methods range from the use of formalized international and national banking systems, informal funds transfer systems (IFTS) such as *hawala*, informal value transfer methods (IVTM) such as commodity exchanges and payments, and traditional cash carried by couriers.[47] All of these systems or methods offer advantages and disadvantages in their use for both terrorist organizations and government monitoring agencies.

The formal banking system is just one of the many methods used by Philippine terror organizations to transfer and store their funds. Even since the improved monitoring measures put in place over the banking system since September 11, 2001, terrorist still move significant amount of their funds through the formal or traditional banks as seen by the number of bank accounts and assets that have been frozen in banks such as *Maybank*, *Al-Shamal Islamic Bank*, and *PCI*

---

45   Abuza, "Funding Terrorism in Southeast Asia," 27.

46   Abuza, "Funding Terrorism in Southeast Asia," 47.

47   Thomas Biersteker and Sue Eckert, *Countering the Financing of Terrorism* (Routledge, London and New York, 2008), Chapter 8.

Bank located in the Philippines and Indonesia, and *Arraji Bank* located in Saudi Arabia.[48] Additionally, governments such as Libya and China have acted as third party negotiators between the Abu Sayyaf Group and the Philippine and other governments and private individuals in arranging for the payments of hostages to transfer through and reside in their financial systems.[49]

Informal funds transfer systems (IFTS) have become particularly important in recent years as terrorists have taken advantage of their low profile and geographic reach. "The informal *hawala* network—an alternative remittance system that functions outside of traditional banking or financial channels and relies extensively on regional affiliations—has provided criminals, insurgents, and transfer funds to third parties."[50] The *hawala* networks, or *padala* as it is known in the Philippines, *phoe kuan* in Thailand, and *fei chien* in China, play a critical role in allowing all of the terror organizations in the Philippines to operate and transfer their illicit funds throughout the world without being detected or disrupted by governments, however it is unknown exactly how much illicit funding is transferred through these networks.

Informal value transfer methods (IVTM) such as in-kind payments and transfers, gift services, trade diversion, stored value or credit cards, and exchanges of cash and commodities are another major method used to transfer and store funds. These methods are often "part of legitimate or legitimate-looking trade transactions, which effectively obfuscate substantial value transfers."[51] Front and shell companies are one way in which terrorist organizations are able to hide and move funds in this way through the legitimate economy. With a minimal amount of capital investment the MNLF and MILF were able to establish commercial business that served to cloak their financial dealings. With assistance from terrorist organizations such as al Qaeda and Jemaah Islamiyah (JI), the MNLF and MILF were able to be linked into the "trading company" network.[52] Trading companies are an easy way to transfer illicit funds because the sources of their initial funds are often unknown and difficult to trace, and the return funds disappear once repatriated.[53] The MNLF and MILF established businesses and company branches of the Pyramid Trading Co., ET Diton Travel, and Khalifa Trading Industries that were tied to business dealings in Saudi Arabia, Dubai, Lebanon, and Indonesia in an effort to transfer their funds without visibility. Additionally, the ASG has

---

48   International Crisis Group, "Southern Philippines Backgrounder."

49   Max Gross, "A Muslim Archipelago: Islam and Politics in Southeast Asia," National Defense Intelligence College, Washington, D.C., March 2007, 212.

50   Chester Oehme III, "Terrorists, Insurgents, and Criminals—Growing Nexus?" *Studies in Conflict & Terrorism*," 31, 2008, 86.

51   Biersteker and Eckert, *Countering the Financing of Terrorism*, 176.

52   International Crisis Group, "Southern Philippines Backgrounder."

53   For more information on trading companies and laundering practices refer to Biersteker and Eckert, *Countering the Financing of Terrorism*, 159-68.

been linked to business such as the Sana-Bell Inc., Sanabil Al-Khair, and Success Foundation Inc.[54]

Vast amounts of funding to the MNLF, MILF, ASG, and NPA is believed to be moved through charities located both in the Philippines and internationally. Because there is poor oversight of how charities spend and allocate their funds, it is easy for terror groups to transfer illicit funds through them. Charity organizations include the Islamic Wisdom Worldwide, FI Sabilillah Da'Wah and Media Foundation, Al-Haramain Islamic Foundation, and the Daw'l Immam al Shafee Center, but it is the International Islamic Relief Organization (IIRO) based out of Saudi Arabia with the widest ties to terror organizations in the Philippines. The IIRO is used to fund legitimate social projects throughout Mindanao, however with reports that "only 10 to 30 percent of the foreign funding goes to the legitimate relief and livelihood projects and the rest go to terrorist operations,"[55] it is inevitable that the IIRO "is being utilized by foreign extremists as a pipeline through which funding for the local extremists are being coursed through."[56] Another important charity established in Mindanao was the International Relations and Information Center (IRIC) run by Abu Omar, an Islamic student and supporter of the MILF from Mindanao State University.[57] Unlike the IIRO and other Philippine charity organizations, IRIC supported or funded almost no social works and was used almost exclusively as a front to move and hold terrorist money.[58]

In the same manner that Islamic terror groups utilize their ties to Islamic charities, the NPA uses its numerous political party organizations to move and store illicit funds. Political organizations that have been linked to support of the NPA in the Philippines include; the KMU Labor Federation (a partner organization of the International Labor Rights Fund), the Karapatan (a Philippine-based human rights organization), the Kilusang Magbubukid ng Pilipinas (a Philippine farmers organization), and Gabriela (a women's organization).[59]

Expenditures

Terrorist groups in the Philippines spend their money in a variety of ways based on their particular strategies and desired end-states. The expenditures have been divided into sustainment costs, equipment and attacks expenses, and costs spent to fund social programs and works projects throughout the Philippines.

54   International Crisis Group, "The Philippines: Counter-Insurgency VS Counter-Terrorism in Mindanao," ICG Asia Report No. 152, 14 May, 2008.
55   Biersteker and Eckert, *Countering the Financing of Terrorism*, 79.
56   Biersteker and Eckert, *Countering the Financing of Terrorism*, 78.
57   Biersteker and Eckert, *Countering the Financing of Terrorism*, 79.
58   International Crisis Group, "The Philippines," 9.
59   International Crisis Group, "The Philippines."

Sustainment expenses vary widely between the numerous terrorist groups in the Philippines and consist of everything from paying leaders and fighters within the MILF and MNLF to political campaign costs and legal expenses of the NPA. The size and needs of these groups dictate the way they spend their funds in order to sustain their operations. For example, the MNLF had a reported 45,000 members[60] at its height and the MILF 10,000 to 15,000,[61] with leaders and fighters earning an estimated $50 to $100 a month. Understandably, not all of these members draw pay, but even with a smaller core receiving these payments, the costs associated with this is substantial. The ASG, which is a much smaller organization with membership numbers ranging from 100 to 280,[62] can afford to pay their fighters and hostage guards more with estimates ranging from $1000 to $2200 a month. Another significant cost to the larger and more expansive groups of the MNLF and MILF are in the sustainment of their military camps throughout Mindanao. The MILF operates a reported fourteen different camps throughout Mindanao[63] ranging in size from smaller outposts costing $1,000 a month, to larger camps such as Camp Abu-Bakr with shooting ranges, mosques, and schools operating on it that can cost upwards of $10,000 and month.[64] Likewise, the NPA is believed to spend vast amounts of money on land and agrarian campaigns aimed at the elimination and reduction in land rents and redistribution rights for tenants, support to clandestine revolutionary committees in thousands of barangays, and defense militias, peasant organizing, health and literacy campaigns in guerrilla operated zones.

Terrorist attacks in most instances are relatively inexpensive to fund and undertake. Although the specific costs of attacks depend on the nature of the operation, they can be categorized by the operational costs such as travel and planning, and equipment necessary to undertake the operation such as weapons and explosives. With the exception of the ASG, terror groups in the Philippines have low operational costs with respect to attacks because they operate locally within the Philippines, usually only throughout the island of Mindanao. Because of this travel costs are almost non-existent. The ASG, although expeditionary in their attacks throughout the islands of Southeast Asia, operate by the use of speedboats, motorcycles, and other relatively inexpensive equipment to conduct their attacks and kidnappings.[65]

All of the groups are estimated to spend considerably more on equipment and weapons costs than on travel. The MILF has a reported armory of over

---

60   International Crisis Group, "The Philippines," 6.

61   International Crisis Group, "Southern Philippines Backgrounder," 5.

62   Council on Foreign Relations, "Abu Sayyaf Group."

63   Peter Chalk and Carl Ungerer, "Neighbourhood Watch: The evolving terrorist threat in Southeast Asia," ASPI Report, Australia, June 2008, 19.

64   International Crisis Group, "Southern Philippines Backgrounder," 15-17.

65   Larry Niksch, "Abu Sayyaf: Target of Philippine-U.S. Anti-Terrorism Cooperation," CRS Report for Congress, Congressional Research Service, Library of Congress, January 20, 2006.

7,000 weapons that include Garand, M16, M14, and AK47 rifles, M203 grenade launchers, landmines, M79 rocket propelled grenades, and .50 and .60 caliber machine guns.[66] Likewise, the ASG is believed to have an arsenal estimated at over two million dollars. With rifles costing between an estimated $200 to $400 and 30 kilos of TNT costing $2,000 on the black market in Southeast Asia, the funds spent on weapons become significant.[67]

With an estimated 65 to 90 percent of Islamic charity funds believed to be siphoned off from charities to fund terrorist activities, it is difficult to determine how much money these organizations put back to fund their own social works projects. Charities such as the International Islamic Relief Organization (IIRO), Haramain Islamic Foundation, and Muslim World League are fully state-funded and based out of Saudi Arabia, as is the World Assembly of Muslim Youth in Southeast Asia.[68] The amount of money from various charities spent on legitimate social work such as mosque construction, support of NGOs, the construction and support of local charities, cultural centers, production of translations of religious texts, and public works projects varies greatly from the ASG to the MILF, and from charity to charity. However, the MNLF, MILF, and NPA do spend significant amounts of money to fund these social works programs in areas of the Philippines that they garner large popular support from local Filipinos, who are often very poor.

Combining these totals to make estimate these groups yearly total expenses is difficult. However, assuming that these categories are fairly stable, it could be estimated that these groups spend anywhere from $8 to $18 million dollars annually (see Figure 9.1). The majority of the funds for each group, with the exception of the NPA, are spent on sustainment with costs between $3 and $7 million, followed by social services for the MNLF, MILF at around $4 million. The ASG spends the most on equipment and attacks at around $5 million.

Countermeasures

Terrorist financing was never seriously considered a problem in the Philippines until the government became aware of the massive foreign funding that both the communists and the Muslim separatists were receiving from abroad. Since the signing of the Peace Agreements with the MNLF in 1976, terrorist groups have relied more on domestic sources such as revolutionary taxes, illegal activities in tandem with organized crime groups, and even legal enterprises. After 9/11, the Philippines actively pursued a policy of obstructing terrorist financing through the use of legal, diplomatic, and information operations mechanisms while working with the international community. The measures include monitoring the sources

---

66   Chalk and Ungerer, "Neighbourhood Watch," 19.
67   International Crisis Group, "Southern Philippines Backgrounder," 18.
68   Biersteker and Eckert, *Countering the Financing of Terrorism*, 77-8.

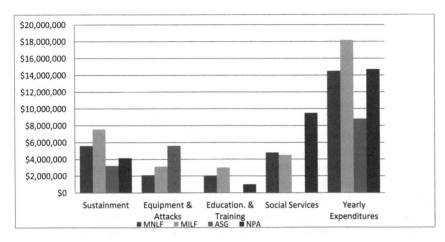

Figure 9.1   Estimates of Annual Philippine Terrorist Expenditures

and how the finances are spent as well as destroying enemy infrastructures and support systems.

Specifically, the Philippines came up with a comprehensive counter-terrorism strategy composed of hard and soft components. The hard strategy seeks to neutralize the armed capabilities of the terrorists, decimate their leadership, disintegrate their organizational networks, stop their finances, and cut their links to foreign support. The soft strategy focuses on separating the terrorists from the rest of the population, addressing the humanitarian and development needs of the populace, reducing the ideological attractiveness of the terrorists, and promoting inter-faith dialog and other forms of consultation to strengthen trust, understanding, and confidence between communities and sectors.[69] In order to synchronize its internal efforts with the outside world, the Philippine government also forged strong counter-terrorism cooperation with its partners in ASEAN and beyond since it recognizes that bilateral, regional, and international cooperation is absolutely vital for its common security.[70]

In September 2001, the government enacted its anti-money laundering law. Initially, the Philippines government was placed on the Financial Action Task Force (FATF) list of non-cooperating countries and territories. Due to the failure of the Philippines to enact legislation to address previously identified deficiencies in their anti-money laundering regime, the FATF recommended that its members impose additional countermeasures against the Philippines.[71] However, the Philippines

---

69 Alberto Romulo, "Philippine counter-terrorism policy," Conference on Counter-Terrorism Cooperation, March 7, 2007, http://www.dfa.gov.ph/archive/speech/romulo/2007/ps014.htm (site discontinued).

70 Romulo, "Philippine counter-terrorism policy."

71 FATF withdraws counter-measures with respect to Ukraine and decides on date for counter-measures to Philippines, Financial Action Task Force on Money

made significant progress by addressing the deficiencies identified by FATF, thus, the FATF removed the Philippines from its list of Non-Cooperating Countries and Territories in February 2005.

The Philippines was also admitted in June 2005 to the Egmont Group, the international network of financial intelligence units. The Egmont Group helps ensure that individuals and entities suspected of financing terrorism are identified and that information is shared freely and rapidly. In the event of the discovery of relevant information, countries should respond through the appropriate channels.[72] The power of financial intelligence lies in financial investigations that provide information on activities, behaviors, locations, associates, and email/phone records. It also provides opportunities for disruption.[73] To further enhance its legal mandates, the Philippines is a signatory to 11 of the 14 international counter-terrorism instruments and supports the adoption of a Comprehensive Convention on International Terrorism that would supplement the Declaration on Measures to Eliminate International Terrorism. The Philippines is also guided by other United Nations resolutions of the General Assembly and the Security Council.[74]

Information operations are also an important component of the counter terrorism financing story. Specifically, the Philippine government has been doing an all-out media campaign to increase public awareness, particularly on the massive extortion attempts by the NPA, MILF, and the Abu Sayyaf. For example, it informs the public about how the NPA exploits, threatens, and requires candidates to pay Permit to Campaign (PTC) fees in order to have free access in NPA-influenced areas.[75] The public should know that the NPA and their legal fronts destabilize and cause trouble to the candidates' campaign through removal of posters, denial of areas, and even denial of audience in case the candidates fail to get the PTC. To reduce this practice, government efforts include encouraging people, including small and large businesses, to cooperate and to report attempts of extortion. Even the church is alarmed about the massive taxation scheme that is being undertaken by the communists.[76]

Laundering, Paris, February 14, 2003, http://www.info.gov.hk/hkma/eng/guide/circu_date/attach/20030225a1.pdf.

72   Counter-Terrorism International Conference, Riyadh, KSA, February 8, 2005, http://www.saudiembassy.net/documents/ctic-workshop-english-feb05.pdf.

73   Gunawan Husin, "Countering the Financing of Terrorism: Key Concepts, Implementation Issues and Counter Measures," Manila, July 7, 2008, http://www.pipvtr.com/pipvtr/files/Manila_CFT_7Jul_For%20circulation.pdf.

74   "Philippines, International cooperation," 142, http://www.interpol.int/Public/BioTerrorism/NationalLaws/Philippines.pdf.

75   Florence F. Hibionada, "Army warns bets of NPA extort scheme Congressmen 'priced' P2M per head, guv at P5M," *The News Today*, April 3, 2007.

76   Jose Aravilla, "Bishops score NPA 'taxation' scheme on candidates," *Philippine Star*, April 17, 2004.

In the case of external funds, putting the terrorist groups on the list of foreign terror organizations has facilitated the monitoring of their financial flows.[77] One problem is that there is still no international consensus on which groups, apart from Al Qaeda and the Taliban, are to be considered terrorist organizations, and have their funding ties cut. This places an increased burden on the U.S. and European intelligence communities to effectively monitor the critical nodes of international transactions.[78] So far, the U.S. and the European communities have tagged both the ASG and the NPA as terrorist organizations. As a result, the flow of money across national borders has been obstructed and the NPA has had to turn to local fund raising efforts.[79] Domestic efforts, however, should be enhanced as authorities estimate that the money raised by the NPA from local sources could run into the hundreds of thousands of dollars.[80] Figures reveal that the NPA was collecting at least $700,000 a month in revolutionary taxes in Mindanao. In a sense, the NPA has morphed into a local extortionist gang victimizing even the poor Filipinos.[81] In the case of the Abu Sayyaf, the group was one of the 27 organizations and individuals whose assets were officially frozen by the U.S. on September 24, 2001.

In 2007, the Philippine government enacted the Human Security Act, or its anti-terrorism law. This legislation strengthens the legal regime for investigating, prosecuting, and bringing to justice terrorists, and their supporters, who are captured in the Philippines. The passage of this legislation demonstrates the commitment of the government of the Philippines to implement comprehensive counter-terrorism financing measures.[82] Now, authorities are more empowered to access bank accounts believed to be used to launder money for terrorist purposes.

In the case of suspected *hawala* operators, the government has enhanced its monitoring and has required business permits. In addition, for remittances coming from abroad, the U.S. Treasury Department and the Philippine Ministry of Finance agreed to work together to improve mechanisms for overseas remittances services to the Philippines. The initiative aims to reduce costs through greater competition and increased efficiency, enhance access to remittance services in the formal financial system, and ensure compliance with counter-terrorist financing and anti-money

---

77   Stephen R. Kroll, "Combating terrorist financing and the 110th Congress," Former Democratic Special Counsel to the Committee on Banking, Housing, and Urban Affairs, United States Senate, January 30, 2007, http://www.eurasianpolicy.org/files/publications/SteveKrollCTConferenceSpeech.pdf.

78   Victor Comras, "Terrorism financing is still big business even if terrorist attacks sometimes are carried out on the cheap," August 27, 2008, http://counterterrorismblog.org/2008/08/terrorism_financing_is_still_b.php (accessed January 13, 2012).

79   "Camiling: Foreign support for NPA dwindles," *Sun Star Davao*, August 27, 2003.

80   "Arroyo to AFP: End NPA taxation," *ABS-CBN Online*, June 22, 2006.

81   "Honesto General, Joma Sison unmasked," *Philippine Daily Inquirer*, September 12, 2007.

82   Alexander Downer, "Government welcomes new Philippine counter-terrorism law," Media release for Australia Foreign minister, March 6, 2007, http://www.foreignminister.gov.au/releases/2007/fa026_07.html (accessed January 13, 2012).

laundering standards. Over seven million overseas Filipino workers sent over $6 billion in remittances to the Philippines in 2001.[83] The Philippine government also continues its efforts at neutralizing crime groups such as kidnap-for-ransom gangs, bank robbers, and drug dealers which have links with terrorist groups.

Moreover, the Philippine government also established an Anti-Terrorism Task Force. As a national agency, it integrates all efforts and ensures interagency collaboration. The military, police and local government agencies operating jointly aim to destroy the insurgent infrastructure down to the village level. The purpose is to neutralize supporters, local intelligence networks, and logistics networks that provide sanctuaries and funds to terrorists. Since the barangays, or villages, are the focal points of the wide-scale building of local NPA organizations at the grassroots level, it is appropriate that the fight and strategy should reach that level.[84]

The Philippines works hand-in-hand with key actors in the region in order to mitigate terror financing. The U.S. so far has contributed $1 billion to enhance the capacity of Philippine agencies not only to neutralize terrorist financing, but also address the root causes of terrorism. In June 2006, Australia and the Philippines conducted inaugural bilateral inter-agency counter-terrorism consultations in Manila, and agreed on a comprehensive plan to deepen counter-terrorism cooperation in areas such as law enforcement, intelligence and anti-terrorist financing, defense and maritime security, and border and transport security. Australia has so far contributed $6 million in a bilateral assistance package worth, and more than $250 million since 2004 through regional assistance packages.[85]

Lastly, vigorous intelligence and monitoring is required in order to obstruct the plans and activities of terrorists. To do so, a public-private partnership is essential to detect terrorist money. Without enlisting the cooperation and collaboration of the banks, the government cannot detect the flow of funds through private financial institutions. The financial sector is the first line of defense. It is the bankers, accountants, and auditors who understand financial systems best and can best detect and bring the suspicious transactions to the attention of authorities.[86]

The crafting of specific laws is a vital component in the fight against terror financing, but success still very much depends on how the laws are implemented. Extortion is a big source of funding in the Philippines, but there were only a few convictions over the past several years, particularly for those supporting the

---

83   U.S. Department of Treasury, "Strengthening Remittance Channels to the Philippines," May 20, 2003, http://www.treasury.gov/press-center/press-releases/Pages/js396.aspx (accessed January 13, 2012).

84   Gilbert Bayoran, "NDF tax collection intensified," *The Visayan Daily Star*, July 29, 2005.

85   Downer, "Government welcomes new Philippine counter-terrorism law,"

86   Rohan Gunaratna, "Singapore's zero-tolerance approach to counter the financing of terrorism," May 28, 2008, http://www.world-check.com/media/d/content_industryvoices_reference/Dr_Gunaratna2.pdf.

terrorists. If the government fails to increase the cost of supporting terrorists, this will result in creating more conditions where terrorists will thrive.

As such, to be more effective, there is still a need to enhance the capacity of Philippine agencies to deal with terrorist financing. Apart from these, there should be enhanced cooperation at the regional level, particularly in securing borders, in order to prevent the movement of terrorists, equipment, and funds from one country to the other. It is also important that the Philippines should be able to synchronize its internal efforts with the global initiatives to fight terror.

In order to gain the cooperation of the people, the government must be able to provide security. Assessing the success of the indirect approach in the Philippines, Hy Rothstein stresses that the "establishment of security and protection of the local population, provide[s] the foundation for all other activities designed to establish stability."[87] Thus, it is critical for any government to establish its legitimacy with the population. For example, businesses will not pay revolutionary taxes if they know that the government will protect them from any retaliatory attacks from the terrorists. Likewise, policies with NGOs need to be revisited and evaluated in the Philippines. NGOs have twice been exposed as channels for terrorist financing during the Khalifa period and the time of Hamoud Al-Lahim with the IIRO and IIC. Thus, there is a need for a serious study on the screening process for these kinds of NGOs and foundations, for their character and orientation makes for easy manipulation for illegal funds generation, and act as fronts for radical groups.[88]

There is also a need to strengthen legal mandates against acts of terrorism. The objective should be to put more terrorists and supporters in jail. After September 11th, many countries accelerated their ratification of pending counter-terrorism conventions. Now, the Philippines is a party to all fourteen existing conventions related to counter-terrorism, and it is trying to persuade countries that have not yet ratified all the conventions to follow suit.[89] Further, international, regional, and bilateral cooperation among states should be strengthened, in order to identify, disrupt, and dismantle the financial underpinnings of terrorism, as well as the activities of organized crime groups, trafficking in illegal weapons and explosives, and the trade of illicit narcotics. States should endeavor to create a framework that allows for a flexible exchange of operational information among the competent authorities, domestically, regionally, and internationally.[90]

Lastly, the Philippines should create 24-hour media operations centers and "multifaceted media campaigns" using the Internet, blogs, and satellite television

---

87   Hy Rothstein, "Less is more: the problematic future of irregular warfare in an era of collapsing states," *Third World Quarterly*, 28:2, 2007, 285.

88   Rodolfo B. Mendoza Jr., "The evolution of terrorist financing in the Philippines," http://www.pipvtr.com/pipvtr/files/Evolution%20of%20Terrorist%20Financing%20PH.pdf.

89   Mizukoshi Hideaki, "Terrorists, Terrorism, and Japan's Counter-Terrorism Policy," Gaiko Forum, Summer 2003.

90   Counter-Terrorism International Conference, Riyadh, KSA, February 8, 2005, http://www.saudiembassy.net/documents/ctic-workshop-english-feb05.pdf.

that "will result in much less reliance on the traditional print press."[91] The general intention should be to pursue policies which contribute to a fast, limited, and decisive operation while maintaining the support of the international community, and contribute to a safe and stable environment to obtain the support of the local population and its leaders, while showing a clear resolution to subdue the adversary.[92]

Conclusion

The nature of terrorist financing in the Philippines, stems from the country's unique and conflicted history. The different terrorist organizations operating in the Philippines today have vastly different goals and ideologies, which greatly affect the sources by which they gain funds, the methods by which they move their funds, the expenditures they spend their funds on. The Philippine government has determined that fighting the financial infrastructure of terrorist organizations is critical to their defeat. Because of this, the Philippine Government has been forced to improve and increase all available methods to counter and combat terrorist financing threats within its borders.

91 Ann Scott Tyson, "Rumsfeld Urges Using Media to Fight Terror," *Washington Post*, February 18, 2006.

92 Raimundo Rodríguez Roca, "Information Operations during counterinsurgency operations: essential option for a limited response," U.S. Army Command and General Staff College, February 14, 2008.

PART IV
Europe

Chapter 10

Financing the Loyalists in Northern Ireland

Stein-Fr Kynoe

> The acquisition of money (and the laundering of illegal money) is an essential component in devising and pursuing an effective and sustained terrorist campaign. Therefore, the imperative in mitigating and disrupting terrorist atrocities and influence is to cut terrorist, and their supporters, off from money.[1]
>
> British House of Commons, Northern Ireland Affairs Committee

Over the decades-long struggle in Northern Ireland, Protestant Loyalist groups used various types of financing to fund their operations. They relied on legal sources, illegal sources, and support from the general populace. This chapter will begin with a brief history of the Irish conflict. The chapter will then analyze the funding of the Loyalists. The discussions will detail their funding activities and the measures used by the government to counter them. The chapter focuses on the period from the late 1960s to the early 2000s, though relevant information from subsequent years will also be included when applicable. The chapter concludes with a summary of key points derived from the analyses.

A Brief History of Conflict in Northern Ireland

Northern Ireland consists of six counties (Antrim, Armagh, Derry, Down, Fermanagh, and Tyrone) within the historic province of Ulster. According to the 2001 census, the total population of Northern Ireland is 1,685,267 people. Approximately 46 percent are Protestant, 40 percent are Catholics, with 14 percent of other religious preferences.[2]

The key players in the struggle in Northern Irelands are the Republicans who wanted to separate from the United Kingdom, the Loyalists who wanted to remain part of the UK, and the governments of both Northern Ireland and Britain.

The Republicans are generally viewed as extreme Irish Nationalists and practically exclusively Catholic. Historically, the Irish Republican Army (IRA), or Óglaigh na hÉireann has been the primary Republican paramilitary group

---

1 House of Commons Northern Ireland Affairs Committee, *The Financing of Terrorism in Northern Ireland* (London: The Stationery Office Limited, June 26, 2002), 9, http://www.parliament.the-stationery-office.co.uk/pa/cm200102/cmselect/cmniaf/978/978.pdf.

2 Answers.com, "Demography and politics of Northern Ireland," http://www.answers.com/topic/demography-and-politics-of-northern-ireland (accessed November 19, 2007).

involved in Northern Ireland. The name Irish Republican Army dates back to April 1916, when it was adopted by the Irish Volunteers who had taken part in the Easter Rising in Dublin that year. The Provisional IRA (PIRA) was established when the IRA split in December 1969 into the Official IRA, known informally as the Officials, and the Provisional IRA, known as the Provisionals (and responsible for the majority of the terrorist acts). Sinn Fein is the political wing of the PIRA. Other organizations associated with the Republicans are the Continuity IRA (CIRA), the Real IRA (RIRA), the Irish National Liberation Army (INLA, also named Peoples Liberation Army, PLA) and the Irish Republican Socialist Party (IRSP).[3]

The Loyalists are usually seen as extreme Unionists and are generally Protestant, and see themselves as British, not Irish. During the so-called Troubles, the Loyalists were the opponents of the IRA, and by 1990, they had begun to match the violence of the PIRA.[4] For the Loyalists, the 1970s was the period of their greatest political popularity and support, while the 1980s were the years of their greatest financial success.

Both the Loyalist and the Republican paramilitaries were part of close-knit neighborhoods. They were locally based within limited areas, with neighbors and friends as their initial supporters. In addition, because both Northern Ireland populations had been physically separated from both the Republic of Ireland and the rest of the United Kingdom, they had developed locally based routines and customs that make their organizations difficult for outsiders to infiltrate. Nonetheless, compared to their Republican counterparts, the Loyalist paramilitary leaders were often more focused on their own personal gain than that of the cause.

The first violent Unionist groups were seen in Northern Ireland after an increase in minor violence in the 1960s. In 1966, the Ulster Volunteer Force (UVF), which traces its roots back to 1912, killed its first Catholics. The UVF, which is linked to the Progressive Unionist Party (PUP), was legalized in May 1974. In 1971, the Ulster Defense Association (UDA), also known as the Ulster Freedom Fighters (UFF), was established as an umbrella organization for various Unionist groups. Its political wing is the Ulster Democratic Party (UDP).[5] The Orange Volunteers (OV), also formed in the early 1970s, was soon the second largest Loyalist organization after the UDA. Though it is believed to have been disbanded some fifteen years later, it reemerged in the late nineties with a wave of attacks on Catholic targets.[6] The Loyalist Volunteer Force (LVF), another significant paramilitary Loyalist group that splintered from the Ulster and Orange

---

3   CAIN Web Service, "Abstracts on Organizations," http://cain.ulst.ac.uk/othelem/ organ/iorgan.htm (accessed November 17, 2007).

4   Andrew Silke, "In Defense of the Realm: Financing Loyalist Terrorism in Northern Ireland—Part One: Extortion and Blackmail," *Studies in Conflict and Terrorism*, 21, 1998.

5   CAIN Web Service, "Background on the Northern Ireland Conflict," http://cain. ulst.ac.uk/othelem/organ/uorgan.htm (accessed August 28, 2007).

6   MIPT Terrorism Knowledge database, group profile, "Orange Volunteers," http:// www.tkb.org/Group.jsp?groupID=79 (accessed November 17, 2007).

Volunteers, existed between 1996 and 2005.[7] Other organizations associated with the Loyalists are the Ulster Resistance (UR), the Loyalist Association of Workers (LAW), and the Ulster Workers' Council (UWC).[8]

Caught between the two sides of the North Irish conflict were the local government of Northern Ireland and the central government of the United Kingdom. During the Troubles, the government of Northern Ireland had the following institutional resources: the Royal Ulster Constabulary (RUC) renamed the Police Service of Northern Ireland (PSNI) in 2002; and the Ulster Defense Regiment (UDR), from 1970 to 1992, when it merged with the Royal Irish Rangers (RIR) and was renamed the Royal Irish Regiment (RIR). The Ulster Defense Regiment replaced the Ulster Special Constabulary (USC). A number of less visible government agencies, such as the British Security Service, MI5 and the Special Air Service Regiment (SAS), supported the administration in Northern Ireland. The British military also patrolled its streets up to 2007, to support the government of Northern Ireland's peace efforts.

For the Republicans, the cause they fought for had three main goals: to unify Ireland under a single Irish flag; to remove British forces from Northern Ireland; and to end the discrimination against Catholics. The cause the Loyalists fought for also had several goals: to keep Northern Ireland part of the United Kingdom; to oppose the so-called Home Rule; to defend themselves against aggression from the Republicans; and to counter IRA violence.[9]

The roots of the struggle over Northern Ireland can be traced back to 1167 with the first Anglo-Norman invasion. Henry II's army invaded in 1171, and gained full control of the island in 1175. For the next 750 years, the British kings and Parliament faced successive waves of Irish violence.[10] When Ireland separated from Britain, the Government of Ireland Act of 1921 created a Protestant dominated "Northern Ireland" that would remain within the United Kingdom. The South, or "The Irish Free State" with the remaining 26 counties, was given a dominion status within the British Commonwealth. Ireland was given its full independence in 1949.[11]

In the early 1950s, the economy in the UK was declining and its impact was felt particularly hard in Northern Ireland, especially among the generally lower-class Catholic communities. Catholics were also politically marginalized

---

7   BBC, "Northern Ireland: The Troubles: Loyalist Volunteer Force," http://www.bbc.co.uk/history/recent/troubles/fact_files.shtml?ff=p10#factfile (accessed November 7, 2007).

8   CAIN Web Service, "Abstracts on Organizations."

9   Ronald J. Terchek, "Conflict and Cleavage in Northern Ireland," *Annals of the American Academy of Political and Social Science*, 433, Ethnic Conflict in the World Today, September 1977, 48, 55.

10   BBC, "Northern Ireland: The Troubles: The Road to Northern Ireland 1167-1921," http://www.bbc.co.uk/history/recent/troubles/overview_ni_article_01.shtml (accessed May 6, 2009).

11   BBC, "The Road to Northern Ireland 1167-1921."

in Northern Ireland. The ways electoral districts were drawn, combined with the single-member constituencies, strengthened Protestant power. Even in areas where there Catholic majorities, Loyalist candidates were often elected to Stormont (the Northern Ireland Parliament).[12] Stormont continued to execute a policy of suppressing the Catholic population, restricting their access to decent housing and equal voting rights.[13]

In 1968, the "Troubles" began, a period of active conflict and terrorist activity that lasted for decades. Initially, the nonviolent, mainly Catholic group, the Northern Ireland Civil Rights Association (NICRA), founded in 1967, addressed injustices in Northern Ireland. When peaceful demonstrations were crushed by the heavy-handed Royal Ulster Constabulary, soon more violent paramilitary organizations emerged. In 1969, when the government of Northern Ireland began to lose control of the situation, the British government sent military troops to support local rule.

In 1971, Stormont was disbanded and taken over by a Secretary of State for Northern Ireland. Internment was implemented, which allowed for the detention of suspects without a sentence. This fueled the conflict and caused the highest yearly levels of loss of life. The internment policy that began in 1971 ended in 1975. Numerous political attempts to establish a lasting peace were made during the 1970s with little success. Nevertheless, in 1976, the special handling and status for paramilitaries in jail, practiced since 1972, was ended. Although paramilitaries viewed themselves as freedom fighters, from 1976 on they were treated like common criminals. This led to what became known as the Blanket Protest. Finally, in 1980-1981, IRA prisoners went on hunger strikes in the Maze prison, during which Bobby Sands and nine others died.

In 1985, the British and Irish governments signed the Anglo-Irish Agreement, which stated that Northern Ireland would remain British as long as that was the will of the majority of six counties in Northern Ireland part of the Ulster Province. Although some initial resistance was seen among the Loyalists, it led to increased cooperation between the actors. However, the violence continued for another decade.

Despite numerous attempts at peace negotiations during the nineties, the violence again increased. Then, in 1998, the Northern Ireland peace talks led to the signing of the Good Friday Agreement on April 10, which had been supported by 71 percent of the population in a referendum in May the same year. Nonetheless, the violence continued into the new millennium.

---

12   BBC, "The Road to Northern Ireland 1167-1921."

13   BBC, "The Road to Northern Ireland 1167-1921;" and John Darby, "Conflicts in Northern Ireland: A Background Essay" in *Facts of the Conflict in Northern Ireland* edited by Seamus Dunn (1995), http://cain.ulst.ac.uk/othelem/facets.htm#chap2 (accessed May 8, 2009).

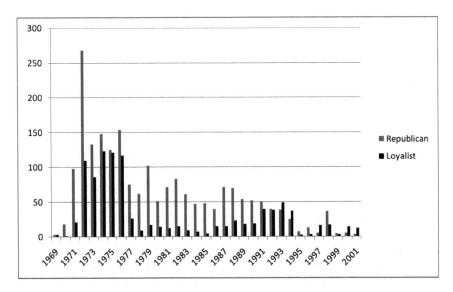

Figure 10.1   Annual Killings in Northern Ireland (1969-2001)

Source: CAIN Web Service, "Revised and Updated Extracts from Sutton's Book," Available at http://cain.ulst.ac.uk/sutton/book/index.html.

In July 2000, the last paramilitary was released from prison and negotiations continued between the actors. In July 2005, the IRA declared an end to armed conflict, and in July 31, 2007, the last British troops left the province.

From 1969 to 2001, the conflict in Northern Ireland claimed a total of 3,524 lives. Of this total, 2,046 were killed by Republican groups, 1,020 by Loyalist groups, 367 by British and Irish Republic armed forces, and 81 by other groups. Figure 10.1 show the number of killings for each of the thirty-three years of this period of the conflict.

Loyalist Terrorist Financing

Loyalist groups remain involved in drugs supply, intellectual property crime, importation and distribution of contraband goods, extortion, money lending, and armed robbery. They are also known to use legitimate businesses, notably pubs, clubs, and taxi-firms as covers for their illegal operations.[14]

During the course of the Troubles, Loyalist groups needed funds for a variety of purposes. The traditional costs are related to weapons, communications, training,

14 Organized Crime Task Force, "Annual Report and Threat Assessment 2006: Organised Crime in Northern Ireland," paragraph 2.7, http://www.nio.gov.uk/octf_annual_report_and_threat_assessment_2006.pdf.

"operational costs," and pay for paramilitaries and their families. During the seventies, as the Troubles developed, the requirement for support of basic needs for Loyalist families increased. The government welfare programs were not enough and so the paramilitary supported the families of the imprisoned as well as unemployed supporters.[15]

As Loyalist activities increased, increasing numbers of militants ended up in prison. In the 1980s, some 225 members, or 35-45 percent of the hard-core Ulster Defense Association and Ulster Volunteer Force were in prison.[16] In addition, as the size of the Loyalist organizations grew during their peak years in the 1980s, this growing prison population and the support required to sustain the families of imprisoned members put an increased burden on the Loyalist organizational costs.[17]

As their operating costs expanded, the traditional collection of money from Loyalist supporters was not enough to cover their day-to-day operations. They needed to establish a continuous, steady flow of cash. The Loyalists were organized into brigades and units with separate areas of operations, but units with high running costs could not depend on support from units that were better off. They were forced to create their own income within their own area of operation or, at least, outside other units' areas. Not surprisingly, therefore, a number of turf wars occurred over control of income streams. In these clashes between units, it was not unusual to see cooperation even between Loyalists and Republicans.

The absence of external support and the expansion of costs led to the creation of a number of avenues to sustain the groups' economic baseline. Some were legal, most illegal, some with popular support, others rejected by the local community. After the renewed peak of violence in the mid-nineties, expenditures on weapons and ammunition decreased, while the costs for supporting Loyalist members probably increased. Large amounts were also pocketed by corrupt leaders.[18]

To give some idea of the amounts spent to purchase weapons and ammunition, Silke found that in 1987 the Loyalists' largest shipment to date cost £325,000. One shipment in 1993 cost about £225,000.[19] The Ulster Volunteer Force and the Ulster Defense Force had attempted to acquire the latter weapons in a joint effort, but the shipment was seized by a joint government sting operation.

In many aspects, the Provisional Irish Republican Army set the standard in Northern Ireland for organizing clandestine paramilitary organizations. Their members were highly specialized, often with a narrow focus, including dedicated fundraising cells. According to Silke's findings, the Loyalists tried to do the same, but were only partly successful in handling their fund-raising activities.[20] In the

---

15   Silke, "In Defense of the Realm," 335.
16   Silke, "In Defense of the Realm," 335.
17   Silke, "In Defense of the Realm," 334.
18   Silke, "In Defense of the Realm," 334, 335.
19   Silke, "In Defense of the Realm," 335. Silke's sources are *Sunday Life*, April 17, 1994); and *Ulster News Letter*, November 23, 1993.
20   Silke, "In Defense of the Realm," 350.

Loyalist paramilitary organizations, there was a significant age difference between the operatives on the street and the fundraisers. On average, the latter were 16 years older than the operatives, and often the senior members and leaders of their units. Often the fund-raisers were also former operatives who had been active in sectarian violence and had done lengthy prison terms but still wanted to be active paramilitary members. When they shifted to racketeering activities, they tended to be less exposed to investigation and normally did less prison time if caught than the violent militants.

The Loyalists had a close relationship with a number of accountants and business people who provided them with financial advice, both in regard to funding sources and to ways to launder the funds gained. While the Republicans had useful contacts in the Republic of Ireland, the Loyalists' contacts were limited to Northern Ireland. Because of that reliance on local support, a number of their accounts were brought in front of the Terrorist Financing Unit (TFU), which attempted to determine the origins of their funding. Apparently, even at the end of the twentieth century, the Loyalists had not been able to create a specialized finance element such as was seen in the Provisional Irish Republican Army. This weakness led to many arrests and less central control of the funding.

Sources of Funding

State Sponsors

The Loyalists never had support from the Irish Diaspora in the United States or from other countries or groups. Their only known external support occurred in 1992, when it was estimated that the Ulster Defense Association and the Ulster Volunteer Force received some £100,000 from Scottish supporters.[21]

Popular Support

While the Republican cause was to change the status-quo, the Loyalist cause was to protect their privileges and avoid a change of status. However, very often, a fight to *change* something is easier to use to unite the population than a fight to *maintain* something. This difference has been evident in the conflict in Northern Ireland through the years. The Loyalists never had as much popular support as the Republicans, and the support they did have diminished as a result of their practices. When paramilitaries' costs increased, corruption among the leadership became more visible and the Loyalist paramilitary leaders' personal use of funds did not go unnoticed. The Loyalists' inability to unite the population was evident

---

21   House of Commons, *The Financing of Terror in Northern Ireland*, 19.

in the government's ability to find and use moles within the Loyalist leadership, as described by Silke and Maguire.[22]

Legal Funding

Although most of the Loyalist revenue came from illegal sources, there were also some legal sources of funds, including drinking clubs and pubs; security firms; and taxi and building firms. However, though the firms were apparently legal at first, as they became more and more involved in illegal activities during the seventies and eighties, the line between legal and illegal activity grew more blurred. When the income from illegal activities increased, those funds were often used to establish legal companies, both to employ supporters and to use for money-laundering purposes.

Drinking Clubs and Pubs   In British culture, there is a long tradition of friends meeting and having a beer or two in a pub or a club. During the sixties, the escalation of violence led to an increase in the number of local drinking clubs, which were preferred because of the risks involved in traveling to more distant pubs. By the end of the 1980s, the income from these establishments became one of the main sources of funds for the Loyalists.[23] Initially, the main difference between a drinking club and a pub was that it was more difficult to obtain a license for pubs and so drinking clubs were less regulated. On the other hand, pub owners did not have to provide the Royal Ulster Constabulary with a copy of their bank accounts/transactions. Anti-racketeering officers estimated that, in 1990, more than £100,000 went missing from one club in Belfast alone, siphoned off in support of terrorist criminal activity. During the early nineties, regulations and oversight were tightened and the government closed a great number of clubs. This new regulations and control had a serious impact on the funding of the Loyalists, and the Loyalists were forced into other avenues to fund their activity.

Security Firms   These companies were legally established and they operated by protecting businesses, estates, and so forth. Incidentally, the business owner could claim the money paid for security as a tax allowance (which essentially meant that the British government, through tax breaks, was indirectly funding the Loyalists). These security firms used harsh measures to protect their clients from common criminals. During the last half of the 1990s, these security firms executed some 1,400 reprisals in support of their clients.[24] Because even the Royal Ulster

---

22   Silke, "In Defense of the Realm," 332; Keith Maguire, "Fraud, extortion and racketeering: The black economy in Northern Ireland," *Crime, Law and Social Change*, 20, 1993, 289.

23   Andrew Silke, "Drink, Drugs, Rock'n'Roll: Financing Loyalist Terrorism in Northern Ireland-Part Two," *Studies in Conflict & Terrorism*, 23, 2000, 108

24   Silke, "In Defense of the Realm," 348.

Constabulary avoided some of the Loyalist areas, the only protection against criminals that was available for some was from the paramilitaries. One famous Ulster Democratic Party leader, James Craig, was the head of three such legal security companies.[25]

Taxi Firms   When the Troubles started, public buses were a popular target for sectarian violence (a method adopted later by the Palestinians in the Middle East, and that is now wide-spread). This created great fear among the local population and the need for more safe taxis increased. The taxi companies were often controlled by paramilitaries, used for money laundering and as employment for their supporters.

Building Firms   According to Silke, at the starts of the Trouble, Belfast contained the worst slums of Western Europe. Therefore, the British Government invested great sums in moving people out of the slums into more spacious, suburban areas.[26] The extortion of building firms will be covered later, but as Maguire argues, these construction branches also saw a number of entrepreneur companies run by the paramilitaries.[27] The intentions of the Loyalist run "front-companies," as well as the Republican ones, were to create avenues of income. These companies might win contracts against regular companies because of lower costs, particularly because they did not have to pay "protection money."[28]

Illegal Funding

Drug Dealing   In Northern Ireland, as in most other places, drug dealing was an extremely profitable and relatively easy way to make money, especially for illegal organizations. However, the constraints against drug dealing were many and could threaten the legitimacy of the groups.

The foundation of the Loyalist and Republican paramilitaries was their local roots and their acceptance by the local populace. Across the Catholic-Protestant religious divide, drug dealing is an activity that is seen as immoral and not in the interest of the people. Thus, according to Silke, the Provisional Irish Republican Army avoided serious involvement in the drug trade. The Republicans made a stronger stand against the drug trade and had more stringent control of their sub-units than the Loyalists, whose commanders were more independent and less "true believers" than the Republicans. The Loyalist involvement began by taking a cut of the regular criminals' drug trade. Once the leadership discovered the volume of money and the low risk involved, they also took over more of the import and distribution.

---

25   Silke, "In Defense of the Realm," 348.
26   Silke, "In Defense of the Realm," 343.
27   Maguire, "Fraud, extortion and racketeering," 283.
28   Maguire, "Fraud, extortion and racketeering," 284.

Within the Loyalist leadership there was less reluctance to being involved in the drug trade. In 1991, the British government estimated that the Ulster Defense Association and the Ulster Volunteer Force made a million pounds from the drug business. During the 1990s it was estimated that the Loyalists controlled some 60 percent of the drugs in Northern Ireland.[29] According to the U.S. Northern Ireland Threat Assessment for 2001, it was believed that half of the groups involved in drug dealing had paramilitary associations.[30]

It is also the case that when the paramilitaries' income from extortion and drinking clubs was reduced due to more effective police work, the drug trade was an easy way to maintain revenue. The drug trade was controversial within the Loyalist movement and never wholeheartedly supported. It became a serious problem for the Loyalist political parties. However, the rate of drug users in the Province in 2006 was only one third of that in the UK as a whole.[31]

During the 1990s, the UVF was a significant actor in this trade, although the senior leadership was against it. For many paramilitary operatives, the drug trade was important to keep the cash-flow safe, which justified the means.[32] Thus was also a major reason why the splinter groups of the Ulster Freedom Fighters and the Loyalist Volunteer Force were established in 1996, in support of the drug trade.[33]

Extortion   In the Northern Ireland Threat Assessment Report for 2001, the Organized Crime Task Force (OCTF) pointed out that among the reports of extortion to the police since the early 1990s, almost all were related to Loyalist groups.[34] It is almost impossible to get accurate figures on the extent of extortion because victims are intimidated from going public. Although an increasing number of incidents are reported to the police service in Northern Ireland, in 2006 it was estimated that only 10 percent of the incidents were reported.[35]

There may be several reasons that extortion activities cannot be traced to the Republicans. The Provisional Irish Republican Army may have been more selective when choosing targets and executing extortion. Also, perhaps the PIRA tried to maintain the moral high ground. In 1993, Gerry Adams went public, saying he would resign as leader of Sinn Fein if the PIRA was indicted for such crimes. A problem the Loyalists faced was that, because their extortion was so

29   Silke, "Drink, Drugs, Rock'n'Roll," 112.
30   Northern Ireland Organised Crime Task Force, *The Threat to Northern Ireland Society from Serious and Organised Crime: Northern Ireland Threat Assessment 2001,* http://www.nio.gov.uk/northern_ireland_organised_crime_threat_assessment_2001.pdf.
31   Organized Crime Task Force, "Annual Report and Threat Assessment 2006," 36.
32   Silke, "Drink, Drugs, Rock'n'Roll," 113.
33   Silke, "Drink, Drugs, Rock'n'Roll," 113.
34   Organized Crime Task Force, "Annual Report and Threat Assessment 2006," 22.
35   Organized Crime Task Force, "Annual Report and Threat Assessment 2006."

well known, regular criminals pretended with great success to be Loyalists and executed blackmail operations.

The targets of extortion comprise four main groups: small businesses, larger companies, building companies, and regular criminals. For small businesses, the Loyalists' protection ensured that the involved business or persons were able to carry out their legal activities without disturbance. The amount they paid would vary from a few pounds to several thousand. Just the presence of two or three well-known paramilitaries in a small shop would "help"—that is, intimidate— the owner to support the Loyalist Prisoners' Association. Such donations were completely legal and could appear in the stores accounts, as could their costs related to security firms. Because of the close relations and personal knowledge between the victim and the offenders, especially small companies could negotiate the amount of money paid. Such negotiations could go on for days.[36]

Within the Loyalist paramilitaries' area few were able to withstand this extortion. Resistance would normally lead to serious damage to the business and even to the owner himself. In 1996, for example, when Clifford Peeples refused to pay blackmailers, the Ulster Volunteer Force set his house on fire while he and his wife were sleeping.[37] For the paramilitary in the extortion business, it was important that they were known as ruthless and brutal against non-cooperative targets.

Larger companies provided opportunities for larger revenues, but were also more difficult to exploit. Access to the decision-makers was usually more restricted, and they were neither as vulnerable nor as locally based as, for example, a shop-owner in Belfast. Because of the distance between the extorter and the top-management, such cases were more often known to the Royal Ulster Constabulary. On the other hand, as Silke explains, by paying for protection, the companies were often also protected against regular criminals. If a problem occurred, they could simply "call the local UVF."[38]

Building contractors have been a main focus of extortionists since the beginning of the Troubles, and are still so today. In the early years of the Troubles, the living conditions of significant parts of the population located around the industrial areas were outdated and depressed. When the central government began to invest in large programs to make improvements, the building industry expanded. The paramilitaries often approached the foreman on a building site because the contractor himself was not usually present. In one case in the late 1990s, when their extortion demands were refused, the Loyalists did more than £400,000 of damage to equipment and machinery.[39] In general, few contractors reported the offenses to the police. If they faced extortion, they just walked away from the contract.

---

36   Silke, "In Defense of the Realm," 340.
37   Silke, "In Defense of the Realm," 346.
38   Silke, "In Defense of the Realm," 342.
39   Silke, "In Defense of the Realm," 344.

Loyalists also targeted organized crime groups with extortion. The Loyalists would either try to force them out of business or extort some of their profits. The increasing activity among criminal franchises gave the Loyalists the desired funding with only minor risks. This form of fund-raising was more common among the Loyalists compared to the Republicans. Normally, the criminals would rather pay on demand than face the well-known harsh consequences of the paramilitaries.[40]

Armed Robbery   Over time, criminals turned away from the more traditional bank robberies of the sixties to robberies of cash in transit; in 2002, 80 such robberies out of a 100 and 20 were successful.[41] Better security by banks and mail providers, combined with better tools for crime science investigators, eventually changed the criminals' focus to less profitable victims.

Although the Republicans executed a number of robberies of money shipments in the Republic of Ireland, the Loyalists restricted their activity mainly to Northern Ireland. All the expertise and necessities required were available within the Loyalist paramilitary ranks. They were trained in the use of brutal force, they had access to weapons, and they had the will to execute operations. Among those who executed robberies, there should be no surprise to find those same individuals who carried out sectarian violence.

In 1996, the Ulster Defense Association carried out a well planned and executed robbery. It began in the home of the security company's driver, where his family were handcuffed and gagged. The actual robbery occurred when armed and masked men outside Lisburn stopped the van, and a million pounds in used banknotes were seized by the UDA. The money was never seen again.[42] It was one of the biggest attacks on a money transport.

Incidents of armed robbery increased during the 1990s, resulting in gains from as small as £600 to £1 million. The huge amounts of money from the robberies led to further corruption of the Loyalist leadership. The 1996 robbery mentioned above illustrates this.[43] The UDA carried out an investigation and later attacked the house of relatives of one of the accused corrupt participants, who at that time was serving a prison sentence for a nonpolitical offense. Since 2000, the paramilitaries have shifted their operations to the hijacking of goods as their most preferred tactic. The risk of robbing a truck carrying alcohol for future resale, for example, is lower than a traditional armed robbery of a bank.

The Loyalists also had close connections to regular criminal gangs, both in Northern Ireland and in the Republic, who worked with them on robberies. The Ulster Volunteer Force, especially, dealt with a criminal gang in Dublin in the

---

40   House of Commons, *The Financing of Terror in Northern Ireland*, 22.
41   House of Commons, *The Financing of Terror in Northern Ireland*, 24.
42   Silke, "Drink, Drugs, Rock'n'Roll," 109.
43   Silke, "Drink, Drugs, Rock'n'Roll," 110.

1980s. Such relationships were not limited to cooperation during operations; they also involved "taxing" of known criminals living in Loyalist areas.

Loan Sharking Banks are normally reluctant to loan money to the unemployed. In the poverty-stricken industrial areas where the paramilitaries had a presence, the Loyalist organizations filled the gap, providing loans ranging over a wide spectrum. Such loans were costly; the interest alone could be as high as 50 percent. Despite how much easier it was to get a loan from the paramilitaries, the consequences for failing to pay back the loan were much different in form and certainly harsher than most people were used to from banks. The use of baseball bats and iron bars were frequent.[44]

Nonetheless, such loans were also a form of local support. They helped sympathizers who were in a difficult situation, while the interest provided income for the paramilitaries, who also at times used the lenders as safe houses or for other support. Even if the profits were low, the risks for the Loyalists were also close to nothing, both in financial terms and in terms of conflict with her Majesty's forces.

Fraud Two of the most popular forms of fraud when the Troubles started were dole and insurance fraud. At the time, many Loyalists were unemployed and were supported by government welfare programs. To be on the dole, an individual had to demonstrate that he had tried to get a job. To achieve this, a number of fraudulent techniques were implemented, including the creation of false job applications and the threatening of social security workers.

In addition to the tax-exemption fraud pertaining to security costs discussed earlier, insurance fraud was also common. On several occasions, for example, the Loyalist paramilitaries were paid to destroy property, so the owner could receive payment for the damages from his insurance company.[45] As the Troubles faded, the government began to do better to counteract fraud. Thus, today, fraud is linked less to the Loyalists and paramilitaries and more to "regular" organized crime.

Counterfeiting Northern Ireland in the late 1960s, with a population marked by poverty and an economy based largely on cash, provided fertile ground for counterfeiters. Although the goods provided have changed over time, counterfeiting has always been seen as a low-risk operation with an acceptable outcome. These illegal activities include, but are not limited to, reproduction of videos and DVDs, designer clothes, perfume, currency, and credit cards.

Many of the counterfeited products sold in the Province, especially videos, DVDs, and clothing, were produced in the Republic, the UK, and the Far East. The paramilitaries established professional distribution lines across borders, and many products were sold directly from trucks driving in the living areas of the Loyalists. According to Silke, at the end of the nineties, the paramilitaries had a market

---

44   Silke, "Drink, Drugs, Rock'n'Roll," 118.
45   Silke, "Drink, Drugs, Rock'n'Roll," 122.

share of 35 percent with a market value of around £3 million, plus whatever they might gain by taxing the regular criminals who were involved.[46] The Loyalist involvement in counterfeiting is no longer as widely seen. Although the Loyalists were involved in video piracy, it was the Republicans and the Provisional Irish Republican Army that were the dominant actors in this business.[47]

Fuel Rackets For many years, there has been a huge price-gap between fuel prices in the Republic and in Northern Ireland. In 2001, out of 700 filling stations, more than 200 sell only illegal fuel, while some 400 were involved in the illegal trade.[48] As HM Customs and Excise says; "In Northern Ireland, the estimated revenue loss from fraud and legitimate cross border shopping of hydrocarbon was £380 million for 2000, up from £140 million in 1998."[49] Although the fuel rackets are remarkable today, their history goes back to before the Troubles. As long as there is a price difference across the border from that in the Republic, there will be fuel rackets. They may involve bringing fuel across the border for resale to paramilitary-owned taxi companies or to fuel stations, and laundering to remove chemical markers and dyes.

Corruption

History offers numerous examples of Loyalist corruption. James Craig, a senior figure among the Loyalists and a member of the Ulster Defense Association's inner council, is an interesting example. According to Silke, at the height of his power in the early eighties Craig was probably the most corrupt leader in the UDA. He involved himself directly in the extortion of businessmen and building contractors, having them pay him directly for sorting out "problems." Craig, though, did not limit himself to skimming off huge amounts. When John McMichael tried to eliminate corruption within the UDA ranks, Craig cooperated with the Provisional Irish Republican Army in a Loyalist power struggle.[50] Silke points out that of the earnings of the UDA in the 1980s were some five to six million pounds, while the running costs were most likely less than two million a year. Some of the funds were probably invested or stored for further use, but the leadership also took vast sums for personal use, which turned the major Loyalist paramilitaries somewhat more into criminal gangs than "legitimate" warriors for the Loyalist cause. When such sums were siphoned off for personal use, less ideologically driven individuals sought leadership positions, the focus

46   Silke, "Drink, Drugs, Rock'n'Roll," 120.
47   House of Commons, *The Financing of Terror in Northern Ireland*, 24.
48   HM Customs and Excise, "The Misuse and Smuggling of Hydrocarbon Oil,"
February 15, 2002, http://www.nao.org.uk/whats_new/0102/0102614.aspx (accessed May 9, 2009).
49   HM Customs and Excise, "The Misuse and Smuggling of Hydrocarbon Oil."
50   Silke, "In Defense of the Realm," 343.

on the cause suffered, and popular support declined. Over time, Loyalist leaders and members seemed to be more concerned with their own interests, and less motivated by the ideological justification of the group.

Summary

While the Republicans were able to execute strong central control over their Brigades and sub-units, the Loyalists were not. The Loyalist organizations' lack of central control led to more local independence, including in fundraising, as individual Loyalist unit commanders depended more on themselves to create income than their compatriots. The lack of adequate central control of Loyalist racketeering and funding made the ground more fertile for corruption, compared to the Republicans. Furthermore, the Loyalists' smaller size and the absence of specialized units led to less advanced methods and made them more exposed to compromises with the government. The Loyalist lack of a specialized business element to handle their finances meant that this task was given to local units, which further provided a fertile ground for corruption.

The legal methods of funding used by the Loyalist cause were not sufficient to fund the organizations and had to be combined with illegal sources. The Loyalists showed great flexibility in changing funding sources. When one approach became closed, the focus changed to others. Nevertheless, the effects of the government's countermeasures also drove the Loyalists into less public-supported criminal activities in order to maintain a constant money stream. As the last century drew to a close, extortion and drug dealing were the most important cash cows and the Loyalist paramilitary had turned practically into pure gangsterism.

State Counter-Actions

Countering Legal Activities

When the paramilitaries' gains from drinking clubs and pubs reached their peak in the late 1980s, the government implemented a number of regulations that had a serious impact on this type of funding.[51] During the 1990s, around one hundred clubs were closed. In 1994, the tax exemption for blackmailing costs was revoked, after costing the government around tens of millions of pounds every year. Although this initially led to an increased cost for business owners, it also led to an increased number of "walk-aways" from extortion attempts.[52]

---

51   Silke, "Drink, Drugs, Rock'n'Roll," 108.
52   Silke, "In Defense of the Realm," 349.

Countering Illegal Activities

Cooperation with the building contractors, when possible, was very successful during the 1990s. Because of their direct approach, it was relatively easy for the Royal Ulster Constabulary to get incriminating evidence. Later, the successor of RUC, the Police Service of Northern Ireland established its own extortion unit.

During the seventies and early eighties, a number of different agencies and units operated on behalf of the government in Northern Ireland. In 1988, coordination of these resources took a giant step forward with the establishment of the Royal Ulster Anti-Racketeering Unit, also called C-13, which proved very successful and had a serious impact on the paramilitaries' fundraising capacity. Following the establishment of the C-13, the Terrorist Finance Unit was established in 1989.[53] The two units merged in 1996. That same year, the Proceeds of Crime (Northern Ireland) Order was issued, which forces suspects to prove that their accounts are legally achieved. If they cannot, the Crown confiscates the illegally achieved values. With the establishment of the Criminal Assist Bureau (CAB) in Ireland, also in 1996, cooperation across the border and the UK's ability to fight the illegal border-crossing funding of the paramilitaries were reinforced. In 2003, the Assets Recovery Agency became operational with its own Northern Ireland Branch. Its goal is to eliminate criminal profits, making suspects prove that the values gained are by legitimate means.[54]

On September 25, 2000, a united Organized Crime Task Force (OCTF) for Northern Ireland was created. Since then, paramilitary activity has been characterized as "serious" and/or "organized" crime. The establishment of the OCTF was a key step forward in the fight against organized crime and the paramilitaries in Northern Ireland. The Task Force consists of representatives from the Criminal Justice Directorate, Northern Ireland Office; British Customs and Excise; the National Criminal Intelligence Service; Organized and International Crime Directorate, Home Office; the Police Service of Northern Ireland; Royal Ulster Constabulary; Policing and Security Directorate, Northern Ireland Office; and other government agencies.[55] Although the paramilitaries' activities are still significant, they are now treated more as "regular" organized and serious crime than terror activity. This change is clearly evident in the number of subsequent publications, strategy documents, and threat assessments produced the recent years by the Northern Ireland Crime Task Force. The establishment of the Serious Organized Crime Agency on April 1, 2006, further reinforced the government's assets.

---

53   Silke, "In Defense of the Realm," 334.

54   The Northern Ireland Organised Crime Task Force, *Strategic Response 2003-2004*, http://www.nio.gov.uk/octf_strategic_response_2003-04.pdf.

55   Northern Ireland Organised Crime Task Force; "Confronting the Threat: Strategy 2001-2," http://www.nio.gov.uk/confronting_the_threat_orgaised_crime_taskforce_strategy_2001-02.pdf.

Conclusion

There are three key conclusions about the financing of terror in Northern Ireland. First, the techniques used by groups such as radical Islamic groups today to finance terrorist campaigns are nothing new. Both the Irish Republican Army and the Loyalists used legal businesses to funnel money to their illegal activities. What al-Qaeda and similar groups are using in the twenty-first century was used in Ireland in the latter half of the twentieth century.

Second, the Republicans had a distinct advantage in terms of external support. External groups that sympathized with the struggle demonstrated how easy it is for people distant from a fight to get involved in it. From the relative safety of their homes thousands of miles away, the American Irish helped fund a struggle that killed thousands in Northern Ireland. However, the Loyalist had only very limited access to this kind of support. Today, as well, terrorist organizations receive funding from supporters all over the world.

Third, the Irish paramilitaries were very adaptive to their situation. In the context of dividing the different areas for financing purposes between the Ulster Volunteer Force and the Ulster Defense Association, the Loyalists and the Republicans were even able to cooperate.[56] As the TV reporter Robert Cook, noted, "Republican and Loyalist paramilitary groups ... cooperate to divide territories. Political ideals come second. Crime comes first."[57] They exploited whatever funding opportunities were available to them. However, while the Republicans were able to retain a certain degree of relative legitimacy in their activities, possibly due to a stronger faith in their cause, the Loyalists lost focus, turned to purely criminal activity, and lost much of their public support. Within the Loyalist paramilitaries, corruption was widespread, especially in the leadership.

The final conclusion concerns the way the government adjusted its strategies as the Troubles developed, changing from a passive to a more proactive role. A House of Commons document, "The Financing of Terrorism in Northern Ireland, 2001-2002," describes the British government's four main strategies for a successful antiterrorism campaign: 1) intelligence, cultural understanding, and the use of available technology; 2) joint working of total governmental efforts; 3) combined strategies, proactive as well as reactive; and 4) legitimacy by continuous updating of key legislation. These four strategies are also applicable in other conflict areas.[58]

---

56   Silke, "In Defense of the Realm," 336.
57   Silke, "In Defense of the Realm," 347.
58   House of Commons, *The Financing of Terror in Northern Ireland*, 28

Chapter 11

The Financing of Islamist Groups in Albania

Eduart Bala

Since the fall of communism, Albania has witnessed a proliferation of radical and militant Islamic groups. As a result, Albania provides a useful case study of the ways in which the ideology of radical Islam is spread by Islamic non-governmental organizations (NGOs), and how weak states have become fertile recruiting grounds and safe havens for Islamic militants.

This chapter will describe the relationships and cooperation between al-Qaeda, other international terrorist organizations, Islamic NGOs, and Islamic legal businesses in Albania, and how the Albania government has responded to this activity. First, a brief overview of Albania at the beginning of the post-communist period will be provided. This will be followed by descriptions of the various Islamic NGOs that emerged during this period and the ways that they have supported terrorist activities in the country. The chapter will conclude with a discussion of the Albanian government's reaction to this threat.

Overview

After the fall of communism in the early 1990s, Albania went through political, economic, legal and social changes. The country was in poor economic condition, had a high rate of unemployment and weak rule of law, and was exploited by Islamic NGOs related to terrorist organizations. Those NGOs gained the cover of legitimacy by claiming their mission was to engage in charity and spread Islam. In fact, for many of them, their aim was to promote Islamic radicalism and to use Albania as a safe haven for their operations.[1]

A number of factors made Albania a welcoming place for these Islamic NGOs and affiliated terrorist groups, allowing them to build a wide logistic base for financing and supporting their activities. These factors included Albania's location, its mix of religions, its poor economic conditions, and the weakness of its legal system and government agencies.

First, the location of Albania in the Balkan region of Eastern Europe allows easy access to Western European countries. For example, the Albanian city of

---

1 Xhavit Shala,"The Assets of Religious Communities and the National Security," *Albanian Center for National Security Studies*, http://www.acnss.com/ang/st/pdf/3/The%20 Assets%20of%20Religious%20Communities%20and%20the%20National%20Security.pdf.

Valona and the Italian city of Bari are only 35 miles apart, a distance that can be covered in an hour by boat.[2] This proximity has been exploited by organized crime groups engaged in human trafficking and the smuggling of drugs, weapons, etc.

Second, the majority of the population of Albania is Muslim. Islam in Albania dates from the arrival of the Ottomans during the fourteenth and fifteenth centuries.[3] When the country gained its independence from the Ottoman Empire in November 1912, Albania was 50 percent Sunni Muslim, 20 percent Bektashi Muslims (Shi'a), 20 percent Roman Catholic, and 10 percent Orthodox Christian. During the period 1924-1933, King Zog I established Albania as a secular kingdom, forcing Muslim congregations to end their relations with Istanbul after 1921. When the Shi'a (Bektashi) community was banned in Turkey in 1925, it moved its world center to Tirana, where it was officially recognized as a separate community in a decree issued that same year.[4]

After its liberation from the fascist occupation that lasted from 1939 to 1944, Albania was ruled for more than 46 years by a totalitarian communist regime led by Enver Hoxha,[5] a xenophobic communist leader who turned the country into the most isolated place in Europe.[6] Distaste for religion was strongly promoted by communist ideology, which saw religion as a conservative custom and an obstacle to the socialist "Cultural Revolution." The communists' campaign against religion culminated in 1967, when all religious practices and literature were banned, making Albania an officially declared atheist country for approximately 25 years.[7]

As the formerly communist countries of East Europe transitioned to democracy in the 1990s, they learned that religious tolerance was a precondition for joining European institutions.[8] This was a particular issue for Albania. The country's ban on all things religious came to an end; religious practices were gradually revived, and religious institutions were rebuilt and restored. This rebirth of religion in Albania affected all faiths, including Roman Catholic, Orthodox Catholic, and Muslim.

When the Islamic NGOs began to appear, much of the Albanian Islamic community welcomed them, and allowed many of them to gradually push the

2 Yossef Bodansky, *Bin Laden: The Man Who Declared War on America* (Roseville, CA: Prima Publishing, 2001), 297.

3 Marvin Gettleman and Stuar Schaar, *The Middle East and Islamic Word* (New York: Grove Press, 2003), 40-1.

4 Olsi Jazexhi, "The Bektashi Tarikah of Dervishes," October 9, 2007, http://www.olsijazexhi.com/bektashi.pdf.

5 Enver Hoxha was the leader of the Albanian Communist Party and the dictator of the Albanian Communist regime.

6 Arshi Pipa, *Albanian Stalinism: Ideo-Political Aspect* (Columbia University Press, New York, 1990), 79-80.

7 Isa Blumi, "Hoxha's Class War: The Cultural Revolution and State Reformation, 1961-1971," *East European Quarterly*, 33:3 (Fall 1999), 303-26.

8 Pirro Misha, "Religious Tolerance or Irresponsibility?" *Shekulli*, January 10, 2003, http://arkiva.shekulli.com.al/ (accessed October 20, 2007).

community towards extremism and radicalism.[9] This turn toward a more radical version of Islam is part of the broader movement of Islamic revivalism in Albania.

The third factor that made Albania especially attractive to Islamic NGOs and terrorist groups was the poor economic situation there, particularly in the rural areas. Unlike the other religious groups that flocked to Albania during this period, the Islamic charities and businesses claimed that their intent was to foster the economy of Albania.[10]

Fourth, the gaps in the legal infrastructure in post-communist Albania made the country particularly attractive to Islamic charity foundations. The new democratic system that came into power was legally and politically weak and had many other problems, such as widespread corruption and a reluctance to rigorously scrutinize foreign investment and foreign companies, especially Islamic NGOs.[11] Additionally, Albanian intelligence and law enforcement agencies lacked the experience and skills necessary to monitor the activity of these NGOs and extremist groups and the individuals who came into the country to work for them.

Islamic Humanitarian Organizations and Charities

Within this context, many radical Islamic organizations and affiliated NGOs moved into Albania, using it as a safe haven, recruiting ground, and logistical base. As was discussed in Chapter 2, one of the sources of terrorism financing is through charities, when funds are either inadvertently or intentionally diverted to finance terrorism instead of benevolent activities. The Islamic charities collect billions of dollars worldwide every year.[12] In the case of Albania, most of them are used for benevolent causes, such as building mosques and Islamic centers, educating and helping the poor, and selecting and sponsoring young Albanians who are sent to study in Islamic countries. Part of the funds, unfortunately, is diverted to terrorists, either by design or through the unwitting exploitation of otherwise legitimate organizations.

Terrorist organizations such as al-Qaeda, Egyptian Islamic Jihad (EIJ), the Algerian Islamic Salvation Front (FIS), and the Islamic Armed Islamic Group (GIA), have used the cover of NGOs and charities to raise and distribute funds in Albania. These extremist organizations managed to infiltrate their people into the

---

9   Genc Myftiu, "Albanian Religions Beliefs," *Albanian Culture Heritage*, available at: http://www.shqiperia.com/tr/besimet_fetare.php (accessed October 20, 2007).

10   Miranda Vickers and James Pettifer, *Albania: From Anarchy to a Balkan Identity* (New York: New York University Press, 1997), 10-32.

11   Robert Looney, "The Mirage of Terrorist Financing: The Case of Islamic Charities," *Strategic Insights*, 5:3, March 2006, http://www.nps.edu/Academics/centers/ccc/publications/OnlineJournal/2006/Mar/looneyMar06.pdf.

12   Rachel Ehrenfeld, *"Funding Evil: How Terrorism is Financed and How to Stop It"* (Chicago, IL and Los Angeles, CA: Bonus Books, 2003), 2-3.

NGOs where they (1) controlled the organizations' funds, using them to support terrorist activities; (2) used the advantages provided by the legitimate status of these organizations; (3) used the cover of Islam to radicalize young Albanians and recruit them into extremist movements against the Albanian government and its institutions; (4) conducted an effective propaganda and recruitment role through the NGOs' offices, schools, cultural centers, newspapers, magazines, and videotapes to disseminate the terrorists' Wahhabi and Salafi extremist ideology; (5) used Albania as a bridge to promote their terrorist activities and operations abroad, especially in other Balkan countries (Bosnia and Kosovo), Afghanistan, Iraq, and Europe.[13]

The following is a description of some of the Islamic NGOs that have been working in Albania and how they have been used for terrorist purposes. Much of the information is based on the author's professional experience dealing with these organizations.

The International Humanitarian Islamic Organization (IIRO), which established a branch in Albania early in 1990, was the first Islamic NGO to be launched after the new democratic government allowed freedom of religion in Albania. The IIRO is a Wahhabi organization, and is sponsored and supported by Saudi Arabia;[14] it has supported al-Qaeda and its terrorist activities around the globe.[15] The IIRO was the main umbrella organization for the other Islamic NGOs that later came to Albania. During the first period of its activity, the organization played an important role in helping the mujahidin in Bosnia with money and logistics.[16] It also supported al-Qaeda and other terrorist organizations such as the GIA and FIS.[17] Muhammad al-Zawahiri, the brother of Bin Laden's deputy, Ayman al-Zawahiri, was employed by the Albanian office of the IIRO, where he assisted al-Qaeda's efforts in the Balkans.[18] During the Kosovo crisis (1999-2000), this organization played an active role in supporting Kosovo refugees

---

13   Sheikh al-Mujahedeen Abu Abdel Aziz, as quoted in Rohan Gunaratna, *Inside Al Qaeda: Global Network of Terror* (New York: Columbia University Press, 2002), 132.

14   CIA, Report on "International Islamic NGOs," January 1996, http://en.wikisource.org/wiki/CIA_Report_on_NGOs_With_Terror_Links (accessed June 21, 2010).

15   Public Hearing, National Commission on Terrorist Attacks upon the United States, July 9, 2003, *Archives*, http://govinfo.library.unt.edu/911/hearings/hearing3.htm (accessed June 21, 2010).

16   Steven Emerson with Jonathan Levin, "Terrorism Financing: Origination, Organization, and Prevention: Saudi Arabia, Terrorist Financing and the War on Terror," *Testimony before the U.S. Senate Committee on Governmental Affairs*, July 31, 2003, http://www.investigativeproject.org/documents/testimony/17.pdf.

17   Treasury Department, "Treasury Designates Director, Branches, of Charity Bankrolling Al Qaeda Network," *Press Release*, August 3, 2006, http://www.treas.gov/press/releases/hp45.htm (accessed June 22, 2010).

18   Dore Gold, "The Kingdom of Incitement," *The Wall Street Journal*, April 14, 2003.

in Albania and Kosovo.[19] However, its main aim was to establish the Wahhabi theology in Kosovo's Muslim community and, later, to create the possibility for mujahidin and terrorist activities.[20]

The al Haramain Islamic Foundation (HIF),[21] an Islamic charity based in Jeddah, Saudi Arabia, was established in Albania in 1992. From the beginning, al Haramain was active in building Wahhabi mosques around the country,[22] opening Islamic cultural centers, and supporting orphans and poor families by helping the children attend Wahhabi theological schools in Saudi Arabia. It has been active in indoctrinating the young Albanian imams with Salafi ideology and providing them with financial help. This charity has also provided financial and logistic support for the mujahidin in Bosnia (specifically, for the battalion in Zenica) and Chechnya.[23] From 1993 until 1998, the al Haramain Albanian branch was penetrated by Egyptian Islamic Jihad (EIJ) members associated with al-Qaeda. The mission of the EIJ cell in Albania was to create many sub-cells by recruiting young Albanians, training them to forge documents, and preparing them to engage in acts of terror in Kosovo and to foment conflict among the different religious groups in Albania.[24] The head of EIJ's Albanian cell, Ahmed Ibrahim al-Nagar, aka Mohamed Ragab Foudah, worked as the head of al Haramain's office in Albania, while Mohamed Hasan Mahmoud Hassan, aka Abu Omar, was the foundation's director. After both men were arrested and deported to Egypt, the al Haramain headquarters decided to continue to support the branch, but assigned young Albanian Muslim extremists to lead it. From 1999 until the Albanian government closed it down in 2005, the organization was led by young Wahhabi and Salafi former religious students who had been trained in Saudi Arabia.[25]

---

19   "Saudi Arabia assesses its aid to Kosovar refugees," The Royal Embassy of Saudi Arabia, Washington, D.C., Archives, June 4, 1999, http://www.saudiembassy.net/archive/1999/news/page230.aspx (accessed June 21, 2010).

20   Loretta Napoleoni, "Slipping with Enemy," http://www.conspiracycafe.net/forum/index.php?/topic/26459-the-house-of-saud-follow-the-money/ (accessed June 22, 2010).

21   9/11 Commission, "Al Haramain Case Study," *Terrorist Financing Staff Monograph*, Chapter 7, www.9-11commission.gov/staff_statements/911_TerrFin_Ch7.pdf.

22   Victor Comras, "Al Qaeda Finances and Funding to Affiliated Groups," in *The Political Economy of Terrorism Finance and State Responses: A Comparative Perspective*, edited by Jeanne K. Giraldo and Harold A. Trinkunas (Stanford, CA: Stanford University Press, 2006), 121.

23   Gunaratna, *Inside Al Qaeda: Global Network of Terror*, 133.

24   U.S. Department of Treasury—Office of Terrorism and Financial Intelligence, "Additional Background Information on Charities Designated under Executive Order 13224: Al Haramain Islamic Foundation-related Designations," http://www.treas.gov/offices/enforcement/key-issues/protecting/charities_execorder_13224-a.shtml (accessed June 23, 2010).

25   U.S. Department of Treasury "Additional Background Information on Charities Designated Under Executive Order 13224."

The Revival of Islamic Heritage Society (RIHS), an Islamic NGO that is sponsored by the Muslim Brotherhood Organization in Kuwait, opened an office in Tirana in 1992. Like al Haramain, the RIHS was penetrated by EIJ and al-Qaeda from 1993 until the end of 1998. Specifically, it was taken over by several operatives, including Ahmed Ismail Othman Saleh, aka Abu Anas, who lived in Albania on a false Sudanese passport in the name of Mohammed Khaled Ahmed Moussa. Abu Anas worked as the representative of the RIHS in the urban areas, where he recruited Albanian students to Wahhabi and Salafi ideology. When he was arrested while attempting to escape from Albania, the police found that he possessed a homemade blueprint of the U.S. embassy in Albania.[26] Affiliated with him was Mosbah Ali Hassannein Azab, aka Saif or Abdel Rahman, a Yemeni national who used a false passport with the name of Fahd Ali Saleh. He was the head of the NGO for North Albania. When the police tried to arrest him, he escaped to Montenegro; from there, he moved to Milan with the help of organised crime groups involved in human smuggling and was subsequently arrested.[27] The final operative from EIJ/AQ to penetrate this NGO was Hossam Ezzat Hossam Nour El Din, aka Alaa, who used an Egyptian passport under the name Salah Mohammed Omar el Sayed. He was killed during a confrontation with police forces.[28] Other EIJ members working for RIHS were arrested and deported to their countries of origin in 1998. In 2005, the RIHS NGO was closed by the Albanian government. The organization was reopened under the name "Call for Wisdom" at the end of 2005, by young Albanian Islamic extremists whom it had recruited and trained. In 2006, the Albanian government discovered that behind this group was the same organization financed illegally by the RIHS headquarters in Kuwait shut it down.[29]

The Muwafaq Foundation (or Blessed Relief Foundation) established a branch in Albania in 1993 as an Islamic charity. This NGO was sponsored by Yassin Abdullah al-Qadi, who is on a list of 39 individuals and groups accused by the U.S. Department of Treasury of financing Osama bin Laden and al-Qaeda.[30] This foundation was very active during the Bosnian War, supporting the mujahidin

26   For more on this issue see Jane's Sentinel Security Assessment "Albania: Internal Affairs," http://jir.janes.com/docs/jir/search.jsp (accessed June 24, 2010).

27   Sharaf al-Din, Khalid "Returnees from Albania' Case Report Ends." *al-Sharq al-Awsat*, March 9, 1999. FBIS Translation, FBIS-NES-1999-0310, http://www.fas.org/irp/news/1999/03/990306-cairo-4.htm (accessed June 24, 2010).

28   For more on this issue see Jane's Sentinel Security Assessment "Albania: Internal Affairs."

29   U.S. Department of the Treasury, "Kuwaiti Charity Designated for Bankrolling al Qaida Network," Press Room, June 13, 2008, HP-1023, http://www.ustreas.gov/press/releases/hp1023.htm (accessed October 15, 2007).

30   Security Council 4976th Meeting (AM), "List of Suspected Terrorist Organizations and Individuals, National Reports Continue to Play Crucial Role in Fight Against Terror, Security Council Told," Press Release SC/8102, http://www.un.org/News/Press/docs/2004/sc8102.doc.htm (accessed November 10, 2007).

and the Kosovo refugees in Albania.Mohammed Jamal Khalifa,[31] one of Osama bin Laden's brothers-in-law and an al-Qaeda financier, visited the Muwafaq Foundation's Albanian office in 1994.[32] Al-Qadi closed the Muwafaq Foundation in 1998 following reports that publicized the organization's ties to terrorism.[33] He used the funds from the foundation to open several businesses, including a sugar importing business, a medical enterprise, and a construction business, as well as a number of commercial companies with names such as "Medicare," "Loxhall," "Karavan," "Alintid Beton," "Albanian Snacks," "Loks Holl," "Cavallo," "Waleed for General Trade," "Emane," and "Kambel."[34] The Albanian government shut down these companies and froze their investments, not only because they were connected with al-Qadi and al-Qaeda, but also because they were fictitious companies with limited commercial activity.[35]

The Project of Benefaction of the Gulf Foundation was established in Albania in 1997. This organization is a Kuwaiti NGO financed and sponsored by Kuwaiti Brotherhood extremists. The founder and director of the foundation was Dr. Abdul Latif Saleh. Saleh was born a Palestinian and has Jordanian citizenship. He was the first director of al Haramain, and the first Arab to take Albanian citizenship. Saleh is closely associated with a number of NGOs in Albania that have links to the Egyptian Islamic Jihad. In 2000, Albanian authorities expelled Saleh from Albania on suspicion of membership in a "radical Islamic Jihad group," and for closely associating with Osama bin Laden, who provided Saleh with $600,000 to encourage the establishment of extremist groups in Albania.[36]

The World Assembly of Muslim Youth (WAMY) has its center in Riyadh, Saudi Arabia, and is financed by the Saudi King. "WAMY was co-founded by Kamal Helwabi, a former senior member of the Egyptian Muslim Brotherhood and by Osama bin Laden's nephew Abdullah bin Laden (who served as WAMY's President through 2002 and is now its Treasurer)."[37] This foundation

---

31   History Commons, "Profile: Muwafaq Foundation," http://www.historycommons. org/entity.jsp?entity=muwafaq_foundation (accessed May 3, 2010).

32   Devlin Buckley, "Ptech owner's assets confiscated in Albania," *The American Monitor*, January 16, 2007, http://www.theamericanmonitor.com/articles/albania_alqadi. html (accessed June 25, 2010).

33   Victor Comras, "Al Qaeda Finances and Funding to Affiliated Groups," 121.

34   Stephen Schwartz, "Saudi Influence in Our Government Ignores Terror," *Dafka*, December 9, 2002, www.dafka.org/news/index.php?pid=4&id=85 (accessed October 15, 2007).

35   Yassin al-Qadi is on the U.S. list of al-Qaeda suspects. At the request of the U.S., Albanian authorities sequestered his investments and blocked his assets. The issue is still under legal review; meanwhile, al-Qadi has fled the country.

36   U.S. Treasury Release JS-2727, "Treasury Designates Bin Laden, Qadi Associate," September 19, 2005, http://www.treas.gov/press/releases/js2727.htm (accessed October 15, 2007).

37   U.S. Government Accountability Office (GAO), "Information on U.S. Agencies' Efforts to Address Islamic Extremism," September 2005, http://www.gao.gov/new.items/

is active worldwide, and the WAMY branch in Albania was registered as a legal organization on November 1, 1993; its stated aim was to construct mosques and provide humanitarian aid. This charity was active in bringing Wahhabi and Salafi ideology to Albania, and in recruiting and sending Albanian students to Saudi Arabia to study Wahhabi and Salafi theology there. In 1999, police forces raided the organization and deported its suspected terrorist elements. Since then, WAMY sponsors in Saudi Arabia continue to support the new leaders of the Albanian branch with money and propaganda material.

The Islamic Relief Foundation was registered as a legal organization in Albania on December 12, 1991. Like the other Islamic charities, its stated purpose was to engage in humanitarian activities: providing aid for poor people and orphans, building mosques, and spreading religious propaganda. In reality, however, the organization was used as a base for Islamic extremists and especially as a place for the members of the Algerian Front of Islamic Salvation (FIS) and its armed branch, the GIA, to hide from Algerian forces. For instance, Qamar el-Din Kharban, a cofounder of FIS and one of its key leaders, stayed in Albania for a year and afterwards went to Bosnia.[38] Other members of the FIS, Algerians Adnan I. Habib and Grinat Belhout, came to Albania at the beginning of 1993; they were deported in 1999 after special law enforcement operations.[39]

Taibah International was an Islamic organization headquartered in and sponsored by Saudi Arabia. The Albania office was established in 1993. Its espoused mission was to support poor Albanian families and orphans and to build schools. However, Taibah International was penetrated by extremist members of the Egyptian Muslim Brotherhood. It opened one school in Tirana, called Drita ("The Light"), which taught Wahhabism and Salafi theology to boys under fifteen. The other school was in North Albania and was called the Abu Hanife Insitute. Students of this "institute" were under the leadership of the Egyptian extremists and instigated violent conflicts with the members of other religions (Christians and Shiia Muslims), not only in the areas around the schools, but also in the places where they went to live and promote Islam after their graduation. After the police shut down this organization in 2005,[40] the foundation changed its name to "Jeta," Albanian for "The Life." The new managers of this Islamic NGO were former students of the Taibah schools and were supported by the same headquarters. As a

---

d05852.pdf.

38   J. Millard Burr and Robert O. Collins, *Alms for Jihad: Charity and Terrorism in the Islamic World* (Cambridge: Cambridge University Press, 2006), 146-9.

39   Michael A. Innes, *Denial of Sanctuary: Understanding Terrorist Safe Havens* (Westport, CT: Praeger Security International, 2007), 144.

40   U.S. Department of State, "Country Reports: Europe and Eurasia Overview— Chapter 5," Office of the Coordinator for Counterterrorism, April 29, 2006, http://www.state.gov/s/ct/rls/crt/2005/64342.htm (accessed June 16, 2010).

result of this connection to the original Taibah International NGO, the government also closed down the new organization.[41]

Al Waqf al Islamia established a branch in Albania in 1992. Sponsored by Saudi Arabia, the organization is headquartered in the Netherlands. The Albanian branch has been penetrated by extremist elements of the EIJ and al-Qaeda. Al Waqf's aim was to recruit young people into the ideology of extremist Islam. It built madrassas in the Albanian cities of Berati and Gjirokaster. For its extremism and connection with EIJ and al-Qaeda the Albanian Government closed foundation and its activity in Albania, but still it exists in Kosovo.[42]

The Qatari Charitable Society, based in Doha, was financed and supported by the Emirs of Qatar. The office in Albania was established in 1993. Its activities have been fairly limited, but it sponsored and supported the mujahidin in Bosnia during the Bosnian War.[43]

The Joint Saudi Committee for Kosovo was established in Albania in 1999; its main aim was to build a terrorist network in Kosovo during the Kosovo War.[44] The organization was sponsored by the Saudis, Osama bin Laden, and al-Qaeda affiliates. It took on the leading role among the Saudi NGOs in Kosovo (IIRO, Al-Haramain, WAMY, al-Waqf al Islamia). The director, Wael Hamza Julaidan, and secretary, Abdal Sadek Kathum, were also representatives of the Rabita Trust Company (a global Salafi charity) in Albania. In 2000, both of them were declared persona non grata; they were deported from Albania, and the NGO was closed.

Global Relief Foundation (a.k.a. Secours Mondial) headquartered in Brussels had an office in Tirana, Albania until 2005. Because of connections its officers and directors had, and provided support for and assistance to, Osama bin Laden, the al-Qaeda network and the Taliban,[45] the foundation and two of its directors were included in the list of terrorist financing in Albania. The Global Relief Foundation was shut down and the bank accounts belonging to foundation and Nabil Abdul

41   Albania Ministry of Finance, "Annual Report of General Directorate of Prevention Standards Money for the Year 2005," http://fint.gov.al/doc/Rap.%20Vjetor%202005-2006%20perfundimtar-final%20me%20foto_revised%20-%201.pdf.

42   Hussein Saud Qusti, "Unsung Heroes," *Saudi Aramco World*, July/August 1999, http://www.saudiaramcoworld.com/issue/199904/unsung.heroes.htm (accessed June 20, 2010).

43   U.S Congress, House Committee on Financial Services, Subcommittee on Oversight and Investigations, *Progress since 9/11: The Effectiveness of the U.S. Anti-Terrorist Financing Efforts*, 108th Congress, 1st session, March 11, 2003.

44   Jean-Charles Brisard, "Terrorism Financing: Roots and Trends of Saudi Terrorism Financing," *JCB Consulting*, December 19, 2003, http://www.investigativeproject.org/documents/testimony/22.pdf.

45   UN Security Council Committee, "Security Council Committee Adds Name of an Entity to Its Lists," Press Release, SC/7543, October 22, 2002, www.un.org/News/Press/docs/2002/sc7543.doc.htm (accessed October 1, 2007).

Salam Sayadi personnel of "Global Relief Foundation") were frozen by the Albanian government on March 10, 2005.[46]

The Islamic World Committee, which is sponsored by the Muslim Brotherhood in Kuwait, was established in Albania in 1993. The foundation was penetrated by extremist elements of the Egyptian Muslim Brotherhood, who used it as an umbrella to allow Egyptian Muslim Brotherhood members to enter Europe clandestinely.[47]

The Kuwait Joint Relief Committee for Charity (KJRC), which has its headquarters in Kuwait, includes some humanitarian associations such as the International Islamic Charitable Organization and House of Zekat. The KJRC has been active in Albania since 1993. The funds for this foundation come from Kuwait, and through sales of books and magazines that promote Wahhabi and Salafi theology. The El Hagri institute in Elbasan, Albania, where young Albanian students learn the extremist Wahhabi and Salafi theology, is part of this organization. The foundation opened a branch in Kosovo during the war there. Overall, this foundation is reducing its activity in Albania and is transferring its main focus to Kosovo.[48]

There were also several small Islamic NGOs that were not very active and did not openly support terrorists, but that did play a significant role in spreading the Wahhabi and Salafi theology among the young Albanians. The organizations provided the students with money to attend Wahhabi and Salafi schools and courses in such countries as Sudan, Pakistan, Saudi Arabia and Libya.

Counterterrorism Policies of the Albanian Government

Originally, Albania lacked a counterterrorism strategy or even the organizational structures for countering terrorism. Over time, however, the government has responded to this threat in various ways and with varying degrees of success. One critical task has been to identify the role of the Islamic NGOs in supporting and financing the terrorist activities of al-Qaeda and other groups.[49] Since the late

46 The Albanian Legislation Order No. 5, dated March 10, 2005 "For seizing the assets of citizens Nabil Abdul Sayadi, which results announced in the list of terrorist financiers," *Orders of the Minister of Finance*, http://www.qpz.gov.al/doc.jsp?doc=docs/Urdher%20Nr%205%20Dat%C3%AB%2010-03-2005.htm (accessed June 16, 2010).

47 History Commons, "Profile: Islamic World Committee," http://www.historycommons.org/entity.jsp?entity=islamic_world_committee_1 (accessed November 10, 2007).

48 U.S. Department of Treasure, Office of Foreign Assets Control, "Recent OFAC Actions," June 13, 2008, http://www.treas.gov/offices/enforcement/ofac/actions/20080613.shtml (accessed November 10, 2007).

49 Mark Basile, "Going to the Source: Why Al Qaeda's Financial Network is Likely to Withstand the Current War on Terrorist Financing," *Studies in Conflict & Terrorism*, 27 (2004), 169-85.

1990s, Albania has taken many steps to identify these NGOs and curtail their activities.

The new Albanian political leadership that came into power after the 1997 economic crisis clearly understood the perils of taking a reactive approach to counterterrorism. The government's new pro-active policy was encouraged by international actors, particularly the U.S. intelligence services, which, in cooperation with the Albanian secret services, and police, marked the change in the official counterterrorism policy. During the period 1998-1999, the CIA and Albanian intelligence conducted a joint operation where they identified an Egyptian Islamic Jihad cell that was allegedly planning to bomb the U.S. Embassy in Tirana, Albania's capital. As a result a number of suspected international terrorists were arrested and extradited from Albania, and a number of NGOs came under the scrutiny of the law.[50]

In the aftermath of September 11, 2001, some international media outlets and neighboring governments portrayed Albania as a haven of terrorism, and made allegations of links between ethnic Albanian insurgents and Islamic terrorism. However, the Albanian government worked to demonstrate its commitment to fighting terrorism. In close cooperation with different western partners, including the U.S., U.K., France, Italy, and Germany, a number of raids were launched against Islamic NGOs in Albania, and several of their principal officers were deported; in addition, the government revoked the visa privileges of the Arab nationals suspected of terrorist or extremist activities.

In the framework of the implementation of the U.N. Security Council counter-terrorism resolutions, the government of Albania took action to freeze or sequester the assets and bank accounts belonging to individuals enlisted in the "Consolidated List"[51] like the Saudi national Yassin al-Qadi,[52] Palestinian-Jordanian Abdul Latif Saleh,[53] and Belgian national Nabil Abdul Salam Sayadi. Foreign Islamic NGOs were shut down, and assets and bank accounts belonging to Al-Haramein, Global Relief Foundation, Taibah International, and Revival of Islamic Heritage Society were frozen. The Albanian Government has frozen 350,000 Euros in total, and they are still frozen and under court procedure.[54]

---

50   History Commons, "Profile: Muwafaq Foundation."

51   The Consolidated List established and maintained by the paragraph 6 of resolution 1267 (1999) Committee with respect to Al-Qaida, Osama bin Laden, and the Taliban and other individuals, groups, undertakings and entities associated with them, http://www.un.org/sc/committees/1267/consolist.shtml (accessed June 16, 2010).

52   Comras, "Al Qaeda Finances and Funding to Affiliated Groups," 121-2.

53   Al-Qadi is thought to support Al-Qaeda and have links with Abdyl Latifi Saleh, a suspected Saudi terrorist who was extradited from Albania in November 1999. See Kristin Archick and Paul Galles, *Europe and Counterterrorism* (New York: Nova Science Publishers, 2003), 41-2.

54   The Albanian Legislation Orders No: 5, 6, 7, 8, 9, 10, dated March 10, 2005 "For seizing the assets of NGO-s and their personnel, which results announced in the list of terrorist financiers," *Orders of the Minister of Finance*, http://www.qpz.gov.al/doc.

The national defense policy of Albania has identified terrorism as one of the nation's main challenges and risks to overall security. The government has acknowledged that the following problems need to be addressed in its counterterrorism efforts: a large informal economic sector, money laundering, a cash economy, weak internal security, lack of border control, and a fragile financial system that allowed Islamic NGOs and terrorist elements to bring in money in the form of cash or electronic wire transfers. The government is taking radical measures to deal with these issues. Albania has signed and ratified all international conventions and protocols against terrorism, and is working continuously to strengthen its legislation in order to suppress any terrorist-related activities in Albania.[55] Consequently, the government suggested and the Parliament approved amendments to the existing Criminal Code and Criminal Procedure Code related to procedures about legal pursue of terrorism and terrorist financing activities. In 2004, a new law entitled "On the Prevention of Money Laundering and Terrorist Financing" was enacted; the law, which was amended in 2008, aimed to further improve the legal framework for the fight against terrorism and money-laundering.[56] It created a legal basis for preventing and punishing economic informality (informal cash-based transactions), money laundering, and the financing of terrorism; furthermore, it strengthened border control in accordance with respective requirements of the new law, other international agreements and UN resolutions in the area of terrorism financing.[57] Moreover, the Albanian government has made every effort to improve national and international co-operation in preventing and fighting terrorism. The 2008 amendments to the law "On the Prevention of Money Laundering and Terrorist Financing" led to the creation of the National Coordinating Committee to Fight Money Laundering and Terrorist Financing, headed by the Prime Minister and composed of the Attorney General, the Governor of the National Bank of Albania, the Ministers of Foreign Affairs, Defense, Interior, and Justice, and the Head of the State Intelligence Service. This Committee determines the national policy that targets money laundering and terrorism financing.[58] New law enforcement bodies were established, such as the General Directorate for the Prevention of Money

---

jsp?doc=docs/Urdher%20Nr%205%20Dat%C3%AB%2010-03-2005.htm (accessed June 16, 2010).

55 Albanian Ministry of Foreign Affairs, "International Conventions & Reports," http://www.mfa.gov.al/ (accessed June 16, 2010).

56 2005 International Monetary Fund, "Albania: Financial System Stability Assessment, including Reports on the Observance of Standards and Codes on the following topics: Banking Supervision and Payments Systems," IFM Country Report No 05/274, August 2005, http://imf.org/external/pubs/ft/scr/2005/cr05274.pdf.

57 The United Nations Office on Drugs and Crime South Eastern Europe Project Office—Albania, "Money-laundering, financing of terrorism and asset forfeiture," http://www.unodc.org/southeasterneurope/en/alb/g70.html (accessed June 16, 2010).

58 IBA Anti-Money Laundering Forum, "Albania," October 23, 2009, http://www.anti-moneylaundering.org/europe/Albania.aspx (accessed June 16, 2010).

Laundering, which consists of the Financial Intelligence Unit (FIU) and the Interagency Technical Working Group; the Directorate's mission is to coordinate Albania's counterterrorism efforts at the operational level and its fight against money laundering at the national level. Among the results have been increased flexibility in governmental interagency cooperation, and additional training for new and existing personnel. As a member of the Egmont Group of Financial Intelligence Units, the FIU exchanges information on financial intelligence with its counterpart organizations around the world.[59] The National Bank of Albania has established a task force to monitor the financial activities of the secondary banks. Under the antiterrorism laws, all banks in Albania are obligated to identify the accounts of individuals suspected of having terrorist ties, and to prevent the withdrawal or transfer of funds.[60]

The Albanian government has made the fight against terrorism one of the priorities on its political agenda. Its counterterrorism policy includes respect for human rights, effective law enforcement, and full international co-operation. The government continually works to strengthen and update its legislation in accordance with respective UN and EU resolutions in order to prevent and suppress any terrorist-related activities in Albania. Moreover, the government is doing its best to ensure that actions targeting international terrorism and terrorist financing are in line with international laws and agreements and the norms and standards of liberal democracy.

Conclusion

Al-Qaeda and the international terrorist organizations associated with it have shown how non-state actors and global networks can support and finance terrorist activities. In the Albanian case, NGOs used the country to build their operations, to raise money to support mujahidin, to recruit new Albanian radicals, to gain legal cover for their operations, and to serve as a springboard for their operations in Europe. Some terrorists have already infiltrated other parts of Europe from bases in Albania, illegally entering Italy by way of speedboats across the Adriatic Sea.

As this case study shows, NGOs adapt their operations as circumstances dictate. After the Arab leaders who founded the Albanian NGOs were arrested and/or deported, the organizations found new leaders among the Albanian students whom they had recruited; the names of the NGOs were changed from Arabic to Albanian; al-Qadi closed the NGO he led and transferred its money to different shadow businesses.

---

59 Egmont Group of Financial Intelligence Units "Albania," http://www.egmontgroup.org (accessed June 16, 2010).

60 Bank of Albania, "Supervision Annual Report-2006," www.bankofalbania.org/previewdoc.php?crd=3226&ln=2&uni=200902241245076579 (accessed June 16, 2010).

This case study highlights the need to not only freeze and seize terrorist-linked assets, but also to detect and follow them. Together, these methods offer the best way to stop and disrupt criminal actions in Albania and beyond as part of a global effort against terrorism.

PART V
Americas

Chapter 12

The FARC of Colombia

Saul Hiram Bandala

The FARC, or Fuerzas Armadas Revolucionarias de Colombia—Ejército del Pueblo (Revolutionary Armed Forces of Colombia—People's Army), is a Marxist group that has terrorized Colombia for decades. As a fairly large insurgent organization, it has relied on several sources of funding, including narcotics trafficking, cattle theft, extortion, and kidnapping for ransom. As a case study, the activities of the FARC and the responses of the Colombian government provide useful examples of the diversity of terrorist sources of income, how terrorist organizations and their finances change over time, and how groups like the FARC can pose serious problems for the state trying to combat them, especially when the state itself has limited resources. The following chapter will first address the background of the FARC and Colombia and then turn to their financial resources and expenditures. The final part will address the government's efforts against FARC finances and explore future options that should be considered.

Background

Drug cartels, terrorist groups, and insurgencies have all taken advantage of Colombia's isolating geography of mountains and jungles to conduct their activities. Coupled with the weakness of the Colombian state, the effort of the military and security forces to counter them has been further complicated by "the pattern of dispersed settlements, poor national integration, and poor communications."[1] President Álvaro Uribe (2002-2010) and his administration fought three concurrent wars against narco-trafficking, paramilitaries, and rebel insurgent groups. This dynamic was made more challenging by social issues and a growing population, concerns common to many Latin American countries. The most significant problems faced by the administration of President Uribe are unemployment, displacement of the population due to violence, violence itself, terrorism and organized crime. The origins of these problems can be traced to the lack of a culture and mentality to effectively identify and integrate the population. Excessive population growth, primarily in irregular settlements around the main

---

1 Gabriel Marcella, "The United States and Colombia: The Journey from Ambiguity to Strategic Clarity," Carlisle: Strategic Studies Institute, May 2003, http://www.strategicstudiesinstitute.army.mil/pdffiles/PUB10.pdf.

urban areas, has hampered the delivery of services to the people, sharpening the differences between social classes and strengthening the frustration and resentment of the marginalized sectors toward the middle and upper classes.[2]

Despite the fact that Colombia is upheld as Latin America's oldest democracy, it is plagued by the longest running civil conflict in the hemisphere. Historically, Colombia's social differences, combined with the interests of local landlords, have prevented the political unification of the country. In 1948, the country became immersed in a violent struggle between supporters of the Colombian Liberal Party and the Colombian Conservative Party. This struggle became known as *La Violencia*. The turmoil generated by *La Violencia* never truly ended; killings just continued at a slower rate. In the 1960s, new guerrilla armies appeared in the country with the assistance of Fidel Castro's Cuba. In part, the current struggle against Latin America's oldest and most powerful guerrilla organization, the FARC-EP, is a continuation of this conflict.[3]

The geography of the country, in addition to the ethnic and social divisions among the population, has represented a constant challenge for the integration and consolidation of the Colombian state. The task for the Colombian government has been further complicated by the pronounced dispersion of power, manifested through extreme levels of localism and regionalism. Additionally, much of the population has strong local values that bond them together and alienate them from the centralized ruling aristocracy. In this context, the most significant and violent challenges to the Colombian state are the FARC-EP, the National Liberation Army (ELN), and the United Self-Defense Forces of Colombia (AUC).

These three actors, what Joseph R. Nuñez named the "Hobbesian Trinity,"[4] plague Colombia and complicate any attempt to resolve the ongoing dilemma. The fight of the Colombian government against its internal enemies has been supported by the United States through the joint United States-Colombian strategic Plan Colombia, which was a six year strategic plan developed by former Colombian President Andrés Pastrana (1998-2002). The purpose of this plan was "to end the country's 40-year old armed conflict, eliminate drug trafficking, and promote economic and social development."[5] Plan Colombia is considered by the Colombian government as:

2   William Ramírez Tobón, Revista Análisis Político, "Violencia y Democracia en Colombia," No. 3 Enero a Abril de 1988, 88, http://bibliotecavirtual.clacso.org.ar/ar/libros/colombia/assets/own/analisis%20politico%2003.pdf.

3   For background, see Alvaro de Souza Pinheiro, "Narcoterrorism in Latin America, a Brazilian Perspective," (Report 06-4, Joint Special Operations University, 2006), 18.

4   Joseph R. Nuñez, "Fighting the Hobbesian Trinity in Colombia: A New Strategy for Peace," Carlisle: Strategic Studies Institute, April 2001, 1, http://www.strategicstudiesinstitute.army.mil/pdffiles/PUB28.pdf.

5   Connie Veillette, "Colombia: Issues for Congress," Congressional Research Service: Report for Congress, January 4, 2006, 4, http://digital.library.unt.edu/ark:/67531/metacrs9352/ (accessed January 13, 2012).

an integral policy that looks to reiterate the commitment that the Colombian government has to look for a negotiated political solution to the conflict, under fundamental basic principles such as democracy, territorial integrity and the defense and protection of human rights.[6]

While the main objectives of the Colombian government have been to "promote peace and economic development, and increase security," within this context, addressing drug trafficking is considered an integral part of these objectives. Nevertheless, despite the huge amount of military resources allocated by the United States to its South American ally, history has proven that defeating the adversaries with a solely military response is not possible. Drug traffickers, paramilitary groups, and terrorist/insurgent organizations continue to represent significant challenges to the Colombian government and its institutions.

It is important to highlight that despite their economic wealth and military power, the insurgents lack the military or popular support necessary to overthrow the government. Nevertheless, despite the fact that violence has been decreasing since around 2002, insurgents continue their attacks against civilians and significant portions of the countryside are under guerrilla influence.

The FARC

The FARC-EP was founded in 1966 as the military wing of the Colombian Communist Party under the influence of fidelista groups, on the basis of the independent peasant republic of Marquetalia.[7] Initially the FARC was organized among the peasant population of the remote and isolated mountainous areas between Bogotá and Cali.[8] Nevertheless, this guerrilla organization has evolved to become Latin America's oldest and most powerful guerrilla organization, also recognized as "one of the largest and most well-funded militant organizations in the world."[9] Since its beginning, the communist ideology has played a very significant part in recruiting sympathizers and followers for the FARC. Nevertheless, since FARC got involved in drug trafficking, economic interests superseded ideological motivations.[10] The

---

6 Mauricio Cárdenas, Revista Cambio, quoted in Omar Pina, "Plan Colombia: How U.S. Military Assistance Affects Regional Balances of Power." Naval Postgraduate School Thesis, 2004, 48.

7 Thomas C. Wright, *Latin America in the Era of the Cuban Revolution* (Westport, CT: Praeger Publishers, 2001), 79.

8 Ricky M. Longhurst and Jesus K. Lopez, "The Forgotten Insurgency: Is there Hope for Colombia?" Naval Postgraduate School Thesis, 2005, 5.

9 Kim Cragin and Bruce Hoffman. *Arms Trafficking and Colombia* (Santa Monica, CA: RAND, 2003), xxi.

10 Paul D. Taylor, ed. "Latin American Security Challenges: A Collaborative Inquiry from North and South," Naval War College, 2004, 32, http://www.dtic.mil/cgi-bin/GetTRD oc?AD=ADA430425&Location=U2&doc=GetTRDoc.pdf.

limited capability of the Colombian state to satisfy the demands of its population has facilitated the evolution of FARC from a guerrilla movement to a criminal institution that apparently represents the only viable option for some people, mainly peasants, to escape poverty and have access to a better way of life.[11] The FARC-EP has an estimated 12,000-18,000 members (approximately 20 to 30 percent of them are recruits under 18 years of age) and is present in 35-40 percent of Colombia, most strongly in the southeastern jungles and in plains in the base of the Andes mountains.[12]

The peak of the FARC's political power was reached during the Pastrana administration [1998-2002], when the government ceded to the demands of the FARC-EP and granted them five FARC-controlled municipalities in south-central Colombia, encompassing 42,139 square kilometers, to create a demilitarized zone known as Zona de Despeje or Distention Zone. In theory, this agreement between the government and the guerrilla was meant to provide an incentive to develop a political and a territorial space for negotiations between both parties.[13] In practice, the FARC used the demilitarized zone as a safe haven for its illicit activities, most significantly drug production, weapon smuggling, hostage holding, training and directing attacks against the Colombian military outside this area.[14] As a result, President Pastrana was severely criticized for the concessions that he made to the guerrillas. The level of disagreement and criticism to Pastrana's policy for peace within his cabinet was evidenced by the resignation of the Colombian Defense Minister Rodrigo Lloreda together with 16 army generals, in disapproval for excessive concessions to the guerrillas and the continued extension of the demilitarized zone.[15] As a result, the experiment with the Distention Zone lasted from November 7, 1998 until February 21, 2002.

FARC Revenues

Like with all terrorist groups, the FARC had many options for financing their activities. Typically, terrorist or insurgent groups rely on some combination of state sponsorship, criminal activities, and legal activities.

---

11 Garry Leech, "Young Women Struggle to Survive in War-Torn Colombia," *Colombia Journal*, June 11, 2001, available at: http://www.colombiajournal.org/colombia67.htm.

12 Nicole Ferrand, "FARC's atrocities," The Americas Report: Center for Security Policy, May 31 2007, http://www.centerforsecuritypolicy.org/p14069.xml (accessed January 13, 2012).

13 Saúl H. Bandala Garza and David Vargas Schul, "Information Operations, An Evolutionary Step for the Mexican Navy," 56, Naval Postgraduate School Thesis, 2007.

14 Cragin and Hoffman. *Arms Trafficking and Colombia*, 13.

15 Nina M. Serafino, "Colombia: Conditions and U.S. Policy Options," CRS Report for Congress, February 2001, 20, https://www.hsdl.org/homesec/docs/crs/nps10-120803-05.pdf&code=afed3073f52ab7c3415c20be66189367 (accessed January 13, 2012).

In terms of state sponsorship, according to the supreme commander Manuel Marulanda Vélez, the FARC never received support from the Soviet Union or Cuba. Apparently, the main reason for this lack of support was that the insurgent leadership did not want to tie itself to the ideas, demands and expectations of outside interests like Cuba or the Soviet Union.[16] Nevertheless, the FARC appears to receive support from some leftist-socialist groups and governments that, in some cases covertly, support their cause. The most relevant support to the FARC from outside Colombia has come from Venezuela during the administration of President Hugo Chávez. According to some reports, the Venezuelan government has been a source of money, weapons, and safe haven for the FARC.[17] As part of his Bolivarian project, Chávez has repeatedly expressed rejection of U.S. policy in Southern America and sympathy for the FARC. In 2007, the position of Chávez as an intermediary with the FARC was strengthened when the Colombian President Alvaro Uribe asked Chávez to negotiate with the insurgents for the release of some hostages.[18]

In the years prior to the early 1980s, the insurgent organization obtained most of their financial resources from illicit activities, such as extortion, bank robberies, and kidnappings.[19] According to McDermott the average ransom demanded by FARC for its hostages is around $75,000 USD. Nevertheless, when the Japanese vice-president of the Yazali-Ciemel, Chikao Muramatsu, was kidnapped on February 22, 2001, the FARC demanded a ransom of 75 million dollars. Eventually, his body was found on November 24, 2003.[20]

In the early 1980s, the FARC got involved with Colombia's drug cartels, as a way to obtain resources to carry out their revolution. As a result, this has become a conflict that is fuelled by the gains of the drug trade. Despite the present

---

16   Paul E. Saskiewicz, "The Revolutionary Armed Forces of Colombia—People's Army (FARC-EP): Marxist-Leninist Insurgency or Criminal Enterprise?" 31, Naval Postgraduate School Thesis, 2005.

17   For more information about support by the Venezuelan government to the FARC, see Martin Arostegui, "Venezuela Aids FARC Rebels," http://newsmine.org/content.php?ol=war-on-terror/venezuela/venezuela-aids-farc-rebels.txt (accessed January 13, 2012).

18   "Delegados de las FARC ya están en Venezuela, Hugo Chávez [Hugo Chávez: FARC delegates are already in Venezuela]," *El Universal*, November 5, 2007 http://www.eluniversal.com.co/noticias/20071105/ctg_nal_delegados_de_las_farc_ya_estan_en_venezu.html (site discontinued); "Otages/Colombie: des représentants des FARC au Venezuela (Chávez) [Hostages/Colombia: FARC delegates in Venezuela (Chávez)]," *Le Monde*, http://www.lemonde.fr/web/depeches/0,14-0,39-33090128@7-60,0.html (site discontinued).

19   Alfredo Rangel Suárez, "Parasites and Predators: Guerrillas and the Insurrection Economy of Colombia," *Journal of International Affairs*, 53:2 (Spring 2000), quoted in Saskiewicz, "The Revolutionary Armed Forces of Colombia," 31.

20   Jeremy McDermontt, "Revelan finanzas de las FARC [FARC finances are exposed]," *BBC News*, February 1, 2005, http://news.bbc.co.uk/hi/spanish/latin_america/newsid_4224000/4224715.stm (accessed January 13, 2012).

involvement of the FARC in drug related activities; this was not always the case. In fact, until 1981, the insurgent leadership forbade the cultivation of coca and marijuana drugs, considering their cultivation as counter-revolutionary. From this perspective, it appears that the involvement of the guerrilla group with drug related activities was the result of the combination of a contest to gain the support of the population and an effort to preserve the social base of the movement.[21] With the level of violence and drug related activities associated with the FARC increasing since the early 1980s, the U.S. State Department identified this group as "the most dangerous international terrorist group based in the Western Hemisphere."[22]

The FARC gains revenue from the drug trade in a variety of ways. They impose "taxes" on the illegal drug trade, run processing laboratories, and even occasionally export drugs. In return, the guerrilla and paramilitary groups (with a total strength of approximately 26,500 men under arms) provide armed protection to illicit drugs plantations, laboratories and airstrips.[23]

According to estimates from the Colombian Ministry of Defense: The FARC has a precise schedule of fees, called *gramaje* or "grammage," for protection and services to drug producers and smugglers. As of October 1999, the FARC fees (in USD) were: production of basic paste, $15.70/kilo; chlorhydrate of cocaine, $52.60/kilo; protection of laboratories, $5263 each; protection of coca fields, $52.60/hectare; protection of poppy fields, $4210/hectare; security of landing strips, $2631 each; cocaine shipments, $10.50/kilo; river transportation of precursor chemicals, 20 percent of shipment value; international drug flights, $5263 each; and domestic drug flights, $2631 each.[24]

In addition to their involvement in coca plant harvesting, protection of crops, and processing of coca leaves to manufacture cocaine, the FARC is also known for having seized "control over various parts of the procurement chain—especially the link between Colombia and various smuggling rings in Brazil, Venezuela, Central America, and Mexico."[25] It is interesting to highlight the fact that according to Sam Logan:

> In the late 1990s, the FARC worked with Mexico's Tijuana Cartel, which controlled access to Southern California. When their middleman, Carlos Ariel Cherry, was captured in 2000, the FARC moved on to the Gulf Cartel. In 2004,

---

21 Angel Rabasa and Peter Chalk, *Colombian Labyrinth: The Synergy of Drugs and Insurgency and Its Implications for Regional Stability* (Santa Monica, CA: RAND, 2001), 26.

22 Asa Hutchinson, "Narco-Terror: The International Connection between Drugs and Terror" The Heritage Foundation, http://www.heritage.org/Research/HomelandSecurity/HL751.cfm (accessed January 13, 2012).

23 Saskiewicz, "The Revolutionary Armed Forces of Colombia," 24.

24 Colombian armed forces briefing, March 2000, quoted in Rabasa and Chalk, *Colombian Labyrinth*, 32-33.

25 Sam Logan, "Mexico's Uppermost Threat is Organized Crime," Mexidata.info, May 1, 2006, http://www.mexidata.info/id869.html (accessed January 13, 2012).

the FARC stopped working with the Gulf Cartel when it again lost connections with trusted middlemen. Now, it appears the FARC is working with El Chapo and the Sinaloa Cartel.[26]

The FARC also uses the legal economy to store funds and invest money for future profits. For example, the FARC invested in the Colombian stock exchange, the *Bolsa de Valores de Colombia.*[27] Among the legal business where the guerrilla has been known to participate are: agricultural cooperatives, transport cooperatives, security companies, as well as cattle and food industries.[28] In 2004, the Colombian military arrested Anayibe Rojas Valderrama aka Omaira Rojas Cabrera and *Sonia*, who allegedly administered the bank accounts that the rebel movement had in Panama. Rojas estimates that 60 percent of the resources obtained from drug traffic are allocated in the international financial system and the other 40 percent returns to Colombia in the form of weapons, munitions, supplies, goods and services for commercialization and as a way to launder money. He also point out that the money obtained from extortion and hostage ransoms paid by transnational corporations, particularly those related to the oil sector, goes directly to accounts that the FARC has abroad, particularly in the Panamanian Stock Exchange, the *Bolsa de Valores de Panama.*[29]

Overall, it is difficult to obtain reliable and accurate information about the sources of financing and the amounts involved, as different sources make their estimates taking into consideration different factors and information. In consequence, estimates of the amounts of money involved vary very significantly according to the different sources. In order to illustrate this, we can compare the following estimates:

1. Manuel Marulanda, leader of the FARC, wrote to its constituency that the group requires $230 million specifically to finance its war against the Colombian state.[30]
2. According to the Center for Defense Information, "drug profits from cocaine and heroin range anywhere from $100 million to $1 billion annually to purchase arms, attract new recruits and fund FARC operations.

26 Logan, "Mexico's Uppermost Threat is Organized Crime."
27 Junta de Inteligencia Conjunta, "Estimación de los ingresos y egresos de las FARC durante 2003 basados en información de inteligencia recolectada por las agencias del Estado," February 24, 2005, http://www.semana.com/documents/Doc-1760_2008926.pdf.
28 "Los negocios de las FARC," *Semana* (Santafé de Bogotá), April 5, 1999, http://www.semana.com/wf_InfoArticulo.aspx?IdArt=37855 (accessed January 13, 2012).
29 Franco Rojas, "Las finanzas de las FARC [FARC finances]," *La Prensa*, http://ediciones.prensa.com/mensual/contenido/2004/04/04/hoy/portada/1609481.html (accessed January 13, 2012).
30 "Los secretos del PC de Reyes," *Semana* (Santafé de Bogotá), March 8, 2008, http://www.semana.com/noticias-nacion/secretos-del-pc-reyes/110107.aspx (accessed January 13, 2012).

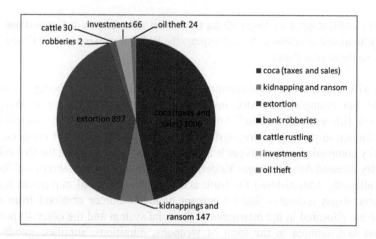

Figure 12.1　FARC Income (US$), 2003, according to the CJIJ

Source: Juna de Inteligencia Conjunta—JIC [Joint Intelligence Junta], "Estimación de los Ingresos y Egresos y Egresos de las FARC durante 2003 basados en la información de inteligencia recolectada por las agencias del estado [Estimate of FARC's income and expenditures during 2003 based on intelligence information gathered by state agencies]," http://usregsec. sdsu.edu/docs/Junta_de_InteligenciaFeb2005.pdf.

>　These profits have made the FARC one of the richest, if *not* the richest, insurgent group in the world."[31]

3. Some Colombian analysts estimate that FARC receives over $300 million annually from narcotrafficking.[32]
4. One of the best sources of information about FARC financing is a document of the Colombian Joint Intelligence Junta (CJIJ). This document estimates the income and expenditure of the FARC during 2003 based on intelligence gathered by different agencies from the Colombian state. According to an estimate from the CJIJ during 2003, the FARC obtained over $2 billion in income. According to the CJIJ report, drugs are the most significant source of income for the FARC, followed by extortion and kidnapping. See Figure 12.1.
5. According to a study made by the Financial Analysis and Information Unit (UIAF), in 2003 the FARC obtained $94 million. See Figure 12.2.

31　"Revolutionary Armed Forces of Colombia (FARC)," Center for Defense Information,　http://www.cdi.org/document/search/displaydoc.cfm?DocumentID=120 4&StartRow=21&ListRows=10&appendURL=&Orderby=Enabled&Program=&Da te_From=&Date_To=08/01/2007&Keywords=farc&ContentType=&Author=　(accessed January 13, 2012).

32　John A. Cope, "Colombia's War: Toward a New Strategy," Institute for National Defense Studies, October 2002, https://www.hsdl.org/homesec/docs/dtic/ADA421906.pdf &code=6775d93a129d79b20ad200db9799a0e0 (accessed January 13, 2012).

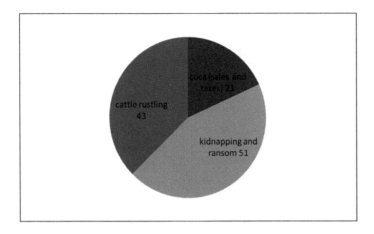

Figure 12.2   FARC Income according to the UIAF

Source: "Las Cuentas de las FARC [The FARC Accounts]." *Revista Semana*, January 30, 2005, http://www.semana.com/wf_InfoArticulo.aspx?IdArt=84475.

FARC Storage, Movement, and Expenditure of Finances

To store its money and to avoid the increasing surveillance by Colombian authorities, the FARC has chosen to hide some of its money underground in what is known as *Caletas* (Creeks).[33] These were used in urban and rural areas to store the huge amounts of money that could not be absorbed by the financial system.[34] During the 1990s, the FARC learned to use more effective ways to launder its finances. According to some estimates, "... as much as 80 percent [of FARC's resources], is not spent immediately on combat activity. Rather, it is invested in diverse ways in the formal economy, on the local, national and international levels."[35] Furthermore, according to Rangel the guerrillas' access to investment resources, has allowed it to develop a "symbiotic relationship with legal economic sectors such as banking and finance, which indiscriminately handle resources from both the formal economy and the underground economy, including finances of the guerrilla groups themselves."[36]

---

33   This term refers to an underground storage facility, a hideout, a compartment or a secret exit. It is used mainly in drug related activities, either to conceal drugs, weapons, or even kidnapped people from the authorities.

34   "¿La economía se libró de la plaga del narcodólar?" *El País*, January 2, 2007, http://www.elpais.com.co/paisonline/especiales/caletas/notas/Enero212007/dolar.html (site discontinued).

35   Suárez, "Parasites and Predators," 579.

36   Suárez, "Parasites and Predators," 584-5.

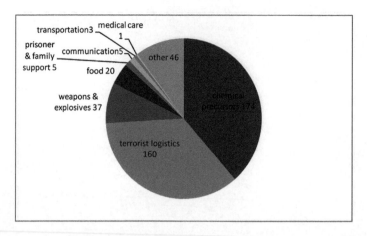

Figure 12.3   FARC Expenses according to the CJIJ

Source: Juna de Inteligencia Conjunta—JIC [Joint Intelligence Junta], "Estimación de los Ingresos y Egresos de las FARC durante 2003 basados en la información de inteligencia recolectada por las agencias del estado [Estimate of FARC's income and expenditures during 2003 based on intelligence information gathered by state agencies];" http://usregsec. sdsu.edu/docs/Junta_de_InteligenciaFeb2005.pdf.

For estimates of how the FARC spends its money, there are several reports with divergent figures. Nevertheless, as the two pie charts that follow show, both the CJIJ and the UIAF estimate that logistics represent the FARC's most significant concern to support its operations against the Colombian government while gaining or sustaining the support from the population.

The following stories are examples of how the FARC conducts its businesses abroad, deals drugs, and obtains weapons. Denis Silva Ruiz, aka El Peruano, was responsible for the purchase of 60,000 AK-47 assault rifles from Jordan between March and August 1999. These weapons were illegally bought in Jordan by members of the Peruvian Military Intelligence, sponsored by Vladimiro Montesinos, head of Peru's intelligence service. Silva Ruiz also bought drugs from the FARC and sent them abroad through routes that went through Venezuela and Brazil.[37]

Brazilian drug lord Luiz Fernando da Costa, aka Fernandinho Beira-Mar, was captured in Colombia on April 20, 2001 while in the company of FARC guerrillas. Colombian and Brazilian authorities have claimed that this constitutes proof of

---

37   "Capturan a enlace de la guerrilla de las FARC con Vladimiro Montesinos [Arrest of liaison between the FARC and Vladimiro Montesinos]," Fuerza Aérea Colombiana, February 20, 2007 http://www.fac.mil.co/index.php?idcategoria=18124&facmil_2007=89 5cab3a8844b63e9f3af174e5cade50 (accessed January 13, 2012).

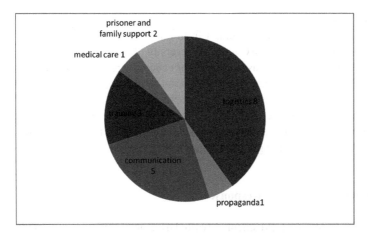

Figure 12.4   FARC Expenses according to UIAF

Source: "Las Cuentas de las FARC [The FARC Accounts]," *Revista Semana*, January 30, 2005, http://www.semana.com/wf_InfoArticulo.aspx?IdArt=84475.

further cooperation between the FARC and the drug lord.[38] According to Colombian sources, Beira-Mar admitted that he paid 10 million dollars monthly to the FARC to obtain 20 tons of coca, which he handed over to distributors in Brazil and exported to Europe via Surinam.[39] When Beira-Mar was arrested by the Colombian military, he declared that on a weekly basis he would buy approximately 600 kilograms of coca from Colombian peasants. He sold each kilogram for $3,500 in Brazil. From this money, he would receive $500 and give another $500 to the FARC. The rest of the money would stay in Brazil. Beira-Mar also declared that he personally handed 150,000 boxes of 20 rounds each (3,000,000 rounds) to Tomás Molina Caracas, aka El Negro Acacio,[40] and estimated that the FARC received approximately $10 million monthly from drug trafficking.[41] According to a report from the Brazilian Parliamentary Commission of Narcotraffic Investigation, Beira-Mar was linked with the ex Paraguayan general Lino Oviedo Silva, who was allegedly involved in drug trafficking. Beira-Mar had also contacts in Surinam, the former Dutch colony, through which he exported cocaine and received weapons from Europe,

---

38   Alain Labrousse, "The FARC and the Taliban's Connection to Drugs," *Journal of Drug Issues*, 35:1 (Winter 2005), 180.

39   Marcella, "The United States and Colombia," 26-7.

40   According to Colombian Ministry of Defense, Tomas Molina Caracas was killed on September 1st, 2007 during an air strike by the Colombian Air Force against the base camp of FARC's front 16. For additional information, see "Caen el 'Negro Acacio' y 16 terroristas más," Ministerio de Defensa Nacional, http://www.mindefensa.gov.co/index. php?page=181&id=6014 (site discontinued).

41   "La confesión de Fernandinho [The confession of Fernandinho]," *Revista Cambio*, http://www.geocities.com/lamorle/articulos-cambio1.html (accessed July 1, 2009).

mainly Russia. One of Beira's associates was Leonardo Días Mendona, related to Dino Bouterse (son of the ex-dictator from Surinam, Desi Bouterse.)[42]

The incursion of the FARC in a vast diversity of activities, most of them illicit, has allowed it to generate vast quantities of economic resources to finance its fight against the Colombian State. The diversification of its operations has allowed the FARC to obtain economic resources from practically all the different levels of the Colombian society, while extending its invisible tentacles practically over all the country's territory and even abroad; consolidating, as Latin America's oldest, most powerful and best funded guerrilla organization.

Colombian Government Response

The administration of President Álvaro Uribe implemented new strategies to respond to the threat of insurgent and paramilitary groups within the country. These strategies diametrically diverged from the strategy of its predecessor, President Ernesto Samper, whose administration was characterized by high levels of corruption and inadequate policies to counter the insurgency. Some of the most significant actions taken by the Colombian government in its fight against insurgency have been to fight corruption, promote intelligence based operations while increasing cooperation among national institutions, and increase international cooperation.

Fight Corruption

In 2002, according to a survey carried out by the Colombian Confederation of Chambers of Commerce, in the most important cities of the country, 70.3 percent of the businessmen who enter into contracts with government bodies "believed that corruption in government had increased in the two years since a prior survey had been taken."[43] As part of the Colombian government's effort to eradicate corruption, the Colombian military has also taken additional measures in order to discourage and fight corruption among its ranks. One of the most publicized actions was the trial of military personnel involved in the illegal disposition of money from the FARC found in Caletas.[44]

---

42   Eleonora Gosman, "Un capo narco reveló lazos con poderosos de Brasil [Druglord reveals links with powerful people in Brazil]," *El Clarin*, April 25, 2001, http://www.clarin.com/diario/2001/04/25/i-02801.htm (accessed January 13, 2012).

43   Luz E. Nagle, "Plan Colombia: Reality of the Colombian Crisis and Implications for Hemispheric Security," Carlisle: Strategic Studies Institute, December 12-13, 2002, http://www.strategicstudiesinstitute.army.mil/pdffiles/PUB13.pdf.

44   "Soldados, no guaqueros," *Semana* (Santafé de Bogotá), August 12, 2006, http://www.semana.com/wf_InfoArticulo.aspx?IdArt=96388 (accessed January 13, 2012).

Promote Intelligence Based Operations

During the initial efforts to consolidate Plan Colombia, the Colombian government emphasized the need to increase the cooperation among its institutions to counter drug related activities and insurgency, based on intelligence based operations. In 1999, as part of the strategy to obtain the support of the United States launching Plan Colombia, the administration of President Andrés Pastrana created the Financial Analysis and Information Unit (UIAF). The UIAF was created under the Ministry of Finance and Public Credit, with experts from different areas from the government on countering money laundering and the financial structures of the drug cartels. This unit has access to all the economic information, public or private, within the country. The advantage of this integrated approach was that the group was able to access information from the armed forces, the police, the Administrative Department of Security (Security Service) and the Office of the Attorney General, while also being able to access information from private companies and corporations in order to conduct significant operations against the infrastructure and financial networks of illegal groups.[45]

Later, during the administration of President Álvaro Uribe and as part of his Democratic Security and Defense Policy, the Colombian Military created the Joint Intelligence Junta (CJIJ) under the Colombian Military Staff D-2. The CJIJ was created to coordinate the different sources of the intelligence from the state to provide the President and the Minister of Defense for information for decision making. The CJIJ is headed by the minister or vice minister of Defense, and it is integrated by the Chief of the Intelligence Department of the Joint Staff, and the directors of the Army, Air Force, Navy, National Police, Administrative Department of Security (which is the Security Service of Colombia—DAS), as well as the director from the Financial Analysis and Information Unit.

In order to integrate and support its actions against insurgent and paramilitary groups, in 2007 the administration of President Álvaro Uribe modified the penal code to define and criminalize direct and indirect financing of terrorism, as well as money laundering. The relevance of this new law is described by the U.S. Department of State in its 2008 International Narcotics Control Strategy Report, as follows:

> The new law allows the UIAF to receive STRs [suspicious transaction reports] regarding terrorist financing, and freeze terrorists' assets immediately after their designation. In addition, banks are now held responsible for their client base and must immediately inform the UIAF of any accounts held by newly designated terrorists. Banks also have to screen new clients against the current

---

45   Andres Saenz, "Intelligence Management and the decision making process: views and comments based on the Colombian experience," Center for Hemispheric Defense Studies Santiago, Chile, October 28-30, 2003, 27, http://www.ndu.edu/chds/redes2003/Academic-Papers/9.Intelligence/1.Intelligence-New-Threats/Saenz-final.pdf.

list of designated terrorists before the banks are allowed to provide prospective clients with services report to the UIAF any accounts held by newly designated terrorists. Banks and financial institutions would also participate more actively in preventing suspicious financial activities, as they would be responsible for screening new clients against the current list of designated terrorists release by the Colombian government and before providing services.[46]

Another significant action taken by the Colombian government to counter illicit terrorist financing has been the increased supervision of charities and non-government organizations activity within the country. Today, the activities of these organizations are more regulated in order to ensure compliance with Colombian law and to guard against their involvement in terrorist activity.

One of the most evident achievements attained through the coordination of the military and the police has been the reduction of kidnappings in the country. Reducing kidnapping represents a major achievement because of the significance it had as a source of financing for insurgency. According to a report from the Presidency of Colombia released this year, kidnappings in the country have dropped very significantly since 2002. This at least gives hope that it is possible to achieve some successes against terror financing and these lessons can be applied to the remaining sources of FARC financing: drug trafficking and cattle stealing.[47]

Increase International Cooperation

The Colombian government has also worked with the international community, mainly the United States, to prevent and counter financial activities of terrorist and insurgent organizations. In this context, Colombia participates actively in international efforts to counter terrorist financing. Among the most relevant international agreements subscribed to by Colombia are: the United Nations International Convention for the Suppression of the Financing of Terrorism; the Financial Action Task Force of South America against Money Laundering (GAFISUD); and the Organization of American States Inter-American Drug Abuse Control Commission (OAS/CICAD) Money Laundering Experts Working Group.[48]

---

46   U.S. Department of State, Bureau of International Narcotics and Law Enforcement Affairs, "2008 International Narcotics Control Strategy Report (INCSR)," 94, http://www.state.gov/documents/organization/100919.pdf.

47   "10 Achievements: Security based on democracy," *República de Colombia*, Presidencia, http://www.presidencia.gov.co/resultados/english/documents/AVANsecurity_090427.pdf.

48   U.S. Department of State, Bureau of International Narcotics and Law Enforcement Affairs, "Colombia, International Narcotics Control Strategy Report," March 2007, 95, http://www.state.gov/p/inl/rls/nrcrpt/2007/vol2/html/80886.htm (site discontinued).

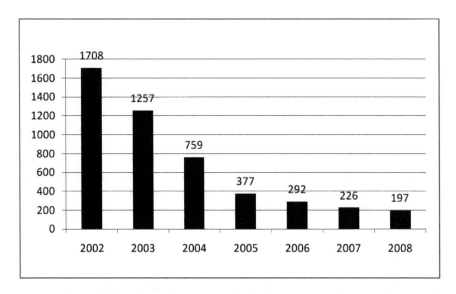

Figure 12.5   Persons Kidnapped in Colombia

Source: Adapted from President of Colombia, "10 Achievements: Security Based on Democracy," March 2009, http://www.presidencia.gov.co/resultados/english/documents/ AVANsecurity_090427.pdf.

As part of this international cooperation to counter illicit financing activities, the U.S. Treasury Office of Foreign Assets Control (OFAC) added the names of FARC and AUC leaders to the list of persons designated under the Foreign Narcotics Kingpin Designation Act. This action prohibits U.S. individuals and companies from doing business with the designated persons and blocks their assets found in U.S. jurisdiction.[49] The official designation of these groups as Foreign Terrorist Organizations also has the effect of increasing public awareness about these terrorist organizations and the concerns that the United States has about them.[50]

Meanwhile, as part of Colombia's ratification of the United Nations International Convention for the Suppression of the Financing of Terrorism, the Colombian and the U.S. governments closely monitor transactions that could disguise terrorist finance activities. Once narco-trafficking and terrorism-related accounts are identified within the Colombian financial system by either government, the Colombian government can take appropriate measures with the

---

49   U.S. Department of the Treasury, "Treasury Targets FARC Financial Network in Colombia," April 22, 2008, http://www.treasury.gov/press-center/press-releases/Pages/ hp938.aspx (accessed January 13, 2012).

50   Mark P. Sullivan, "Latin America: Terrorism Issues," CRS Report for Congress, January 22, 2007, 5, http://fpc.state.gov/documents/organization/81364.pdf.

country's financial institutions in order to block these assets.[51] It is interesting to highlight the fact that in early 2007, the Colombian Congress passed a law making terrorist financing a crime in its own right.[52] As a result, financial institutions within the country are required to cooperate with Colombian authorities providing necessary information to investigate suspicious accounts. Under this law, financial institutions are also required to take appropriate steps to verify the identity of new clients and to file "suspicious transactions reports" about doubtful financial activities. Also, as part of this regulation, financial institutions that operate within the country are required to maintain their records of financial transactions for a period of five years. Additionally, Colombian banks have taken measures, working with government and private consultants, to ensure the integrity of their operations.

Conclusion

Throughout its history the FARC have taken advantage of Colombia's geostrategic location, the weaknesses of the Colombian state and its willingness to resolve the conflict while protecting the population and its interests.

The interaction of these circumstances has been further exploited by the FARC as it diversified its activities, both legal and illegal, to obtain resources for its fight against the Government. The profits from these activities have grown to such levels that serious questionings have risen as to whether FARC's struggle is still driven by ideological reasons or has evolved to rest solely on economic interests.

Considering the large economic and material capabilities of its foe, the Colombian Government, supported by the United States, implemented Plan Colombia as the integral policy to guide its efforts to find a negotiated solution to the conflict while acting within the rule of law, democratic principles and total respect to the defense and protection of human rights.

The administration of President Álvaro Uribe has endorsed intelligence based operations, together with national and international cooperation, and the attention to social issues as the most important tools in the Colombian Government's fight against guerrilla organizations. This holistic approach to counter insurgency has proved more successful than the efforts made by previous administrations. Nevertheless, the issue of insurgency in Colombia will not be completely settled while these types of organizations have access to large amounts of economic resources to finance their struggle, and the support of some sectors of the population.

Thus, denying insurgent groups access to the financial system while gaining the support and credibility of the population have consolidated the fundamental

---

51 Bureau of International Narcotics and Law Enforcement Affairs, "2008 International Narcotics Control Strategy Report," 90.

52 Bureau of International Narcotics and Law Enforcement Affairs, "2008 International Narcotics Control Strategy Report," 94.

strategy of the Colombian State to counter these groups. So far, important progress has been made in this fight, nevertheless, the Colombian government must continue to innovate and consolidate its strategy to counter this ever-mutating enemy.

Chapter 13

The Finances of the National Liberation Army (ELN)

Celso Andrade-Garzon

Although the FARC is probably the best known terrorist group in Colombia, the National Liberation Army (ELN) has also been responsible for violence and mayhem. The ELN initially received much of its funding from the Soviet Union and Cuba, but transitioned to using extortion, kidnapping for ransom, and taxes on the drug trade to finance their operations. Since the early 2000s, violence associated with the ELN has decreased. This change, it could be argued, it a result of a greater effort by Colombia to address its terrorism and insurgency problem through international cooperation in the legal and financial realms, negotiations with the ELN, and better training and higher levels of aid from the United States through Plan Colombia to the Colombian security forces.

An Overview of the ELN

The ELN is Colombia's second-biggest Marxist insurgent guerrilla group with an estimated size of 3,500 to 5,000 rebels at its peak in 1998-2002. It has been operating in several regions of Colombia, especially in the southwest and near the Venezuelan border. The ELN was created in 1964 by Fabio Vasquez Castano, who introduced the main principles of Fidel Castro's Cuban Revolution and, at least at the beginning, was strongly influenced by a "liberation theology."[1] The ELN was founded by multiple, distinct groups. One group was comprised of

---

1   James D. Warrant, "The FARC and other Terrorist Groups in Colombia and South America: Are We Moving Closer to the Next Phase in the War on Terror?" *Military Intelligence Professional Bulletin*, October-December, 2002, http://findarticles.com/p/articles/mi_m0IBS/is_4_28/ai_94538591/?tag=mantle_skin;content (accessed January 13, 2012). According to the Vatican: "The theological and pastoral movement known as 'Liberation Theology' was born, first in the countries of Latin America which are marked by the religious and cultural heritage of Christianity, and then in other countries of the third world, as well as in certain circles in the industrialized countries... 'Theology of Liberation' refers first of all to a special concern for the poor and the victims of oppression, which in turn begets a commitment to justice." See Joseph Cardinal Ratzinger, "Instruction on Certain Aspects of the 'Theology Of Liberation'," http://www.vatican.va/roman_curia/congregations/cfaith/documents/rc_con_cfaith_doc_19840806_theology-liberation_en.html (accessed January 13, 2012).

urban, left-wing intellectuals with strong ties to rural farmers. They co-founded the ELN with a second group made up of radicalized oil-sector unionists. Additionally, radical members of the Catholic clergy joined the group in late 1965.[2] This was the first time that Christians and Marxists had joined together in a Colombian revolutionary movement.[3] It is important to highlight that this legacy of priestly influence played a significant role in initially limiting the involvement of the ELN in drug related activities on moral grounds. Nevertheless, as time passed and the strong religious influence diminished, the group has become increasingly involved with drugs. In terms of its history, analysts agree that "the ELN's trajectory can be divided roughly into four periods: rise and expansion (1964-74), crisis (1974-80), reconstitution (1980-90), and strategic adaptation (1990-2002). Although it has been through numerous crises and changes, important lines of continuity exist to this day."[4]

The ELN started its territorial expansion mainly in five areas: northeastern, northwestern, northern, southwestern and central Colombia. The territorial expansion of this group has focused on zones with natural resources such as oil, coal, gold and emeralds, and, especially in the south, coca.[5] In the past, the ELN has also attempted to benefit from the Colombian government's struggle with the Revolutionary Armed Forces of Colombia (FARC). The ELN tried to follow the precedent set by the FARC and negotiated with the Pastrana administration to obtain a demilitarized zone from the Colombian government. However, in this case civil resistance played a significant role and ultimately prevented the government from ceding any region to the ELN.[6] In 2005, the ELN began preliminary talks in Cuba with the Uribe administration, but they did not agree to a cease-fire.[7]

Insurgent groups in Colombia, which includes the ELN, as well as the FARC and the United Self Defense Forces of Colombia (AUC), are inextricably tied with the drug trade. Colombian terrorist groups, with "close to 30,000 well-armed, drug-financed terrorists," supply the U.S. with more than 80 percent of the cocaine and

---

2   Among the priests that joined the group where Camilo Torres, Aurentino Rueda, Domingo Laín, and others. "The ELN under the shadow of the Cuban Revolution," *El Colombiano*, 2002, http://www.elcolombiano.com/micolombiano/violencia/eln.htm (site discontinued).

3   MIPT, "National Liberation Army (Colombia)," http://www.tkb.org/Group.jsp?groupID=218 (site discontinued).

4   International Crisis Group, "Colombia: The Prospects for Peace with the ELN," October 4, 2002, 5.

5   Colombian Government and the United Nations Office on Drugs and Crime, *Colombia Coca Cultivation Survey, June 2004*, http://www.unodc.org/pdf/colombia/colombia_coca_survey_2003.pdf (site discontinued).

6   Anders Rudqvist, "ELN and the current peace talk scenario in Colombia," The Collegium for Development Studies, Uppsala University, February 2006, http://www.kus.uu.se/pdf/publications/Colombia/Intro.ELN.pdf, 5-6, 8.

7   Hugh Bronstein, "Colombia accuses ELN rebels of drug smuggling," *Reuters*, April 3, 2007, http://www.reuters.com/article/latestCrisis/idUSN03252737 (site discontinued).

as much as 70 percent of its heroin, and therefore is the focus of a significant share of the U.S. government's international counter-drug effort.[8] Colombia is Latin America's oldest formal democracy and a major U.S. partner in the fight against international narcotics trafficking and terrorism.[9] The Colombian government today focuses on defeating drug traffickers and insurgents by eliminating the coca crops and cocaine production that are the main facilitators of regional violence perpetrated by the ELN, FARC, and AUC.

In 1989, the Bush Administration began funding, with an average of $700 million per year, the Andean Counter-Drug Initiative (ACI), whose initial purpose was to decrease illicit drug crop cultivation and trafficking to reduce the impact of the illegal drug trade in America.[10] Furthermore, in 1999, the Colombian government proposed *Plan Colombia* as an integrated strategy whose successful implementation would end Colombia's civil war, strengthen its democratic pillars, revive the nation's economy, and negatively affect the narcotics industry.[11]

After the attacks of September 11, terrorism became the main concern of the U.S. Government. Since the U.S. recognized that terrorism and the illicit narcotics trade in Colombia are linked, the Bush Administration used the terrorism threat as a justification for keeping this plan going. Thus, the U.S. funded *Plan Colombia* as part of its counter drug and counter terrorism policies with an estimated $5 billion over the last seven years. Furthermore, in August 2002, U.S. Congress passed P.L. 107-206 (Public Law), which allows the Colombians to use U.S. aid for counter-terrorist and counter-insurgency as well as counter-narcotics purposes.[12]

Sources of Income

Before the 1990s, the ELN "largely depended on assistance from other leftist groups in Central America and Cuban leader Fidel Castro, and the Soviet Union."[13]

---

8   Roger F. Noriega, "U.S. Policy and Programs in Colombia," Testimony Before the House of Representatives Committee on Government Reform, Bureau Of Western Hemisphere Affairs, Washington, D.C., June, 2004, http://www.state.gov/p/wha/rls/rm/33676.htm (site discontinued). U.S. State Department, Bureau of Western Hemisphere Affairs, "Background Note: Colombia," March 2007.

9   Tina Rosenberg, "The Great Cocaine Quagmire: Can Bush resist expanding Clinton's Colombian Drug War?" *Rolling Stone*, April 12, 2001, 51.

10   The White House, "The Andean Counter-drug Initiative Assessment," http://www.whitehouse.gov/omb/expectmore/summary/10002210.2004.html (accessed January 13, 2012).

11   Garry Leech, "Plan Colombia: A Closer Look," The Information Network of the Americas (INOTA), July 2000, http://www.colombiajournal.org/plancolombia.htm (site discontinued).

12   Public   Law   107–2066,   http://frwebgate.access.gpo.gov/cgi-bin/getdoc.cgi?dbname=107_cong_public_laws&docid=f:publ206.107.pdf.

13   Liz Harper, "Colombia's Civil War: National Liberation Army (ELN)," PBS, Online NewsHour, August 2002, http://www.pbs.org/newshour/bb/latin_america/colombia/

Before the Cold War ended, "Cuban aid long sustained the organization."[14] Today, Cuba has been involved in the peace process, provides the ELN some degree of safe haven, medical care, and political consultation, but no direct funds.[15] Once the Soviet and direct Cuban financing stopped, the ELN looked for other sources of income.[16] The ELN has gone from a heavy reliance on extortion during the 1980s, to kidnapping during the 1990s, to a mixture of other illegal activities; however, getting accurate data related to the amount of income that the ELN gets from conducting illicit activities is difficult.[17] Nevertheless, some available numbers will provide a general idea of how much has been involved in the ELN finances.

The group is recognized as the organization responsible for many of the kidnappings that happen in the country.[18] In 2000, Alfredo Rangel Suarez argued that the ELN obtained "60 percent of its income through extortion, 30 percent from kidnapping, 6 percent from drug trafficking and 4 percent from cattle theft."[19] Today, Colombian officials estimate that drug-related income represents approximately fifty percent of total terrorist groups' revenue, with kidnapping ransoms, extortion, robberies, assassination, attacking petroleum installations, pipelines, and exploratory drilling sites—mostly owned or operated by foreign companies—completing the difference.[20] The ELN also has "legal" businesses such as transport companies, food, and gasoline distributors that allow them to launder money, to give liquidity in cash, to fix supplying difficulties, and to facilitate an effective intelligence network.[21] People that work for and profit from

---

players_eln.html (accessed January 13, 2012).

14   Robert Villa, "IRA/Cuban/Venezuelan Involvement in Colombia," *Newsmax.com*, August 20, 2001, http://archive.newsmax.com/archives/articles/2001/8/19/211055.shtml (accessed January 13, 2012).

15   U.S. Department of State, "Country Reports on Terrorism," The Office of the Coordinator for Counterterrorism, April 30, 2007, http://www.state.gov/s/ct/rls/crt/2006/82738.htm (site discontinued); "Colombia's Civil Warriors," PBS, Wide Angle, http://www.pbs.org/wnet/wideangle/shows/colombia/handbook2.html (accessed January 13, 2012); and LaVerle Berry et al., "A Global Overview of Narcotics-Funded Terrorist and Other Extremist Groups," Library of Congress, May 2002, 119.

16   Harper, "Colombia's Civil War: National Liberation Army (ELN)."

17   María Eugenia Pinto, Ivette Altamar, Yilberto Lahuerta, Luis Fernando Cepeda and Adriana Mera, *El Secuestro en Colombia: Caracterización y Costos Económicos* (National Planning Department, June 2004), 38.

18   Warrant, "The FARC and other Terrorist Groups in Colombia and South America."

19   Alfredo Rangel Suarez, "Parasites and predators: Guerrillas and the insurrection economy of Colombia," *Journal of International Affairs*, 53:2 (Spring 2000), 35.

20   Tom Marks, *Colombian Army Adaptation to FARC Insurgency*, Army War College Strategic Studies Institute, Carlisle Barracks, 7-9.

21   Nazih Richani, "The Political Economy of Violence: The War System in Colombia," *Journal of Inter-American Studies and World Affairs*, 39:2, Summer 1997, 3-4.

Table 13.1   Guerrilla Taxes on Colombian Cocaine and Heroin Industry, 1994-1995 (850 to 910 Colombian pesos=1 USD)

Activity	Tax Amount
Cultivation	10,000 pesos per hectare per month
Processing	5,000 pesos per kilo produced
Export from trafficking zone	20,000 to 30,000 pesos per kilo shipped
Operation of laboratory	Up to 12 million pesos per month
Use of airstrip	10 million pesos per month
Import of chemicals into zone	1,000 pesos per liter
Import of gasoline into zone	1,000 pesos per 55-gallon drum

Source: Patrick L. Clawson and Rensselaer W. Lee III, *The Andean Cocaine Industry* (New York, St. Martin's Press, 1996), 179.

ELN businesses develop a tight association and are available for supporting the organization either in logistic activities or for operational actions.[22]

Drug Trafficking and Drug Taxes

Estimates of narcotics-related revenue generated for the three Colombian guerrilla groups (FARC, ELN, and AUC) vary widely. An Institute for National Strategic Studies report published in 1997, estimated between U.S. $500 million to $1.5 billion in annual income for the three groups combined. A subsequent report estimated the drug-related income as low as U.S. $30-$100 million, but most reports settle on the U.S. $400-$600 million per year figure.[23] According to some estimates of Colombian analysts, the ELN receives over $200 million annually from narcotics trafficking.[24]

Although the ELN Central Command systematically denies any involvement in the drug business, a commonly acknowledged source of income for the organization is known as "weight," which is a tax that is levied between coca and poppy growers in return for "protection." According to Colombian governmental

---

22   Constanza Vieira, "Colombia: Uribe Prepared to Sign Agreement with ELN," Inter Press Service, August 15, 2007, http://ipsnews.net/news.asp?idnews=38905 (accessed January 13, 2012).

23   "El nuevo narcotráfico," *Semana*, September 23, 2002, http://www.semana. com/wf_InfoArticulo.aspx?IdArt=65574 (accessed January 13, 2012); Nina M. Serafino, "Colombia: Conditions and U.S. Policy Options," Congressional, Research Service (CRS) Report for Congress, Updated February 12, 2001, 12.

24   John A. Cope, "Colombia's War: Toward a New Strategy," *Strategic Forum*, No. 194, October 2002, 3, https://www.hsdl.org/homesec/docs/dtic/ADA421906.pdf&code=67 75d93a129d79b20ad200db9799a0e0 (accessed January 13, 2012).

sources, the ELN earned, in 1995, approximately $5 million from weight. Table 13.1 lists the taxes imposed in the drug industry by the guerillas. The figures amply support the view that income received from narco-trafficking as of the mid-1990s provides for a significant amount in guerrilla groups' revenues.[25]

Kidnapping

The NGO Pax Christi Holland states that the ELN obtained about $1 billion by kidnappings in the 1990s.[26] Similarly, the Colombian Administrative Department of Security (DAS) estimates that the FARC and the ELN obtained $1.5 billion from abduction during the period 1991-1999 and that "in 1998 alone, the ELN obtained U.S. $84 million from ransoms and U.S. $255 million from extortion."[27] In 1998, the ELN agreed to no longer kidnap pregnant women, children, and the elderly, but requested $40 million from the government to maintain its fighters for the envisaged six-month ceasefire. The Pastrana administration denied the request because they saw the ELN's relevancy and strength decreasing.[28]

Of a total of 3,041 kidnappings registered by the foundation "Free Country" in 2001, 800 were carried out by the ELN. Most of these "financing" actions have targeted employees of foreign petroleum corporations, which the guerillas view as exploitative apparatuses of hostile interests.[29] Such victims often are "sold" to crime organizations, which then negotiate the payment of ransom to the relatives of their hostages. In 2001, Jeremy McDermott stated that "there is one abduction every three hours in Colombia—the majority carried out by the FARC or the country's second rebel force, the National Liberation Army."[30] According to other sources, between January and July of 2002, the ELN kidnapped 470

25 Cited in Gernot W. Morbach, "Terrorism and Organized Crime: The Alliance of Tomorrow? How to Counter a Possible Future Threat," Naval Postgraduate School thesis, June 2, 1998, 105.

26 "¿Quién es el enemigo?" *Semana*, June 9, 2003, http://www.semana.com/especiales/quien-enemigo/70787-3.aspx (accessed January 13, 2012).

27 Global Defense Group, "National Liberation Army (ELN) – Colombia," MIPT Terrorism Knowledge Base, http://www.globaldefensegroup.com/terrorist-networks/national-liberation-army-eln-colombia.html?Itemid=35 (site discontinued).

28 International Crisis Group, "Colombia: The Prospects for Peace with the ELN," 2002, 2

29 Shawn Choy, "In the Spotlight: The National Liberation Army," Center for International Policy, Colombia Project, June 21, 2002, http://www.cdi.org/terrorism/eln.cfm (accessed January 13, 2012); Jeremy McDermott, "Colombia's rebel kidnappers," *BBC News*, January 7, 2002, http://news.bbc.co.uk/1/hi/world/americas/1746914.stm (accessed January 13, 2012).

30 Jeremy McDermott, "Colombian rebels 'stronger than ever'," *BBC News*, May 28, 2001, http://news.bbc.co.uk/1/hi/world/americas/1355513.stm (accessed January 13, 2012).

people.[31] In 2003, government sources estimated the ELN received $74 million annually from kidnappings.[32]

While the ELN "conducted 3,931 kidnappings between 1996 and 2001, the number dropped to 1,458 kidnappings between 2002 and 2006. The ELN has gone from 797 abductions in 2002 to 66 in 2006."[33] According to Colombian officials, the ELN is having increasing difficulties in carrying out abductions, due to logistical and operational problems in keeping the individuals hidden from the Colombian military and other illegal armed groups.[34] This is why government sources believe that between 2005 and 2007, drug trafficking gradually replaced kidnapping as the ELN's main source of income.[35]

Extortion and Theft

Table 13.2 shows how Colombian terrorist groups—including the ELN—have attacked oil pipelines (especially the Caño Limón Coveñas pipeline) for extortion and theft. From 1986 onwards statistics show that oil pipelines have been bombed over a thousand times and hundreds of oil-company employees have been kidnapped.[36] In 2002, the weekly Colombian magazine *Semana* asserted that the ELN has benefited more from oil than all the oil multinationals. "Pipelines are like as an automatic teller for ELN ... they learned to milk the cow without killing it."[37]

---

31   International Crisis Group, "Colombia: The Prospects for Peace with the ELN," 10-11. See also Marianne Moor and Liduine Zumpolle, *The Kidnap Industry in Colombia: Our Business?* Pax Christi (Netherlands), 26, 33-4, www.ikvpaxchristi.nl/catalogus/uploaded_file.aspx?id=167 (accessed January 13, 2012).

32   United Nations Development Program (UNDP) and Colombian Observatory of the Presidential Program for Human Rights and Vice-President of the Republic, *Informe Nacional de Desarrollo Humano Colombia – 2003: Conflicto Callejón con Salida*, Bogotá, 2003, 285.

33   International Crisis Group, "Colombia: Moving Forward with the ELN?" Latin American Briefing No. 16, October 11, 2007, 7, http://www.crisisgroup.org/en/regions/latin-america-caribbean/andes/colombia/b016-colombia-moving-forward-with-the-eln.aspx (accessed January 13, 2012).

34   Mauricio Rubio, "Kidnapping and Armed Conflict in Colombia," Paper presented at the PRIO Workshop on Techniques Of Violence In Civil War, Oslo, August 2004, 13, http://uniset.ca/terr/art/colombiakidnapping.pdf.

35   International Crisis Group, "Colombia: Moving Forward with the ELN?" 7; and Hugh Bronstein, "Interview, Colombia accuses ELN rebels of drug smuggling," *Reuters*, April 3, 2007, http://www.reuters.com/article/latestCrisis/idUSN03252737 (accessed January 13, 2012).

36   N. Feiling, "Plan Colombia and violence in the country," 2004, http://www.termpapergenie.com/Columbiaandviolence.html (accessed January 13, 2012).

37   "El nuevo narcotráfico," *Semana*.

Table 13.2   Attacks on Oil Pipelines, 2001-2004

	2001	2002	2003	2004
All Pipelines	263	74	179	103
Caño Limón Coveñas Pipeline	170	41	34	17

Source: Ministry of Defense, Government of Colombia.

The ELN also controls 20 percent of the national gold and coal production, which generates an annual income of $20 million. The companies that mine these minerals pay their "vaccination" fees either in cash or with mines that the ELN itself works."[38] Furthermore, the Colombian Department of Administrative Security (DAS) estimates that the ELN obtained $255 million dollars from 1999 to 2002 from fuel theft.[39]

The ELN also puts people up for election in controlled areas so they can control the politicians once they win office in order to profit from municipal budgets.[40] In areas of ELN control, there is not a governor who does not have his position without the backing of the ELN and most of the business contractors are sponsored by narco-guerillas. Moreover, although the Constitution establishes a separation of powers, these politicians also promote the appointment of public prosecutors proposed by insurgents. "Here the candidates are from the FARC or the ELN," states an unidentified citizen.[41]

When the ELN controls a region, they collect a monthly protection fee or "vaccination" from property and business owners. For example, contractors often must pay the ELN between 5 and 15 percent of the contract.[42] The ELN also collects monthly "taxes" on property owners, with each property greater than 50 hectares required to pay $25 dollars; coca growers, $2 dollars per hectare; and all transactions of land worth more than $10,000 dollars have to pay $350 dollars.[43] If the targets refuse to pay it, they are eligible for kidnapping or other some sort of violent attack.

---

38   "ELN: Fidel Castro's personal project," *Executive Intelligence Review*, 22:45, November 10, 1995, http://larouchepub.com/other/1995/2245_eln.html (accessed January 13, 2012); Richani, "The Political Economy of Violence," 3-4.

39   "El Gran Negocio de la guerrilla," *Semana*, August 3, 1992, http://www.semana.com/wf_InfoArticulo.aspx?IdArt=49638 (accessed January 13, 2012).

40   "ELN: Fidel Castro's personal project."

41   "ELN: Fidel Castro's personal project;" "El nuevo narcotráfico," *Semana*; and Virginia M. Bouvier, "New Hopes for Negotiated Solutions in Colombia," United States Institute of Peace, September 25, 2007, 25, http://www.usip.org/files/resources/Sept2007.pdf.

42   "La sombra de Martín Llanos, *Semana*, October 6, 2007, http://www.semana.com/wf_InfoArticulo.aspx?IdArt=106720 (accessed January 13, 2012); and "El Gran Negocio de la guerrilla," *Semana*.

43   "¿Quién es el enemigo?" *Semana*.

Storage and Transfer of Funds

Various rebel groups in Colombia are said to have laundered millions of dollars using many different methods. Procedural difficulties and limited resources for anti-money laundering programs constrain the effectiveness of the Colombian government's efforts. Corruption, as well as the high demand for laundering funds related to criminal activity, all contribute "to keep Colombia a major money laundering country."[44] For example, Colombian authorities say they have identified 800 suspect bank accounts allegedly used by left wing rebels to launder millions of dollars.[45] The unregulated electronic financial environment is also a concern regarding terrorist fund transfers and money laundering. Using the internet, for example, cross border transfers can be done in seconds. As such, "illegal transactions made for terrorist organizations and organized crime are inevitably lost among the thousands of legal transactions made within the complex global financial network."[46]

There is an increase in human smuggling of U.S. and other foreign currencies and an increase in the number of shell companies operating in Colombia. Smart cards, internet banking, and the dollarization of the economy of neighboring Ecuador represent some of the growing challenges. Debit cards are used "outside of Colombia and the transfer of funds out of and then back into Colombia by wire through different exchange houses to create the appearance of a legal business or personal transaction."[47]

Expenditures

A percentage of the money raised goes to front commanders to pay remittances and to support other costs of operation. The ELN spends an estimated $100 to 150 per month for each rebel. However, according to the 2002 head of Colombia's anti-drug police, "the guerrillas can pay their troops the equivalent of $300 to $400 a month, while professional soldiers in the Colombian army make a little more than $200 a month."[48] Moreover, according to several anonymous rebels and intelligence officials and a fieldwork conducted by the Colombian weekly *Semana* in 2003, "money can buys arms, logistic, corrupts governments and silences

---

44   U.S. Department of State, "Country Reports, Part II," INCSR 2004, 156, http://www.state.gov/documents/organization/30188.pdf.

45   "Colombia targets rebel finances," *BBC News*, August 29, 2002, http://news.bbc.co.uk/2/hi/americas/2222626.stm (accessed January 13, 2012).

46   Patrick S. Tibbetts, "Terrorist Use of the Internet and Related Information Technologies," U.S. Army Command and General Staff College, 2001, 21.

47   U.S. Department of State, "Country Reports, Part II," 156.

48   David Scanlan, "Colombian Rebels Cost Nation $12.5 Billion since 1990, Study Finds," *Bloomberg Business, News*, January 1996, 2.

witnesses." Further, the same unidentified sources stated that "it is easier to knock down an airplane with tiles than with a missile ... Instead of spending million in armament we [narco-guerillas] can buy a maintenance technician to do 'the job' almost spending nothing." Finally, the same article concludes that narco-money is "the substitute for popular support."[49]

Countermeasures

Colombian based terrorist groups have been weakened as a result of aggressive actions by the military and police, but these groups continue to murder, kidnap, and terrorize the local population. Governmental authorities have to expand counter-narcotics and counter-terrorist group operations to confiscate resources in Colombia and globally; and gain control of the drug producing regions.[50] They must disrupt terrorists' financial infrastructures, specifically their formal and underground methods for transferring funds across borders.[51] The Uribe and Santos administrations focused on defeating and demobilizing Colombia's terrorist groups through its "democratic security" policy. The government of Colombia and the ELN conducted several rounds of peace talks, but still no agreements were reached. "The ELN remained in the field, but with limited resources, a dwindling membership, and reduced offensive capability."[52]

Enforcement of terrorism financing laws continues to be a challenge for Colombia. Limited resources for prosecutors and investigators have made financial investigations problematic. Continued difficulties in establishing the base predicate offense further contributes to Colombia's limited success in achieving terrorist financing convictions. Congestion in the court system, procedural impediments and corruption remain continuing problems.[53] Thus, the Colombian government should move promptly to eliminate procedural impediments and

49 "¿Quién es el enemigo?" *Semana*.

50 International Crisis Group, "Colombia: President Uribe's Democratic Security Policy," Latin America Report No. 6, November 13, 2003, 7-8, http://www.crisisgroup.org/en/publication-type/media-releases/2004/latam/colombia-president-uribes-democratic-security-policy.aspx (accessed January 13, 2012).

51 The White House, "National Drug Control Strategy," FY 2003 Budget Summary, February, 2002, http://www.whitehousedrugpolicy.gov/publications/pdf/budget2002.pdf.

52 U.S. Department of State, "Country Reports on Terrorism, Chapter 2— Country Reports: Western Hemisphere Overview," The Office of the Coordinator for Counterterrorism, April 30, 2007, http://www.state.gov/s/ct/rls/crt/2006/82735.htm (site discontinued).

53 "International Narcotics Control Strategy Report," Bureau for International Narcotics and Law Enforcement Affairs, March 2006, http://www.state.gov/p/inl/rls/nrcrpt/2006/vol2/html/62143.htm (site discontinued).

take other necessary steps to additional strengthen its anti-money laundering and counterterrorist financing programs.[54]

Vanda Felbab-Brown has examined the relationship between counter-drug and counter-terrorism efforts by explaining how the production and trafficking of drugs fuels militarized conflicts. She says that in addition to financial profits, drugs also bring political and military benefits. She challenges the prevailing rationale behind U.S. drug policies (which argue that a suppression of illicit crops will decrease the strength of those Colombian terrorist groups that have turned to drugs) by arguing that suppression strategies may backfire as peasants involved in the cultivation of coca leaves and the drug process give their support to the insurgents.[55] Colombia's internal conflict shows the interdependence that exists between terrorist groups and peasants, both of whom rely on drug trafficking for their survival. This interdependence blocks any attempt to improve plans of social development and border integration.[56]

Colombia Efforts

Colombia is a member of institutions that pursue terrorist and financial crimes such as the Financial Action Task Force of South America against Money Laundering (GAFISUD), the Organization of American States Inter-American Drug Abuse Control Commission (OAS/CICAD), the Money Laundering Experts Working Group, the UN International Convention for the Suppression of the Financing of Terrorism, the UN Convention Against Transnational Organized Crime, and has signed, but not ratified, the UN Convention Against Corruption.[57]

Colombia has a strong banking system that has been cooperative with law enforcement activity based on judicial orders. Banks and other financial sector entities are also mindful of U.S. Patriot Act provisions that require action against criminals that fall under the jurisdiction of that act. Most obligated entities are required to establish "know-your-customer" provisions and are held responsible for their client data base and must maintain records of financial transactions for five years. Charities, alternative remittance systems, and NGOs are regulated to

---

54   U.S. Department of State, "International Narcotics Control Strategy Report: Colombia," Bureau of International Narcotics and Law Enforcement Affairs, March 2007, http://www.state.gov/p/inl/rls/nrcrpt/2007/vol2/html/80886.htm (site discontinued).

55   Vanda Felbab-Brown, "The Coca Connection: Conflict and Drugs in Colombia and Peru," *The Journal of Conflict Studies*, 25:2, Winter 2005.

56   Julia E. Sweig, "What Kind of War for Colombia?" *Foreign Affairs*, September/ October 2002.

57   Virginia M. Bouvier, "Evaluating U.S. Policy in Colombia," A Policy Report from the IRC (International Relations Center) Americas Program, May, 2005, http://americas. irc-online.org/reports/2005/0505colombia.html (site discontinued).

ensure compliance with law and to guard against their involvement in terrorist activity.[58]

Furthermore, there is cooperation between European countries (through the European Police Office [EUROPOL]) and Colombia, which together have undertaken measures such as: "the freezing of funds and other financial assets and economic resources [attributed to those organizations]; ensuring that funds, financial assets or economic resources or financial and other related services are not made available, directly or indirectly, for the benefit of [these] entities; and police and judicial co-operation between the EU Member States."[59] Additionally, France signed a separate security cooperation agreement with Colombia in July 2003. Also, cooperation in combating the flow of drugs is provided for in a port control agreement that was concluded with the Netherlands.[60]

U.S. Efforts

Julia E. Sweig, the 2002 Deputy Director for Latin America Studies at the Council on Foreign Relations, stated that there are several policies that the U.S. should pursue. She argues that:

> Washington needs to conduct a serious debate over how to decrease demand for drugs in America. Colombia's problems will not be solved while U.S. consumption continues to fuel a massive narcotics industry. Meanwhile, the Treasury Department should enforce the financial sanctions that apply to the Colombian terrorist groups on the State Department's terrorist list, seizing their bank accounts and other assets. Likewise, the American private sector should declare a moratorium on paying bribes to grease the wheels of investment in Colombia and throughout the Andes. And the U.S. should appoint a bipartisan figure as a special envoy to begin the process of knitting together support and participation from Colombia's neighbors, the International Monetary System, the EU, Canada, and Mexico into a comprehensive regional diplomatic initiative.[61]

Today, the U.S. provides Anti-Terrorism Assistance (ATA), training, and equipment to Latin American countries to help improve their capabilities in

---

58   Martin J. Manning, "Terrorist Organizations, Freezing of Assets," Encyclopedia of Espionage, Intelligence, and Security, 2004, http://www.espionageinfo.com/Te-Uk/Terrorist-Organizations-Freezing-of-Assets.html (accessed January 13, 2012).

59   An Vranckx, "European policies on Colombia," IPIS, March 2005, 28-29, www.ipisresearch.be/download.php?id=69 (accessed January 13, 2012).

60   Vranckx, "European policies on Colombia."

61   Vranckx, "European policies on Colombia;" Sweig, "What Kind of War for Colombia?"

countering terrorism financing.[62] The Treasury Department has set up a Terrorist Tracking Task Force (TTTF), the diplomatic arm of Treasury's enforcement effort, which works with foreign governments in blocking terrorists' access to funds. Within the State Department, a new Counterterrorism Finance Unit (CFU) has been established to oversee international information-sharing and technical assistance programs relating to terrorist finances. As part of its integrated inter-agency strategy, the U.S. has the National Money Laundering Strategy (NMLS) which is composed of U.S. agencies, as well as foreign country partners and other actors from the private sector, whose mission is to identify appropriate financial targets through technology, intelligence, investigative resources, and regulations to locate and freeze the assets of terrorists, wherever they may be located.[63]

Combined U.S. and Colombian Efforts

First, the U.S. has maintained lines of communication, shared resources, exchanged information and new ideas, provided positive and negative feedback in a bottom up, top down, bilateral, and multilateral flow, and promoted Colombian institutions that embraced the idea of a joint effort to reduce illegal activities.[64] To expand counter narcotics and counter insurgent groups operations, the U.S. provided advice, assistance, training, equipment, and intelligence to support the Colombian government's objectives to locate, interdict, and isolate resources;[65] freeze, confiscate, and close accounts both in Colombia and globally; and gain control of the drug producing regions.[66]

Second, since the end of the Cold War, the Pentagon has conducted specialized training exercises using U.S. Special Operations Forces (SOF) with every army in the Andean region.[67] The U.S. provides Anti-Terrorism Assistance (ATA), training, and equipment in Latin America.[68] Building on the U.S. ATA, Colombia is improving its counter terrorism capabilities and strengthening its political will to combat terrorism in its own country.

Third, the U.S. Foreign Internal Defense program (FID) is designed to help foreign nations defend against existing or potential internal threats. According to the U.S. military, "while anti-drug operations are a sustained focus of the SOF

---

62 Mark P. Sullivan, "Latin America: Terrorism Issues," Foreign Affairs, Defense, and Trade Division, CRS Report for the Congress, January, 2007, http://www.fas.org/sgp/crs/terror/RS21049.pdf.

63 Manning, "Terrorist Organizations, Freezing of Assets."

64 Noriega, "U.S. Policy and Programs in Colombia."

65 "Andean coca spat exposes growing rift over Washington's drug war," *International Herald Tribune*, December 22, 2006.

66 The White House, *National Drug Control Strategy*, February 2002, 4, 40, 121, 158, 198, http://www.whitehousedrugpolicy.gov/publications/pdf/budget2002.pdf.

67 Douglas Farah, "A Tutor to Every Army in Latin America: U.S. Expands Latin American Training Role," *Washington Post* July 13, 1998, A01.

68 Sullivan, "Latin America."

effort in Latin America, the priority mission is military-to-military engagement."[69] Section 2011 of Title 10 governs SOF training with foreign militaries; it is widely applied in Colombia, where SOF participate mainly in counter narcotics operations, training and intelligence gathering. The SOF mission is oriented to stop "ungoverned areas" from becoming sanctuaries for terrorists and drug traffickers.[70]

Fourth, the U.S. Congress has authorized financing for training, security and infrastructure essential for Colombian judges, prosecutors, politicians, and witnesses. Extradition to the U.S. is still the sanction that drug criminals fear most and public acceptance of this measure is increasing.[71] Colombia exchanges information with U.S. law enforcement agencies and is working to overcome several weaknesses in its own court system.[72] There is also a possibility Washington might request extradition of ELN commanders wanted for kidnapping U.S. citizens.[73]

Fifth, the Washington-Bogota axis works to disrupt terrorists' financial infrastructures, specifically formal and underground methods for cross-border funds transfers through banks, businesses, financial companies, currency exchangers, and NGOs that channel funds for terrorist groups.[74] Working with the Department of Homeland Security's Office of Immigration and Customs Enforcement (ICE), Colombia has established a prototype Trade Transparency Unit (TTU) that examines anomalies in trade data for signs of customs fraud and trade-based money laundering.[75] The Treasury Department has also set up a Terrorist Tracking Task Force (TTTF) to work with foreign governments to block terrorists' access to funds.[76]

Sixth, the U.S. has been funding Plan Colombia since 2000. In August 2002, Congress passed Public Law 107-206 allowing Colombia to use U.S. aid for counter-terrorist and counter-insurgency as well as counter-narcotics purposes.[77] According to the Latin America Working Group, between 1997 and 2007, Colombia's police and military will have received "almost exactly two out of

69   Dana Priest, "U.S. Military Trains Foreign Troops," *Washington Post*, July 12, 1998, A01.

70   Linda Robinson, *Master of Chaos* (New York: Perseus Books Group, 2004)

71   Aldo Civico, "Rethinking U.S.-Colombia Policy, The U.S. and Colombia Can Break Cycles of Violence and Repression," Center for American Progress, May 2007, http://www.americanprogress.org/issues/2007/05/pdf/colombia_us_report.pdf.

72   Bouvier, "Evaluating U.S. Policy in Colombia."

73   "Extradition of ELN guerrilla leaders prompted U.S.A., says FBI chief in Colombia," *El Tiempo*, July 15, 2007.

74   The White House, *National Drug Control Strategy*.

75   International Crisis Group, "Colombia: Presidential Politics and Peace Prospects," Latin America Report No. 14, June 16, 2005, http://www.crisisgroup.org/en/publication-type/media-releases/2005/latam/colombia-presidential-politics-and-peace-prospects.aspx (accessed January 13, 2012).

76   Manning, "Terrorist Organizations, Freezing of Assets."

77   http://frwebgate.access.gpo.gov/cgi-bin/getdoc.cgi?dbname=107_cong_public_laws&docid=f:publ206.107.pdf.

every three dollars of U.S. security assistance for the entire region. Thanks to Plan Colombia, aid to Colombia today is about six times what it was in 1997."[78]

Lesson Learned

In order to succeed in disrupting terrorist financing activities, some lessons should be learned from what has been done in the past when dealing with terrorist organizations:

- Any regional policy must be instituted only if the U.S. is willing to make the required commitments to see it through. Good policy is a product of a comprehensive interagency effort at the national level and must have total "buy-in" by the agencies partners and partner nations that develop it.
- Tacit support given to strengthening the rule of law and institutions should go along with increasing the capacity to deliver services such as education, health, and infrastructure.[79]
- Policy and strategy must be weighed against these realities rather than based on U.S. ideology, politics, or immediate threats.[80]
- Because problems do not occur in a vacuum, solutions need regional approaches or the U.S. runs the risk of failure or of creating more problems in neighboring countries. Drug cartels quickly adapted to Colombian interdiction efforts by expanding their operations to other countries in the region. U.S. policy should focus properly on regional issues vice seeking a single solution to a narrowly defined problem.[81]

The U.S. policy has to support the Colombian government's efforts to defend and strengthen its democratic institutions, free the country from narcotics and terrorism issues, promote the rule of law and respect for human rights, address immediate humanitarian needs, and foster socio-economic development and investment.[82] Besides U.S. Congressional support, any policy should include the President's

---

78 "Below the Radar: U.S. Military Programs with Latin America, 1997-2007," A joint publication from the Center for International Policy, the Latin America Working Group Education Fund, and the Washington Office on Latin America, March, 2007, 3, http://www.lawg.org/storage/documents/below%20the%20radar.pdf.

79 House of Representatives, "Plan Colombia: Major Successes and New Challenges," Committee on International Relations, 109 Congress, First Session, May 11, 2005, 16, http://commdocs.house.gov/committees/intlrel/hfa21204.000/hfa21204_0f.htm (accessed January 13, 2012).

80 House of Representatives, "Plan Colombia," 40, 51

81 Martha Crenshaw, "Terrorism, Strategies, and Grand Strategies," in *Origins of Terrorism*, edited by Walter Reich (Washington, D.C.: Woodrow Wilson Center Press, 1998), 84-86

82 Noriega, "U.S. Policy and Programs in Colombia."

guidelines, objectives, actions, ways, and means required, the expected financial costs to the U.S., Colombia, and any other country or entity to achieve those aims, and the expected time schedule for achieving the objectives.

Conclusion

Colombia has had some recent successes against the ELN. According to Colombian government sources, from 2002 to 2007 ELN military actions, including combat with security forces, ambushes, piracy and acts of terrorism, have gradually fallen from 195 per year to 19. Acts of terrorism dropped from 79 in 2002 to two in the first seven months of 2007. Combat with security forces dropped from four in 2002 to one each in 2006 and the first half of 2007. Ambushes dropped from eight in 2002 to five in 2006 and one in 2007.[83]

The ELN does not exclusively dominate any part of Colombian territory, unlike the FARC, which controls an estimated 35 percent or more of the national territory, mainly in rural, sparsely populated areas.[84] Both the FARC and ELN say they are fighting for land reforms to narrow the wide gap that separates rich and poor. But even left-wing Colombian politicians say the groups have almost no popular support.[85] In the past, the public's attitude toward the rebels was not a strong enough factor to shift the balance, but that has changed since Uribe and Santos have made progress in improving the security situation and has carefully cultivated leverage to use against the rebel groups. The degree of this change is evident in ELN's statement about giving up kidnapping; in 2004 and 2005, the group refused to cease kidnappings as part of cease-fire negotiations. The talks collapsed with no significant progress, in no small part because of this refusal. The ultimate goal of the negotiations for the ELN is some form of limited amnesty, such as the demobilization agreement the government reached with the paramilitaries.[86] The movement risks implosion or fragmentation as well as the possibility that it could not fully implement a ceasefire, since its internal cohesion is weak.[87]

Despite these recent successes, future success against terrorist financing activities in Colombia demands a U.S. policy that promotes Colombian institutions to embrace the joint effort concept in order to break down illegal financing activities. Colombian terrorist groups have so far found ways to continue to fund their fight by adapting and finding new sources of income. Through either "taxing" the lands of drug lords, or by directly participating in drug trafficking, "groups in

---

83   International Crisis Group, "Colombia: Moving Forward with the ELN?" 2.

84   Vieira, "Colombia: Uribe Prepared to Sign Agreement with ELN."

85   Bronstein, "Interview-Colombia accuses ELN rebels of drug smuggling."

86   "Colombia: An End to ELN Kidnappings and a Greater Focus on FARC," Stratfor, August 4, 2007, http://intellibriefs.blogspot.com/2007/08/colombia-end-to-eln-kidnappings-and.html (accessed January 13, 2012).

87   International Crisis Group, "Colombia: Moving Forward with the ELN?" 14.

Colombia have demonstrated how a connection to a narco-economy can lead to that group's self-perpetuation."[88] Future success will depend on whether Colombia can adapt their strategy and focus as well.

---

88   Juan Camilo Chaparro, Michael Smart, Juan Gonzalo Zapatas, "Intergovernmental transfers and municipal finance in Colombia," November 18, 2003, 30, http://www.chass.utoronto.ca/~msmart/wp/iib.pdf.

PART VI
Conclusion

PART VI
Conclusion

Chapter 14

Thinking Critically about Terrorist Financing

Michael Freeman

How should scholars and policymakers think about the issue of terrorist financing? Is money the lifeblood of terrorist groups, or are the amounts too small and too difficult to intercept? How much money do terrorists need to operate and where do they get the money? How much priority should we give to counter-terrorist financing efforts? How should we be organized to optimize the creation and implementation of counter-terrorist financing efforts? Should the focus of these efforts be on stopping the flow of money, or on following the money to better understand the terrorist groups or networks? Can financial flows into, within, and from a terrorist group provide information on questions regarding the group's organization, operations, alliances, and legitimacy?

This chapter will address these and other issues. Specifically, it will first draw out several themes regarding how terrorist groups create portfolios of funding sources. This will include recapping some examples of the diversity of resources; discussing why and how most terrorist groups diversify their funding streams; and exploring why terrorist groups rely on different sources of funding (e.g. why do some groups turn to the drug trade and others do not). Second, this chapter will address some of the challenges of trying to counter the sources of terrorist financing. Third, this chapter will raise questions about the overall regime of counter-terrorist financing, with an emphasis on how various actors think about issues of priorities, strategy, organization, coordination, and measures of effectiveness. Lastly, this chapter will offer an alternative approach to thinking about terrorism financing—one that looks less at stopping the sources and movement of funds and more on the informational value of understanding terrorist financing as a window into a terrorist group's organizational structure, operations, alliances, and ideology.

As described in the chapter on sources and demonstrated by the various case studies, terrorist groups find sources of income from a wide range of activities, which can be grouped into state sponsorship, illegal activities, popular support, and legal activities. For state sponsorship, the most dramatic example is that of Hezbollah and the financial and material support provided to it by Iran and Syria. In addition, the case studies showed several other examples of state sponsorship, including Iranian support for Iraqi insurgents, Pakistani support to the Taliban and to LeT, Indian support for the LTTE in its early years, Libyan support to the MNLF, and Cuban and Soviet support to the ELN. Interestingly, the Loyalists and FARC never received any significant state-sponsored funding.

Illegal activities—spanning extortion, smuggling, involvement with drugs, theft, kidnapping and ransom, and more—are used by almost every terrorist group to raise funds to some degree or another. For example, extortion is used by Iraqi insurgents, the Taliban, the LTTE, the PKK, the MILF, the Loyalists, and ELN. Smuggling oil is used by Iraqi groups while the LTTE profits from human smuggling. Ties to the drug trade remain an immensely profitable source of income for groups like the Taliban, PKK, FARC, the Loyalists, and the ELN in its early years. Theft, counterfeiting, and fraud helped groups like Hezbollah (in the Tri-Border Area), the LTTE, and the Loyalists. Kidnapping and ransom is widely used by many groups, including Iraqi insurgents, the Taliban, the Abu Sayyaf Group, the FARC, and the ELN.

Popular support—in the form of charities and donations—is an important source of funding for several of the groups described in the case studies. While the use of charities to fund groups like al-Qaeda and Hamas (not discussed in the case studies) is fairly well known, charities were also an important source of funds for the LeT, and for a time, Iraqi insurgent groups. Groups like Hezbollah, the PKK, and the LTTE also rely on donations from the Lebanese, Kurdish, and Tamil diaspora communities around the globe (as did the Provisional IRA in the 1980s).[1] Sometimes these funds are given voluntarily, and sometimes they should be more accurately categorized as extortion. In Albania, charities are not funding terrorist acts, but are promoting hardline Salafist or Wahhabist principles through the sponsorship and support of various Islamist institutions in the country.

The case studies also highlighted how terrorists groups use legitimate businesses for raising money. In Iraq, for example, insurgents would sell their property. Also, the NPA in the Philippines would profit from government contracts. Lastly, the Loyalists in Northern Ireland established various legal enterprises, like drinking clubs, security firms, taxi firms, and building firms, to raise money. Many of these, of course, were often tied to some of their illegal activities. For example, security firms were often, not surprisingly, tied to extortion operations.

The range of sources of income for terrorist groups is clearly broad and gives any terrorist group many options when they assemble their "portfolio" of sources. As seen by the case studies, practically every terrorist group utilizes several fundraising methods simultaneously. Even Hezbollah, which receives perhaps 50 percent of their funding from Iran, still engages in illegal activities in Lebanon and the Tri-Border Area in South America, and encourages donations from the Lebanese diaspora community. Likewise, groups like the FARC and the Taliban that rely heavily on the drug trade for revenue, still engage in other activities, like kidnapping and ransom, extortion, and smuggling for funding revenue.

Despite the wide variety of options for terrorist groups, the portfolios of terrorist groups have different combinations of funding sources. For example, the Loyalists became involved in the drug trade in Northern Ireland, while the Provisional IRA mostly did not. Likewise, the Provisionals received financial

---

1   James Adams, *The Financing of Terror* (New English Library, 1986), Chapter 6.

support from Irish diaspora communities in the United States and Ireland and safe-havens and sanctuary from the Republic of Ireland (at least in the first few decades of the Troubles), while the Loyalists never received much state or popular support. Some of this can be explained by the organizational controls exerted by the IRA, in contrast to the more decentralized Loyalist groups. And some of the differences can be explained by the different ideologies of each group and the level of support they received from their constituent communities. Overall, it seems that if groups are to receive some measure of popular or state sponsorship, they must have an ideology or grievance that has external legitimacy. Similarly, groups that use drug profits must either be geographically close to their origin (coca or heroin from Colombia or Afghanistan) or ideologically willing to sell drugs at the end of their supply chain.

Besides the variation in the financial portfolios between terrorist groups, there is also variation over time within a terrorist group's portfolio. For example, groups like the ELN and the LTTE received some initial support from state sponsors, but when this dried up, they turned to other, often illegal methods, like drugs, extortion, or kidnapping for ransom.[2] Along the same lines, the insurgency in Iraq has shifted its sources of income, relying less on the assets of foreign regime elements and foreign fighters bringing cash, and more on illegal activities. These shifts in financing sources often could indicate, for example, a change in the group's level of ideological support. (This will be discussed more below.)

Ultimately, as the cases show, targeting the sources of terrorist finances is often difficult. Cutting into state sponsorship of terrorist groups is probably the most challenging because states, in general, do not easily or quickly change their policies. For example, what pressure or incentives could the international community place on Iran to stop their sponsorship of Hezbollah? Sanctions and embargoes may be justified against Iran to try to stop them acquiring nuclear weapons, but is their sponsorship of terrorism enough of a priority to justify such harsh measures? Even if these measures were justified, there is no guarantee that Iran would reverse its policies. Addressing other sources of terrorist financing is only marginally easier. States already devote significant resources to countering the types of criminal activities exploited by terrorist groups. These countermeasures are effective at reducing the levels of criminal activity to what still occurs, but in a world of scarce resources, states cannot be expected to do much more. There have been some successes at countering the popular support (charities, specifically) of terrorist groups. However, as long as a terrorist group has some external legitimacy, they can easily create new organizations and charities to replace those that have been banned or prosecuted.

These challenges are especially salient for states trying to proactively deny funding to terrorist groups. However, states can also use financial intelligence

---

2 Jeanne Giraldo and Harold Trinkunas, "The Political Economy of Terrorism Financing," in *Terrorism Financing and State Responses*, edited by Jeanne Giraldo and Harold Trinkunas (Stanford, CA: Stanford University Press, 2007), 7.

to prosecute terrorists after an attack. In fact, many terrorist cases prosecuted in the United States involve at least some measure of financial evidence to prove connections between individuals and either terrorist groups or terrorist attacks.

Despite some of the inherent challenges in dealing with terrorist finances (opaqueness, flexibility, relatively small sums of money), to some degree states also create challenges of their own making. If states are to better counter terrorist finances, questions of priorities, strategy, organization, and measures of effectiveness need to be addressed.

How much of a priority should countering terrorist financing be? Where should it rank among a list of other national security priorities? Take, for example, Iranian support for Hezbollah. Should ending this relationship take precedence over Iran's attempt to acquire nuclear weapons? Differences in priorities become especially problematic when multiple countries confront a common problem. In the Tri-Border Area of Latin America (where Hezbollah gets some funding and planned the 1992 and 1994 attacks in Argentina, but which is also a smugglers paradise), Brazil, Paraguay, Argentina, and the United States all have different priorities. Brazil's priorities are to keep the region stable and safe enough for all the economic tourists travelling there for cheap goods and for the sightseeing tourists headed for the Iguazu Falls. Paraguay benefits economically from the free-trade zone encompassing the TBA and therefore does not want to do anything—like confronting corruption or smuggling—that would undermine the economic dynamism of the region. Argentina's priorities are similarly tied to tourism and economics, but they also are more concerned with the terrorism-related issues connected to the region. The United States, unlike the other countries, has an almost exclusively counter-terrorism interest in the TBA. With all of these different priorities, agreeing to a common strategy among the interested states is understandably difficult.

One of the most striking challenges in fighting terrorist financing is the absence of an overall strategy against any particular terrorist group. What, for instance, is the U.S. strategy to counter the Taliban's finances? Or al-Qaeda's? Or the FARCs? While there are guidelines and agencies that coordinate many of the various efforts that organizations take against these various groups, there is no central strategy that thinks about matching ends, ways, and means and that thinks about how to use scarce resources in the most productive ways (and this means making decisions about what *not* to do as well as decisions about what *to* do).

Organizationally, the U.S. counter-terrorist financing effort is marked by redundancy, insufficient collaboration and coordination, and inadequate information sharing. In terms of redundancy, the agencies involved in countering terrorist financing would include at least the Treasury Department, the State Department, the Federal Bureau of Investigation, the Department of Defense, the Central Intelligence Agency, the Department of Homeland Security, the Drug Enforcement Agency, and more. Of course, each organization has their unique skill set and legal mandates to address different aspects of the terrorist financing issue, but the multipronged approach makes coordination and collaboration even more difficult. However, based on personal conversations with representatives from many of these organizations, coordination seems to be improving. Yet, inevitably, just as states often have competing priorities, so too do all of the domestic organizations. For example, Treasury might want to designate an individual or entity—like a bank—as affiliated with terrorism, but the CIA might resist because it wants to follow the trail of money for intelligence purposes, or State might resist because of the potential negative diplomatic fallout. This organizational structure also makes information sharing more difficult as every organization keeps their own databases and has incentives to not fully disclose all of their information. Nevertheless, information sharing seems to be improving over time, according to some conversations with members of some of the aforementioned organizations.

Another internal challenge in countering terrorist financing is defining and measuring what we mean by success or failure. What would count as a success? There is a wide range of outcomes that could be considered: disruptions could delay an attack or make it less destructive, efforts could make terrorist groups spend more of their own internal resources acquiring funds, efforts could force terrorist groups to turn to less legitimate sources of income, or is the defeat of the terrorist group the only way to define success? Whichever of these, or other, ways that success is defined, there is still a notable absence of anyone truly measuring success. Instead, what counts as a "success" is the seizure of terrorist assets, or the confiscation of drugs, or charities that are prosecuted, or something analogous to the number of Vietcong killed. While all of these actions may be useful, we must not confuse operational outcomes with successful strategies. For strategies to be successful, they must have a noticeable effect on the group that is targeted. So while we might have "successfully" interdicted some drugs coming into the United States, this does not necessarily mean that these efforts were truly successful at undermining the level of illicit drug use within the United States. Ultimately we cannot confuse actions for effects.

Despite all of these challenges—both from terrorists and from our own making—much more can be done in relation to terrorist financing. Instead of focusing on stopping the flow of money into and within terrorist groups (which is often difficult to impossible to do), instead we could be focusing on what the financial flows tells us about the terrorist groups themselves.[3]

Most directly, financial flows can often indicate the location and general timing of future attacks. For example, before the attack on the MV Limburg oil tanker of the coast of Yemen, al-Qaeda affiliates moved approximately $200,000 to its affiliates in Yemen to buy weapons, boats, safe houses, and other equipment in the several months before the attack.[4] The transfer of such a large sum of

---

3 Phil Williams, "Warning Indicators and Terrorist Finances," in *Terrorism Financing and State Responses*, edited by Jeanne Giraldo and Harold Trinkunas (Stanford, CA: Stanford University Press, 2007), 79, discusses many of these issues.

4 *Yemen Times*, June 3, 2004; *Yemen Observer*, June 5, 2004; *Yemen Times*, August 30, 2004.

money could have been an indicator or warning of both the location (Yemen) and the timing (within several months) of a future attack.[5] More broadly, the financial flows of terrorist groups, especially on the expenditure side, might give some information concerning changing priorities or strategies. Taliban finances moving to a particular province or district in Afghanistan where they had not previously gone, for example, would probably indicate that that area is of particular importance to them and might be the location of not just a future attack, but of a future front in the insurgency.

The movement of finances within a terrorist group can also be used to construct an organizational structure for the group. As Phil Williams points out, "mapping a terrorist network is an enormously complex task." However, financial flows can connect "known and unknown parts of a terrorist network," just as much as other types of communication can.[6] In this case, it does not matter how much money is being transferred—what matters is who is transferring money to whom. For example, financial flows could indicate how leaders of a group order financiers to direct money to local commanders or cell leaders. Additionally, following the money also allows the state to gain a better understanding of the particular type of organizational structure of the terrorist group, specifically if it is more decentralized or hierarchical. Following the money could also provide intelligence on the nature of the alliances between different groups, particularly if these alliances entail financial support from one group to another.

Financial flows can also be an indicator of the overall legitimacy or support that the terrorist group enjoys amongst its constituent population. This is especially relevant when groups have to change their sources of financing over time. In Iraq, for instance, the shift in financing sources from foreign fighters coming with cash to the use of kidnappings and extortion probably indicates some decreasing legitimacy of their ideology both within Iraq and externally in the region. Moreover, the turn to criminal activity—especially the types that target their own potential constituency—can also further erode the legitimacy of terrorist groups. In this sense, changes in sources can be both a factor and indicator of changing support for the terrorist group's cause.

As the case studies show, countering terrorist financing is often a difficult task. Terrorist groups have a wide array of possible sources of revenue and are often adept and flexible actors. Additionally, states face their own internal challenges in dealing with this threat. Nevertheless, there is room for optimism. Understanding our adversaries is always paramount and this volume hopes to increase our knowledge of how various terrorist groups raise, move, and spend money. Additionally, the issue of terrorist financing is relatively new and organizations tasked with fighting this phenomenon have improved their

---

5   See Michael Freeman, David Tucker, and Steffen Merten, "Pathways to Terror: Finding Patterns Prior to an Attack," *Journal of Policing, Intelligence and Counter Terrorism*, 5:1 (2010) for more on the patterns and timing of activity before an attack
6   Williams, "Warning Indicators and Terrorist Finances," 80.

coordination, collaboration, and information sharing over time. However, more critical thinking needs to be done, especially in regards to issues concerning priorities, strategy, and organization.

Index

For Product Safety Concerns and Information please contact our
EU representative GPSR@taylorandfrancis.com Taylor & Francis
Verlag GmbH, Kaufingerstraße 24, 80331 München, Germany